CONCISE COLLEGE TEXTS

GCSE LAW

OTHER BOOKS IN THIS SERIES

AUSTRALIA
The Law Book Company
Brisbane ● Sydney ● Melbourne ● Perth

CANADA
Carswell
Ottawa ● Toronto ● Calgary ● Montreal ● Vancouver

AGENTS
Steimatzky's Agency Ltd., Tel Aviv;
N.M. Tripathi (Private) Ltd., Bombay;
Eastern Law House (Private) Ltd., Calcutta;
M.P.P. House, Bangalore;
Universal Book Traders, Delhi;
Aditya Books, Delhi;
MacMillan Shuppan KK, Tokyo;
Pakistan Law House, Karachi, Lahore

CONCISE COLLEGE TEXTS

GCSE LAW

By

W. J. BROWN
LL.B. (Hons.), F.C.I.S.

FIFTH EDITION

LONDON • SWEET & MAXWELL • 1993

First Edition 1978
Second Edition 1982
Third Edition 1986
Fourth Edition 1989
Fifth Edition 1993

Published in 1993 by
Sweet & Maxwell Ltd. of
South Quay Plaza, 183 Marsh Wall,
London E14 9FT
Computerset by PB Computer Typesetting, Pickering, N. Yorks.
Printed in England by
Clays Ltd., St. Ives plc

A CIP catalogue
record for this book
is available from
the British Library

ISBN 0–421–487208

Preface

The aim of this book is to help candidates prepare for the GCSE examinations in law.

At the end of each chapter there is a revision test, a list of examination questions and suggested coursework titles, which may be helpful to teachers and candidates as class tests, homework or coursework assignments.

I wish to convey my thanks to the Football Association for kindly providing a copy of a professional footballer's contract; to Ken Andrews for his illustration of the Crown Court in session; and to the Southern Examining Group, for giving permission to reproduce their past GCSE examination questions. The Minors' Contract Act 1987 and the Lord Chancellor's Department Form N201 are Crown Copyright; these and the Jury Summons 5221 form are reproduced with the permission of the Controller of Her Majesty's Stationery Office. The Legal Aid symbol is reproduced with permission of the Legal Aid Board.

I also wish to thank friends and old colleagues for their helpful comments and advice, and to Linda for her help in preparing the manuscript.

And finally I wish to thank the staff at Sweet & Maxwell for their help in checking the page proofs, preparing the Tables and Index and for maintaining efficient and friendly communications.

January 1993   *W.J.B.*

Contents

Table of Cases

Table of Statutes

Chapter 1
The Nature of Law

WHAT IS MEANT BY LAW

It is difficult to be precise as to what law is, but it may be defined as a code of conduct for the people in a given community, which controls their activities towards each other, with respect to their private and business lives, and to their relationship with the State.

It is generally agreed that law must be accepted by the majority of the community. Most road-users recognise the necessity for all drivers travelling on the same side of the road, or stopping at traffic lights when they show red. Even if there was no punishment for these offences, the majority of drivers would still follow the Highway Code because they know it is the sensible thing to do.

Most associations and sports are governed by laws or rules. The laws of cricket are observed by cricketers throughout the world, but they are not "law" in the context we are discussing. To be effective, law must be binding on the whole community and must be enforceable. Members of a community do not have to play cricket, and those who do play may agree to change the rules for their own benefit or convenience, but people in this country may not ignore or change the law to suit themselves. Holidaymakers, for example, could play cricket on the beach and ignore the cricket law relating to "leg before wicket," and also create a law that a hit into the sea is "six and out." They could not, however, ignore the criminal law and decide to have gunfights as seen in western films on television most Saturday nights. In *R. v. Moloney* (1985) two men staged a friendly shooting contest to see who had the faster "draw." Although there was no intention for either to be hurt, one was shot and died. The survivor was found guilty of manslaughter. It is against the law to kill or attempt to kill, and members of the community have no choice as to whether the law applies to them or not.

1

Law often reflects a country's moral values. Generally, it is very difficult to define moral conduct, because one person might consider an act to be moral while another person might consider the same act to be immoral. A person might contribute to a lottery which will result in someone winning a large sum of money and the net profits of the lottery being donated to a charity. Another person, however, may consider the lottery to be gambling and therefore immoral and wrong, although recognising that the aim of benefiting a charity is worthwhile.

The difficulty with a moral attitude to law is that moral values change with time and locality. The country's attitude to homosexuality, prostitution, suicide, censorship of plays and pornography has changed drastically over recent years and the law has changed accordingly. There are many people who still consider such things to be immoral, but Parliament has probably considered that the attitude of a large part of the community has changed and has consequently passed the appropriate legislation to make certain conduct lawful which was previously unlawful.

Until a few years ago public-houses in Wales did not open on Sundays, but several counties in the Principality changed this law because the community's attitude had changed. On the Continent most sporting activities take place on a Sunday with little restriction, but in this country it is difficult to ascertain the real position of the law. Horse racing is widely organised on Sundays on the Continent, but as yet not in this country, yet professional cricket and football is played on Sundays. It could be argued that in this respect a previous society's morals are being forced on today's society which in the main does not have the same attitude. In 1986 the Government considered changing the law with regard to Sunday trading, which would have allowed shops to open for business on Sundays. However, there was a powerful lobby from various sections of the community, such as the churches and trade unions, and Parliament did not pass the Bill. The law on Sunday trading is, at present, in some doubt due to an E.C. ruling, and some large retailing companies now open on Sundays, although it appears to be against the law. This is an area of law which could change in future legislation, so students should look out for any developments.

Moral and religious attitudes do have a great effect on our law. "Thou shall not kill," "thou shall not steal" are not only religious commandments, they are also legal commandments. This is because the community as a whole considers it wrong to steal or to kill, and it would still be against the law for a starving person to steal food or to kill for food (see p. 246).

Since the end of the Second World War, legislation dealing with the community's welfare has been introduced on a huge scale. The State has decided that in many aspects of life, it must provide for the needy. The benefit of this legislation is available to all who qualify. The lowest-paid worker and the managing director of the largest company may be entitled to the same State pension when they reach the age of 60 for women and 65 for men. The community has recognised the need to help the less fortunate and Parliament has passed laws to comply with this attitude.

It might be considered that everything a person does is affected by some element of law. If you attend school, college or work, there are Acts of Parliament which govern the condition of the buildings, the hours of attendance, etc. Law affects you when you travel, buy a newspaper, play a radio, enter a football ground, go to the pictures and so on. It is important, therefore, that we should have some knowledge of our law and how it works and is administered.

It should be noted that this book deals with English law, and that it affects the people who live in England and Wales. Scotland has its own system of law.

How good or effective is English law? If you ask a person who has just won a legal case, the answer may be "English justice is the best," but if a person has lost a case on a technical point of law, the reply to the question could be "The law is an ass."

The aim of law should be justice, but as a legal system becomes advanced and sophisticated it is possible that the "letter of the law" becomes more important than the "spirit of the law." It is then possible for a decision of the courts to be legally correct, but not to have achieved justice. In *Re Bravda* (1968) a will had four witnesses, although a valid will only requires two. The last two witnesses were to benefit under the terms of the will and the testator only wished them to be aware of the existence of the will and its contents. However, because the Wills Act 1837 provided that witnesses of a will cannot benefit from the will, the court ruled that they could not receive their inheritance.

In this case the letter of the law was followed, but the intentions of the testator were defeated and the outcome for the last two witnesses was certainly not justice. It should be noted that Parliament quickly changed the law to provide for such an occurrence (Wills Act 1968), but it did not help the two persons concerned in the case.

The difficulty in defining law and the nature of law is that it concerns cultural, moral, religious and egalitarian values, together with political policy and philosophy. But whatever the nature of law, if it is to be effective, it must encompass and bind the whole community, and it must be enforceable. A law that cannot, or will not, be enforced, is in effect no law at all.

THE NECESSITY FOR LAW

"Bank Clerk Shot."
"Armed Gang Steal Wage Roll."
"Terrorists Bomb London Pub."
"Soccer Fans Run Wild."
"Woman Raped in Park."

Headlines such as these are commonplace and their like can be seen in newspapers most days of the week. If there was no system of law, the persons responsible for the above events would be under no fear of punishment or sanction by the State or community in general. Murder is considered by modern society to be a terrible, heinous offence. It is, therefore, essential that there is an established procedure for providing that murder is a crime and that murderers will be punished. It is essential in a civilised community that there is a clearly defined criminal law which may be enforced, and a system of law for determining commercial and private disputes, and providing a means of compensation for injured parties.

If a community did not have a system of law which was capable of being enforced, the strongest person, or group of persons, could dominate with arbitrary and unfair rules, or there could be anarchy, with no form of establishment and individuals following the dictates of their own conscience. If a community is to develop as a fair and free society, law must be present to ensure that an individual's rights and freedoms are protected. As a community develops its industry and business, its law must similarly develop and create a system which will ensure that transactions may take place with reasonable certainty, that disputes will be settled and that breaches of law will be enforced or compensated. It is not a coincidence that as business in the world has developed over the last 100 years, so has mercantile and company law, and the law dealing with insurance, revenue and taxation, consumer protection, industrial relations and similar matters.

Law is not only needed to ensure that offenders will be punished, it creates a code of conduct which a community wishes to follow. The Factories Acts and the Health and Safety at Work Act 1974 created laws to protect workers from injury by placing a duty on an employer to provide a safe place of work. Drivers of motor vehicles are required to be insured, so that a third party injured in an accident will be compensated for any loss suffered. Shopkeepers have to refund the cost of goods which customers return because they are not of merchantable quality, and manufacturers may be liable for damage caused by defective products.

A community has its own values and its law should reflect these values. Laws are not made to be broken, but to be followed.

All breaches of civil or criminal law are not necessarily deliberate. The examples mentioned above could result in a breach of law which was not intentional; an employer may have created a dangerous place of work by accident; a motor accident could have been caused by the negligence of the driver, and a shopkeeper may not have known that the goods were unsatisfactory. Yet all three may have committed an offence or a breach of law. There have been breaches of law because the community created the laws and requires individuals to behave or conduct themselves accordingly for the benefit of the community as a whole.

DIVISIONS OF LAW

English law is usually classified as being either public or private law.

1. Public law

Public law is the law which governs the relationship between the State and individual members within the State, and between one State and another. This division of law comprises several specialist classes of law such as:

(a) Criminal law

Crime affects the whole community and as offences are considered to be against the State, they are punished by a system laid down and administered by the State.

Criminal law is designed to protect the public from attack on their individual property or person, and to enable any individual or group of individuals to perform their rights and duties under the law. Although a crime is against the State, an individual may suffer from the offence, so, as will be seen below in "Private law," in addition to the punishment laid down by the State, the individual will be able to obtain compensation for personal loss.

(b) Constitutional law

This branch of law deals with the method of government within the State. Constitutional law affects the general public, in that it provides for the structure of the legislature (in this country the Houses of Parliament), the formation of the Executive (the Cabinet), the courts and legal system (the Judiciary) and the system of administration for both local and central government. The laws created and administered by these bodies affect the rights, duties and freedoms of each individual within the State. Ideally, there should be a separation of the powers of Executive, legislature and judiciary, but in this country only the latter exercises a separate power.

(c) Administrative law

As the Government has legislated for the provision of a large number of benefits for individual members of the State (e.g. welfare benefits), the courts and administrative tribunals (usually set up by the Government) have developed a body of laws and principles to regulate and control the agencies which administer the legislative provisions.

Administrative law is usually concerned with appeals and complaints from individuals against the ministerial agencies.

2. Private law

This division of law is sometimes called civil law and is contrasted with criminal law. The latter deals with offences against the State, while civil or private law concerns the dealings between individual members of the State. When the State starts an action the case is usually called in the name of the monarch. Regina is used when a Queen is on the throne and Rex when there is a King. For convenience, a criminal case is usually written as *R.* v. *Brown*. In civil cases the names of the individual parties are used: *Smith* v. *Brown*. The first named is usually called the plaintiff (the person bringing the action) and the second name is the defendant.

Because civil law only affects the individuals involved, it does not mean the State is not concerned or involved. In many instances the State will have created the law which regulates the conduct between the individuals, and will also administer the courts to hear disputes which have arisen. The main distinction may be that in a criminal case, the State brings the action, and stipulates and administers the punishment, while in civil cases an individual starts the action and the courts award the wronged individual the remedy best suited to the situation. For example, in breach of contract or negligence a sum of money called damages may be sufficient compensation but if a trespasser refuses to leave another person's land, an injunction may be needed to ensure the trespasser leaves the land.

Civil remedies are discussed on p. 79.

The main classes of civil law are as follows:

(a) *Law of contract*
An agreement between two or more persons which is intended to be legally binding.

(b) *Law of tort*
A recognised civil wrong other than a breach of contract or trust. Torts cover such wrongs as trespass, negligence, nuisance and defamation.

(c) *Law of property*
The rights of individuals to ownership and possession of their property, both land and personal property (chattels). The law of succession deals with wills and how property is distributed after death.

(d) *Family law*
The law concerning marriage, divorce and separation, and the responsibilities, and duties of parents to each other and to their children.

(e) *Welfare law*
As administrative law (see above) deals with disputes arising from the provision of State benefits, welfare law is concerned with the rights of individuals to obtain State benefits, and the rights and duties of parties with respect to housing and employment.

HOW THE LAW HAS GROWN

It was the Norman conquest of 1066 which established the basis of the English common law. Before William the Conqueror arrived the laws and courts varied from area to area, and there was no system which applied to the country as a whole. It was not the intention of the Normans to introduce new laws, their aim being to discover the laws that existed and make them uniform and applicable to the whole country.

The Normans set up the *Curia Regis* (the King's Council) which had judicial powers, as well as being the administrative centre for making laws and raising finance. The importance of the *Curia Regis* in the development of English law was that it probably led to the establishment of Parliament, and it allowed the creation and development of the various common law courts.

The court was composed of the tenants-in-chief of the Crown, who were high-ranking persons and barons. All the land of the country belonged to the King, and the tenants-in-chief were those who received the land directly from the King. Other members of the court were the chief officers and officials of State.

The aim of the Normans was to establish a system of law which would cover and apply to the whole country. Common law means that it is the same law for all; that it is shared by and affects all persons alike; common in this meaning does not mean low, cheap or inferior.

Although William I established the *Curia Regis*, it was in the reign of Henry II (1154–1189) that great steps were taken to develop common law. Judges were sent out to tour the country to settle disputes and administer justice, and eventually to deal with criminal matters. The judges would return to discuss their cases and problems and from these discussions they were able to create a uniform common law. As law developed, the jurisdiction of the *Curia Regis* gradually diminished as new courts were introduced. The principal common law courts were:

(a) The Court of Exchequer

This was so called because the table or bench of the court was covered with a black and white chequer (like a chessboard). This court was usually concerned with financial and revenue matters.

(b) The Court of Assize

This was concerned with criminal and civil matters, although later it dealt mainly with criminal cases. The country was divided into areas (circuits) and the itinerant judges travelled the country to administer the law. This court was in existence until 1971, when it was replaced by the Crown Court.

(c) *The Court of Common Pleas*

This was a civil court, dealing mainly with cases concerning disputes over land, between subjects other than the King.

The court was established to hear cases in Westminster while the King travelled the country. It was staffed by full-time judges who had been serjeants-at-law (barristers). The cost of legal actions was high and the costs for this court in particular were very expensive, therefore only the wealthy could afford to take legal action, and as the main source of wealth was ownership of land this court was very important. The court was abolished by the Judicature Acts 1873–1875 and its jurisdiction was eventually transferred to the Queen's Bench Division of the High Court.

(d) *The Court of King's Bench*

This court had criminal and civil jurisdiction and could hear appeals. Originally the court had civil jurisdiction, dealing mainly with the tort of trespass and the law of contract.

The court was the last of the three main courts to leave the *Curia Regis*, and the King's close association with the court gave it jurisdiction to issue the prerogative writs of *mandamus*, prohibition and *certiorari* (see p. 117). The court used a legal "fiddle" to take cases from the Court of Common Pleas by means of the fictitious Bill of Middlesex procedure. The court had power to hear cases when a defendant was in custody therefore the Sheriff of Middlesex would arrest a defendant on a fictitious trespass action, and then the court would hear the real cause of action and drop the other. A defendant was usually pleased because it meant the case was not heard in the Common Pleas with its expensive costs. The court was abolished by the Judicature Acts and most of its jurisdiction was transferred to the Queen's Bench Division of the High Court.

(e) *The Courts of Exchequer Chamber*

The first court of this name was established in 1357 to hear appeals from the Exchequer. A later court was created to hear appeals from the King's Bench, and in 1830 a court was created to hear appeals from all the common law courts. The court was abolished by the Judicature Acts 1873–1875 and its jurisdiction was transferred to the Court of Appeal.

In addition to the above, other courts were established to deal with the growth of trade, both national and international. The Courts of the Law Merchant, the Pie Powder Courts and the Courts of Staple, administered instant justice at markets and fairs, but eventually the work of these courts was taken over by the Common Law Courts.

THE WRIT SYSTEM

Henry II also developed the writ system. A writ was a royal command to attend court and it had the effect of centralising the jurisdiction of the courts. If a person wished to start an action, it was necessary to obtain a writ from the King's Chancellor, which meant that the royal courts acquired more power. The Judicature Acts 1873–1875 abolished the forms of action, but it is still necessary today to obtain a writ to start certain actions, although the wording of the claim is left to the plaintiff, and there is no danger of the case being lost because of a mistake in the format of the claim.

Writs originally began with a statement of the claim which was common for all writs of a similar nature. The wording on the writs was prepared beforehand for only a limited number of actions, and if a plaintiff had a new or different claim it would be difficult to bring an action before the courts. The clerks began to issue new writs for actions not previously covered, thereby widening the scope of the writ system and helping the development of the common law.

Because the barons considered that the issue of new writs took away their power the Provisions of Oxford 1258 was passed which provided that no writs were to be issued for any new actions. This statute had the effect of severely restricting the development of the common law. To alleviate the harshness and inconvenience of this law the Statute of Westminster 1285 provided that new writs could be issued which were similar (*in consimili casu*) to existing writs. The effect of this statute was that the common law saw further development, but it could still be very difficult to bring a claim before the court if it was for an action that could not easily be adapted into an existing writ.

In addition to the difficulty of obtaining a suitable writ, an action could fail for a minor or simple mistake in the wording of the claim in the writ.

EQUITY

The writ system became very formal and as previously explained could only be issued for particular forms of actions. If there was

NEWLAND CHILD CARE

In Caring Company

Newland, situated in the heart of Hull, is a residential care resource for children. We continue to expand - we need more Carers to add to the Care Team.

Could you become a:

Senior Care Worker

Working to an Assistant Director you will be responsible for supervising and directing day to day care operations. You will need to be experienced in child care work, qualified if possible, and very flexible. Salary £19,175 per annum.

or

Care Support Worker (Grade 1 and 2)

Working directly with children as part of a House Care Team. You will need to be therefore, relevant experience will be needed.

Salary: Grade 1 - £15,500 per annum, Grade 2 - £14,680 per annum

Salaries for all posts include a recognition for unsocial hours. No other allowances are payable. Pension and Health Care Plans are available. Annual leave is generous.

You will need to be exceptional person to join us - we hope you are out there. If so, send a CV and sell yourself to The Director, Sailors' Families' Society, Newland Child Care, 10, Newland Avenue, Cottingham Road, HULL, HU6 7RJ.

Closing date 14 days from this advert.

NEER

specialist equipment
d healthcare
clude the
ed in pharmaceutical
nagement of special

HNC standard and
asiCad.
d application form

no writ for a particular complaint, or one could not be adapted, there was no cause of action and, no matter how justifiable the complaint, an injured party could not obtain a remedy. If there was no writ there was no remedy.

To overcome the harshness of the writ system, appeals were made directly to the King, who made decisions on the facts of the case. As appeals grew in number, the King passed them to his Lord Chancellor. The earlier Chancellors were also the King's chaplain (often referred to as the "Keeper of the King's conscience"), and because of their ecclesiastical calling, their decisions tended to ignore the formal rules of law and were based on conscience and natural justice.

A separate Chancery Court was eventually established to hear the many appeals that were referred to this form of justice. In many instances decisions were contrary to those made in the common law courts and this led to disputes between the two courts. In the early seventeenth century, James I, on the advice of Sir Francis Bacon, ruled that in cases with contrary decisions, equity should prevail. This decision saw an extension of the work of the Chancery Court and new concepts of law were introduced such as the law of trusts (common law would not recognise a trust or the duties of trustees), and new remedies were provided.

Damages was the only common law remedy. Equity offered new remedies such as injunctions, specific performance and rescission (see pp. 153-154). The main problem was that the courts could only award their own particular remedy. If a person bringing an action for trespass was asking for damages and an injunction to stop the other party from continuing the trespass, the litigant would have to go to the common law court for damages, and then start another action in the Chancery Court for the injunction. This situation existed until the middle of the nineteenth century when piecemeal legislation enabled both courts to award each other's remedies.

The main disadvantage of equity was the difficulty of foreseeing with any certainty the result of a case. Decisions varied from judge to judge, and the uncertainty of the outcome of cases led to the opinion at that time that the Chancellors' decisions varied as did the length of their feet.

Equity eventually became a formalised system, but procedure was very slow and, consequently, very expensive, as Dickens criticised in "Bleak House."

It must be noted that common law was a complete system of law; equity was not. Equity was considered as the polish, "the gloss on the common law," which helped to improve the legal system and fill in any deficiencies. The Judicature Acts 1873–1875, whilst confirming that in matters of conflict equity should prevail, fused the administration of the Chancery Court with the common law courts. It is unlikely that any new equitable concepts would be created today.

As a result of the Acts, the common law courts and the Court of Chancery were joined together under the Supreme Court of Judicature, which comprised the Court of Appeal and the High Court of Justice. For convenience, the High Court was divided into three divisions: Queen's Bench; Chancery; and Probate, Divorce and Admiralty.

REVISION TEST

The questions in the revision test sections usually require short answers of a few words. Answer the questions, preferably on a separate sheet of paper and check your answers from within the pages of the chapter. The correctness (or otherwise) of the answers should indicate your understanding of the chapter. If you find the questions difficult, read the relevant section again.

1. Name two specialist classes of public law. *Criminal Constitutional.*

2. Name three classes of civil or private law. *Law of Contract Law of TORT.*

3. To which class of private law does negligence and trespass belong? *TORT*

4. Name the system whose harshness led to the establishment of Equity. *WRIT SYSTEM.*

5. Name the Acts which fused the administration of the Chancery Courts with the common law courts. *Judicature Acts 1873 - 75.*

SPECIMEN EXAMINATION QUESTIONS

1. Explain what is meant by Equity, and explain how defects in the common law lead to the introduction of Equity.

2. What were the changes to the legal system introduced by the Judicature Act 1873–1875? Draw a diagram of the structure of the courts as a result of the Acts, and compare it with the present-day structure.

3. If Parliament did not have the power to make law would the United Kingdom have a system of law?

4. Describe the early writ system and explain how it led to the growth of Equity.

5. Comment on the statement, "a law that cannot be enforced is in effect no law at all."

SUGGESTED COURSEWORK TITLES

What is law? Why do you think it is necessary for a community to have a settled system of law?

Explain how Equity came into English law and discuss its role in today's legal system. Do you consider judges should have the right to give equitable decisions?

Chapter 2

Sources of Law

Many new students of law have difficulty at first in understanding the meaning of the phrase "sources of law." If asked,
however, to locate the source of the River Nile, or the Thames,
or the Mersey, most students would realise that the answer
would be the place at which the river started.

The phrase "sources of law," has a similar meaning. Where
does the law come from? Where does it start? Who makes it? In
English law the law comes from two main sources, legislation
(Acts of Parliament) and judicial precedent (the decisions of
judges), and from subsidiary sources such as custom and books
of authority. It must be emphasised that in modern times only
very occasionally does law arise from the subsidiary sources.

If a person is accused of breaking the law, it is essential that
all interested parties know the source of the law. For example, if
a person takes goods out of a supermarket without paying, the
shopkeeper, the police, the judge and the shopper will need to
know the law that applies if the shopper is to be brought before
the court. This particular offence arises from legislation.
Parliament passed a law in 1968 (the Theft Act) which makes it
a crime for a person to "dishonestly appropriate property
belonging to another with the intention of permanently depriving
the other of it." The sources of law concerning theft or stealing
are the Theft Acts 1968 and 1978 and law reports which record
decisions taken in court on the interpretation of these Acts (*e.g.*
R. v. *Morris* (1983)).

There is a maxim in law "that ignorance of the law is no
excuse," which means that everyone is presumed to know the
law. Obviously no single person knows all the law of the land.
Even judges, barristers and solicitors have to look up the law,
but because of their training they know where the law originated
and are able to go to the source.

The details of the different sources of law are as follows:

15

Judicial Precedent

Judicial precedent, or case law as it is often called, is the source of a large part of common law and equity. The law is "judge-made," in that when a judge makes a decision in a court case on a particular aspect of law, other judges may be bound to follow this decision in subsequent cases. Once the law has been established, the example or the precedent is binding on other judges, who must make a similar decision in cases concerning this aspect of law.

The doctrine of judicial precedent became firmly established by the late nineteenth century, although a system of precedent existed for hundreds of years before that. It was not until a reliable system of law reporting was started in 1866, and the administration of the courts was reorganised by the Judicature Acts 1873–1875, that judicial precedent became an established source of law.

Stare Decisis (The Standing of Decisions)

Not all decisions of judges create a precedent. Some courts are more important than others. The higher the court which creates a precedent, the greater the authority the decision will have. A general rule is that lower courts are bound by decisions of higher courts, and some courts are bound by their own previous decisions. The hierarchy or standing of the courts is as follows:

1. The House of Lords

The House of Lords is the highest appeal court in civil and criminal matters, and decisions of this Court are binding on all lower courts. Unlike most other courts, the House of Lords is not bound by precedent and may depart from its own previous decisions if it wishes to do so, but if a precedent is to be reversed consideration should be given to the effect it would have, particularly on criminal law and commercial and business transactions.

In recent years the House of Lords has overruled its own previous decisions. For example, in R. v. *Shivpuri* (1985), a criminal case, the Court overruled its previous decision made only a year before, and in *Murphy* v. *Brentwood District Council* (1990), a claim for negligence, the Court overruled a 1978 decision.

2. The Court of Appeal (Civil Division)

The Court is bound by decisions from the House of Lords and, although it has been suggested in court that the position should be otherwise, the Court is bound by its own previous decisions. This principle was established by the Court of Appeal in *Young* v. *Bristol Aeroplane Co.* (1944), although it was laid down that the Court may depart from its previous decisions under certain circumstances:

(a)   where it considers that a decision was made *"per incuriam,"* that is, in error;

(b)   where there are two previous conflicting decisions, the Court may choose which decision is correct and overrule the other decision;

(c)   when a later House of Lords decision applies, this must be followed.

Decisions of the Court of Appeal (Civil Division) are binding on all other lower courts, but do not bind the Criminal Division of the Court of Appeal.

However, in *Derby & Co. Ltd.* v. *Weldon (No. 3)* (1989) the judge held that a court at first instance is not bound in every case to follow a Court of Appeal decision, but may take into consideration the possibility that the decision may be reversed in the House of Lords. The Court of Appeal had given leave, for the case in question, to appeal to the House of Lords.

3. The Court of Appeal (Criminal Division)

Decisions of the House of Lords are binding on the Criminal Division, but unlike the Civil Division of the Court of Appeal, this court is not always bound to follow its own previous decisions. The Court will probably follow decisions of its predecessor, the Court of Criminal Appeal, unless that would cause an injustice.

The decisions of this court bind all lower criminal courts and may bind inferior courts hearing civil cases. Decisions of this court are not binding on the Civil Division of the Court of Appeal nor is it bound by decisions of the Civil Division.

4. The Divisional Courts of the High Court

These courts are bound by the decisions of the House of Lords and Courts of Appeal. The civil divisional courts are bound by their own previous decisions, but the Divisional Court of the Queen's Bench Division (which deals with criminal matters) is not so strictly held to its previous decisions. Decisions of the

Divisional Court are binding on judges of the same division of the High Court sitting alone, and on the inferior courts.

5. The High Court
Decisions of cases of first instances, where the judge sits alone, are binding on the inferior courts but are not binding on other High Court judges. A previous decision of a High Court judge will be treated as a persuasive precedent but will not be binding in other High Court cases. It is suggested that this also applies to High Court judges sitting in the Crown Court, but does not apply to Circuit judges or recorders, and they would be bound by previous decisions of a High Court judge. Decisions of the House of Lords, Courts of Appeal and Divisional Courts of the High Court are generally binding on these courts.

6. The inferior courts
The county courts and the magistrates' courts are bound by decisions of the superior courts. The inferior courts are not bound by their own decisions as they cannot create a precedent.

BINDING AND PERSUASIVE PRECEDENTS

It is not the entire decision of a judge which creates a binding precedent. When a judgment is delivered the judge will give the reason for his decision (*ratio decidendi*), and it is this principle which is binding and must be followed in future cases.

On occasions, judges make general comments in the course of their judgment to explain a particular point. Remarks made "by the way" are known as *obiter dicta* and are persuasive authority, not binding precedent. If, however, the judge is well known and respected for previous judicial decisions, such comments may be followed as persuasive authority in cases where there appears to be no existing binding precedent. Other sources of persuasive authority are writers of outstanding legal works and decisions from courts of other countries such as the United States, Australia and New Zealand.

1. Ratio decidendi
Ratio decidendi is the vital part of case law. It is the principle upon which a decision is reached, and it is this principle which is binding on subsequent cases which have similar facts in the same branch of law.

2. Obiter dicta

The second aspect of judgments, *obiter dicta*, are things said "by the way," and do not have to be followed. Decisions of the Judicial Committee of the Privy Council are only persuasive authority because the Council is not part of the English legal system. However, because the Privy Council is mainly composed of the Law Lords, its decisions have great influence on subsequent cases with similar facts.

Court of Appeal cases have three or more judges and the result is given on the decisions of the majority. A judge who disagrees with the decision of the other judges gives a dissenting judgment, which is *obiter dictum* and never binding. If the judge who dissented is respected, the dissenting judgment might be used as a persuasive authority if the case proceeds to the House of Lords. There have been instances of judges giving a dissenting judgment in the Court of Appeal, and later, when sitting as Law Lords in the House of Lords, hearing a completely different case, overruling the precedent created in the earlier Court of Appeal case. In these instances the Law Lords have been "persuaded" by the dissenting judgment to overrule an existing precedent.

3. Distinguishing

Although the facts of a case appear similar to a binding precedent, a judge may consider that there is some aspect or fact which is not covered by the *ratio decidendi* of the earlier case. The judge will "distinguish" the present case from the earlier one which created the precedent.

4. Overruling

A higher court may consider that the *ratio decidendi* set by a lower court is not the correct law, so when another case is argued on similar facts, the higher court will overrule the previous precedent and set a new precedent to be followed in future cases.

Note that in such cases the decision does not affect the parties in the earlier case, unlike a decision which has been reversed on appeal (see below).

5. Reversal

When a court is hearing an appeal, it may uphold or "reverse" the decision of the lower court. For example, the High Court may give judgment to the plaintiff, and on appeal the Court of Appeal may "reverse" the decision and give judgment to the defendant.

6. Disapproval

A superior court may consider that there is some doubt as to the standing of a previous principle, and it may "disapprove," but not expressly overrule, the earlier precedent.

Advantages and Disadvantages of Precedent

1. Advantages

(a) Certainty

When a precedent has been established the law becomes settled. Lawyers and laymen know and recognise the law and can act accordingly.

(b) The existence of a wealth of detailed, practical knowledge

All case law arises from a practical situation, and the law reports give detailed information of actual cases. In English law there are never "theoretical cases." The case before the court must be on facts in which one party claims a legal right from the other party.

(c) Flexibility

We live in a changing world, and a law which was relevant 50 years ago may not be suitable now. The doctrine of precedent allows the law to grow according to the needs of the community and move with the times. For example, as we shall see later (p. 98) a person under 18 is known as a minor. A minor is bound by contracts for goods which are necessaries. Fifty years ago a motor car or motorcycle would certainly have been considered a luxury, but today the court would probably take the opposite view, particularly if a student or young employee lived a long distance from college or work.

Flexibility is probably the most important advantage.

2. Disadvantages

(a) Rigidity

Although it is considered an advantage for law to be certain, a binding precedent may mean that the law is difficult to change. The House of Lords, however, may change a precedent by overruling a previous decision, and Parliament can legislate for a change of the law.

(b) Danger of illogical distinctions

Judges may look for a justification for not following a precedent, particularly if it is considered to be a bad decision, and a case may be distinguished from another for illogical reasons, so that a different decision may be given.

(c) The complexity and volume of the law reports

Law reports date back many hundreds of years and it may be difficult to find an appropriate case, as there are more than 400,000 reported cases.

THE LAW REPORTS

The basis of judicial precedent is the reporting of cases. Without a reliable system of reporting, it would be impossible for case law to be a source of law.

An extract of a law report, *Re Jones (Deceased)* [1981] 2 W.L.R. 106 is reproduced on the following pages.

E

[FAMILY DIVISION]

In re JONES, DECD.

1980 July 17   Sir John Arnold P.

F

Will—Soldier's will—"In actual military service"—Soldier shot while on patrol in Northern Ireland—Oral declaration that personal effects to be given to fiancée—Whether noncupative will to be admitted to probate—Wills Act 1837 (7 Will. 4 & 1 Vict., c. 26), s. 11

During a period when the armed forces had been asked by the Northern Ireland authorities to assist the civil power in maintaining law and order there, the deceased, a soldier, was serving in Northern Ireland and, on March 16, 1978, he had been sent out on a military patrol with an officer and a warrant officer. An unknown assailant shot him and, before he died, he made an oral testamentary declaration to the two soldiers with him leaving his possessions to the applicant whom he was to have married the following week. She applied to have the declaration admitted to probate as a privileged will under section 11 of the Wills Act 1837.

G

On the question whether the soldier was on actual military service within the meaning of the section: —

Held, that it was the nature of the duties a soldier was called upon to perform which determined whether he was on actual military service; that, provided the service was both active and military, it could be either within the United Kingdom or abroad against a force that need not be organised on conventional military lines and, therefore, when the soldier

H

2 W.L.R.   **In re Jones, decd. (Fam.D.)**

A   was called upon to go out on patrol at a time when there was a
clandestinely organised insurrection, he was on actual military
service and his oral declaration would be admitted to probate
(post, pp. 108E, 110D–E, 111H—112B).
In the Will of Anderson (1958) 75 W.N.(N.S.W.) 334
applied.

The following cases are referred to in the judgment:

B
Anderson, In the Will of (1958) 75 W.N.(N.S.W.) 334.
Attorney-General for Northern Ireland's Reference (No. 1 of 1975) [1977]
    A.C. 105; [1976] 3 W.L.R. 235; [1976] 2 All E.R. 937, H.L.(N.I.).
Booth, In re, [1926] P. 118.
Drummond v. *Parish* (1843) 3 Curt. 522.
Tweedale, In the Goods of (1874) L.R. 3 P. & D. 204.
Wingham decd., In re [1949] P. 187; [1948] 2 All E.R. 908.

C
The following additional cases were cited in argument:

Hiscock, In the Goods of [1901] P. 78.
Limond, In re [1915] 2 Ch. 240.
Rippon, In the Estate of [1943] P. 61; [1943] 1 All E.R. 676.
Spark decd., In the Estate of [1941] P. 115; [1941] 2 All E.R. 782.
D   *Thorne, In the Goods of* (1865) 4 Sw. & Tr. 36.

MOTION
The applicant, Anne Mannering, formerly Anne Newport, of Pudsey,
West Yorkshire, applied for an order that the oral statement made by
David Anthony Jones on March 16, 1978, be admitted to probate as a
privileged will under section 11 of the Wills Act 1837. The hearing was in
E   chambers. Judgment was delivered in open court.
The facts are stated in the judgment.

Colin Braham for the applicant.
John Mummery for the Attorney-General as amicus curiae.

F   SIR JOHN ARNOLD P. This is an application in connection with an
alleged will of David Anthony Jones deceased, who was killed in Northern
Ireland while on a military patrol on March 16, 1978. He was fired upon
by unknown hands and died on the following day. He was in the company
of an officer and a warrant officer of his battalion, and to those two men
he made a declaration, and it was in these words: " If I don't make it,"
he said, " make sure Anne gets all my stuff." Anne was his fiancée; Anne
G   Mary Newport, as she then was; Anne Mannering, as she has now become;
and it is plain enough that if that was an effective will it was one which
contained a universal bequest of personalty in favour of Anne. The question whether it was an effective will depends upon whether there extended
to the deceased the privilege afforded by section 11 of the Wills Act 1837 to
make a nuncupative will in the sense of an oral testamentary declaration;
H   and in accordance with the language of the section, that depends upon
whether the right view is that the deceased was at the time of making that
testamentary declaration in " actual military service."
The evidence in the case includes this authoritative statement emana-
ting from an officer of the Ministry of Defence, that in 1969 a request was
made by the Northern Ireland authorities for the deployment of the armed
forces to assist the civil power in the maintenance of law and order in
Northern Ireland; and it was in pursuance of that request that the deceased's

The Year Books were probably the first kind of law reports. They were compiled in the period from approximately 1272–1535 and dealt with pleading and procedure. It is likely they were used as early textbooks by young lawyers and were probably written by students as guidelines in procedure and pleadings. In the main they dealt with civil cases.

Abridgements were a collection of cases from the Year Books. They were written by judges and lawyers, and for convenient reference the cases were grouped in subject-matter, rather than in date order. Some Abridgements were published, the most important and best known being by Fitzherbert (1516) and Brooke (1568).

Private reporting came into fashion when the Year Books were no longer written. The most notable of these reports were Plowden's Reports (1550–1580), Coke's Reports (1572–1616) and Burrow's Reports (1756–1772). The last named established a particular reputation for good reporting of judgments. The value of the private reports depends on the reputation of the reporter, and while many of them were regarded highly, others have no standing and judges have refused counsel permission to quote from them. It has been said of one reporter named Barnardiston, that he often slept through court cases and other reporters would write nonsense in his notebook, which he later printed.

Modern law reporting started when the Inns of Court created the Council of Law Reporting in 1865 to ensure a satisfactory standard of reporting of cases of legal significance. In 1870 the Incorporated Council of Law Reporting was established. The reporters, who are barristers, must present the report which is to be published, to the judge of the case who may revise the wording before publication.

The Council publishes the Law Reports and Weekly Law Reports. The latter were first published in 1953 and replaced the "Weekly Notes." The Weekly Law Reports are consolidated for each year and issued in volumes, so that at the end of a year, there are usually about three or four volumes of the reports.

Reporting of cases is not the monopoly of the Council and other companies and private organisations publish reports which have equal authority. The best known are the All England Law Reports, started in 1936, while reports from *The Times* are frequently cited in court.

Students should know how to refer to a law report. Cases are quoted, for example, as *Rapley* v. *Rapley* [1983] 1 W.L.R. 1069. The reference after the names of the parties means that a student must consult the first volume of the Weekly Law Reports of 1983 and at p. 1069 details of the case are reported. It would be an interesting exercise for students to look up some of the cases quoted and listed in this book. If your college or school does not have law reports in the library, you may find them in the nearest large public library. *Rapley* v. *Rapley* is referred to in this book on p. 269.

LEGISLATION

Legislation is law enacted by Parliament, and when an Act of Parliament, known as a statute, is passed it becomes the law of the land. (A recent Act is reproduced on p. 28.) A statute is superior to all sources of law and judges must enforce this law in the courts, even if it is contrary to an existing binding precedent. This supremacy of Parliament over all other sources of law is called the "Sovereignty of Parliament," and it means that Parliament may make laws which have to be enforced and cannot be challenged on the grounds that they are illegal. In the United States of America this is not so. The Constitution of the United States is very rigid and not easily changed, and the Supreme Court of the United States may rule that a law passed by the Senate is unconstitutional and illegal.

The Process of a Statute

Parliament consists of the House of Commons and the House of Lords, and a statute has to pass through a series of debates in both Houses before becoming law.

Approval of the House of Lords is not essential for measures dealing with finance. There is a set procedure which has to be followed and until this has been finally completed the "statute" is called a Bill (see below). The procedure which follows usually starts in the House of Commons before going to the Lords, but it may be reversed. For example, the Cheques Act 1992 was introduced in the House of Lords as a Private Bill by Lord Harmer-Nicholls.

1. First reading
The Bill is formally presented and there is little debate. The purpose is to inform members of the Bill's existence and to indicate that printed copies will be available.

2. Second reading

There is usually a debate on the general principles of the Bill. If the vote is in favour, the Bill goes to the next stage. It is not necessary to vote at this reading unless 20 members object.

3. The committee stage

The Bill is examined in detail. Each clause is debated and may be amended or even excluded. As the name suggests, the examination may be by a "select" or "standing" committee, or it may be discussed by the entire House acting as a committee. The examination at this stage is very important. Select committees and standing committees (20–50 members) are appointed on the basis of the political parties' numerical strength in the House of Commons.

4. The report stage

Its purpose is to inform the House of changes that have been made to the Bill and to give an opportunity for further discussion. The House may make additional amendments.

5. Third reading

Generally only verbal amendments to the Bill may be made at this stage. It now passes to the other House.

6. The House of Lords

The above procedure is repeated in the House of Lords, unless it started in this House, when it would pass to the Commons.

7. The Royal Assent

After a Bill has passed through Parliament, it does not become law until it has been signed or authorised by the Queen. The Assent is a formality, and by convention cannot be refused. Immediately the Royal Assent is given, the Act of Parliament becomes law, unless another starting date has been provided for in the Act.

A Bill lapses if it has not completed all the above stages by the time a session of Parliament has been ended by Prorogation, or when Parliament is dissolved for a general election. It may be introduced in another session of Parliament but the Bill must pass through all the stages once again.

An Act of Parliament is printed and may be purchased by the general public from Her Majesty's Stationery Office, or its agents.

On p. 28 is a reproduction of the Minors' Contract Act 1987.

Bills

A Bill is a draft of the provisions which are proposed to become law and be submitted to Parliament (see p. 24).

There are different types of Bills.

1. Public Bill

Public Bills are usually drafted by civil servant lawyers under the control of the Prime Minister. They may be introduced by the Government or by a private member, and they alter or amend the law for the country at large.

2. Private Member's Bill

A private member may introduce a Bill, although it is not likely to be successful in passing through the necessary stages, unless it is adopted by the Government. The opportunity to present a Private Member's Bill is limited and a ballot is held early in the session to decide the order in which members may introduce a Bill.

In February 1992 Andrew Hunter, M.P. for Basingstoke, introduced a Private Member's Bill which required sellers of timeshares to allow buyers a "cooling-off" period of 14 days, in case the buyers wish to change their minds. The Timeshare Act 1992, received the Royal Assent on March 16, 1992.

3. Private Bill

These are Bills for special interest or benefit of a person or persons. The most common presenters of these Bills are local authorities wishing to widen the scope of their activities or powers.

Codification and Consolidation

Codification entails bringing together all the existing legislation and case law into a restatement of the law. Codification may be of either the complete law of a country or a particular branch of law. The law of most continental countries is codified, but in this country and other common law countries (mainly the United States and Commonwealth countries) there is little codification. At the end of the nineteenth century there was an attempt to codify commercial law, and as a result there were enacted the Partnership Act 1890, the Sale of Goods Act 1893 and the Bills of Exchange Act 1882. It has been suggested that the law of contract would be a suitable area for codification, but it is unlikely to be so affected in the near future.

Consolidation occurs when all the provisions of several Acts of Parliament, dealing with a common topic, are brought together into one Act. It is becoming very popular because, although it does not alter the law, it makes it easier for lawyers and laymen to find. Areas of law which have recently been consolidated include company law, marriage, taxation and employment protection.

Interpretation of a Statute

It has been explained that Parliament is supreme, and that the courts cannot challenge the legality of a statute. The courts, however, do have some effect on the law created by legislation. An Act of Parliament may have been drafted badly, in that the words used may be ambiguous, or not clear in meaning or may not provide for every eventuality.

For example, if an Act was passed ordering "every dog to be destroyed" by a certain date, what would be the law relating to hounds or bitches? An owner of a bitch may contend that the law only concerns male animals of the canine species, and does not affect bitches. In such an event the dispute would go to the courts for the "legal" interpretation of the word "dog," as used in the Act.

It must be noted that it is the courts which usually interpret the meaning of statutes, not Parliament, although many Acts include an interpretation section on words and phrases used in the particular Act. In addition, the Interpretation Acts interpret many general words and terms that are used in Acts, unless a contrary intention appears. One example provides that "words in the singular shall include the plural and words in the plural shall include the singular."

When the courts have to interpret the wording of an Act, there are certain rules to follow, but it is left for the judge to decide which rule is appropriate to the particular case. The rules are as follows:

1. The literal rule
If the words used are clear and unambiguous, the judge will interpret the words in their ordinary, plain, grammatical meaning. In *Fisher* v. *Bell* (1961), the court followed this rule when deciding that "offering for sale" was plain English, and

ELIZABETH II   c. 13

Minors' Contracts Act 1987

1987 CHAPTER 13

An Act to amend the law relating to minors' contracts.
[9th April 1987]

BE IT ENACTED by the Queen's most Excellent Majesty, by and with the advice and consent of the Lords Spiritual and Temporal, and Commons, in this present Parliament assembled, and by the authority of the same, as follows:—

1. The following enactments shall not apply to any contract made by a minor after the commencement of this Act—

(a) the Infants Relief Act 1874 (which invalidates certain contracts made by minors and prohibits actions to enforce contracts ratified after majority); and

(b) section 5 of the Betting and Loans (Infants) Act 1892 (which invalidates contracts to repay loans advanced during minority).

Disapplication of Infants Relief Act 1874 etc.
1874 c. 62

1892 c. 4.

2. Where—

(a) a guarantee is given in respect of an obligation of a party to a contract made after the commencement of this Act, and

(b) the obligation is unenforceable against him (or he repudiates the contract) because he was a minor when the contract was made,

the guarantee shall not for that reason alone be unenforceable against the guarantor.

Guarantees.

3.—(1) Where—

(a) a person ("the plaintiff") has after the commencement of this Act entered into a contract with another ("the defendant"), and

Restitution.

2   c. **13**   *Minors' Contracts Act 1987*

   (b) the contract is unenforceable against the defendant (or he
       repudiates it) because he was a minor when the contract was
       made,

the court may, if it is just and equitable to do so, require the defendant to
transfer to the plaintiff any property acquired by the defendant under the
contract, or any property representing it.

(2) Nothing in this section shall be taken to prejudice any other remedy
available to the plaintiff.

4.—(1) In section 113 of the Consumer Credit Act 1974 (that Act not
to be evaded by use of security) in subsection (7)—

   (a) after the word "indemnity", in both places where it occurs, there
       shall be inserted "or guarantee";

   (b) after the words "minor, or" there shall be inserted "an indemnity
       is given in a case where he"; and

   (c) for the word "they" there shall be substituted "those
       obligations".

(2) The Infants Relief Act 1874 and the Betting and Loans (Infants) Act
1892 are hereby repealed (in accordance with section 1 of this Act).

5.—(1) This Act may be cited as the Minors' Contracts Act 1987.

(2) This Act shall come into force at the end of the period of two months
beginning with the date on which it is passed.

(3) This Act extends to England and Wales only.

(marginal notes:)
Consequential
amendment and
repeals.
1974 c. 39.

1874 c. 62.
1892 c. 4.

Short title,
commencement
and extent.

PRINTED IN ENGLAND BY J. A. DOLE
Controller and Chief Executive of Her Majesty's Stationery Office and
Queen's Printer of Acts of Parliament.

applied the meaning of this term which was generally used and understood in the law of contract. See p. 128 for details of the case.

2. The golden rule

This principle follows on from the literal rule, in that the plain, ordinary meaning of the words is taken, unless it would be absurd or repugnant to the law. In *Re Sigsworth* (1935), it was held that a man who murdered his mother could not benefit from her estate. The ordinary meaning of the word "issue" would have included the son, but as it would have been repugnant for a murderer to benefit from the estate of the person killed, the court deviated from the ordinary meaning of the word.

3. The mischief rule (the rule in Heydon's Case (1584))

In this rule, the courts try to discover the reason for the Act. The courts look for the defect, or the mischief which the Act was trying to remedy, and they then interpret the words accordingly.

Gardiner v. *Sevenoaks R.D.C.* (1950). An Act required film to be stored in premises under certain conditions. G. kept his film in a cave and claimed that as a cave was not "premises" he was not bound by the requirements of the Act. The court held that the purpose of the Act was the safety of workers or other persons and therefore the cave was "premises" for the requirements of the Act. The court looked for the mischief the Act was designed to protect.

4. The "ejusdem generis" rule

It is a principle of interpretation that where general words follow specific words, the general words must be applied to the meaning of the specific things. If an Act was worded "dogs, cats and other animals," the general words (and other animals) would have to be interpreted in the light of the specific words (dogs and cats). It would be obvious that the Act referred to domestic and not to wild animals.

Evans v. *Cross* (1938). The appellant was charged with ignoring a traffic sign. He claimed that a white line on the road was not a traffic sign for the purposes of the Act, which read, "... warning signposts, direction posts, signs or other devices." The court held that the general words (or other devices) must relate to the preceding words and in this case they did not.

5. The express mention of one thing implies the exclusion of another

If specific things are mentioned and not followed by general words, only these specific things are affected by the Act. A statute referred to "quarries and coal mines," and it was held that as there were no general words, the Act did not cover any kind of mine other than a coal mine.

If we look back at our hypothetical case of the dogs (see above), it can be seen that the literal rule and the golden rule would be unsuitable as the word "dog" has an ambiguous meaning.

If the mischief rule was applied, and it was shown that the reason for the Act was to stop dogs fouling the footpaths or pavements, or to stop the spread of rabies, then the interpretation might be all dogs of the species, whether they be male or female.

In addition to the rules of interpretation, the courts may use external aids such as:

(a)   the Oxford English Dictionary;
(b)   textbooks;
(c)   Law Commission Reports;
(d)   guidelines in the Act (but not margin notes);
(e)   delegated legislation; and
(f)   Hansard. It was a rule that judges may not refer to Hansard (a publication which records the debates in Parliament) to help interpret a statute. However, the House of Lords in 1992, reversing a decision of the Court of Appeal which dealt with a tax dispute with the Inland Revenue, referred to Hansard before reaching their decision.

DELEGATED LEGISLATION

1. What is delegated legislation?

Parliament may give Ministers, Government departments and other bodies the power to make laws which are binding on the community and the courts. Generally, Parliament lays down the framework of the law in an enabling Act, and then delegates to subordinates the authority to make laws and rules for specific purposes within the Act. This form of legislation is increasing every year and has become a very important source of law.

2. Why is there a need for delegated legislation?

(a) Because of the increasing volume of legislation, Parliament does not have the time to consider and debate every small detail needed for the routine administration of an Act.

(b) In an emergency, Parliament may not have the time to deal with the situation, or in fact may not be in session.

(c) Although Parliament has passed a statute, the members may not have the technical expertise or local knowledge to deal with the necessary details, so they are delegated to experts.

(d) It is a difficult procedure for Parliament to amend a statute. Delegated legislation is more flexible and elastic, and if experience shows that a regulation or procedure is not achieving its purpose, or is inappropriate to the aims of the statute, it can easily be amended or revoked.

3. Who has the power to make delegated legislation?

(a) Orders in Council

The Government, usually in times of emergency, may be given the power to make laws in this way. Such an Order requires a meeting of the Privy Council and the signature of the Queen.

(b) Ministers of the Crown

Ministers are given the power to make rules and Orders under statutes which affect their own departments. For example, the Minister responsible for transport has the power to change the maximum speeds allowed on motorways and roads.

(c) Bye-laws

Parliament gives power to local authorities and certain other public and nationalised bodies to make laws within the scope of their own areas of activity. These laws have to be approved by central government.

4. Publication

All delegated legislation is technically made public by "statutory instrument," but this term usually refers to rules and Orders made by Ministers of the Crown.

Control of Delegated Legislation

There are certain safeguards which ensure that delegated legislation is controlled.

(a) Parliament has the right to inspect every statutory instrument, and has a select committee to scrutinise certain legislation considered likely to be oppressive. Parliament also has the ultimate safeguard, in that it may revoke or rescind the delegated power.

(b) The courts may declare a statutory instrument to be *ultra vires* and void. *Ultra vires* means "beyond the power," and if a court considers that the statutory instrument has gone outside the scope of the Act under which it was issued, it may make such a declaration. In *Att.-Gen.* v. *Fulham Corpn.* (1921) an Act allowed the Corporation to build a wash-house, but the Corporation decided to open a laundry. The court held that it was *"ultra vires"* the Act, and issued an injunction restraining the Corporation. In *Bromley L.B.C.* v. *Greater London Council* (1982), the Transport (London) Act 1969 provided that the G.L.C. had a general duty for the provision of integrated, efficient and economic transport facilities and services for Greater London. The G.L.C. reduced fares by 25 per cent. and required London boroughs to increase rates to pay for the cost. Bromley L.B.C. claimed that this was invalid and the House of Lords agreed that the action of the G.L.C. was *ultra vires* the 1969 Act.

(c) Before certain delegated legislation may be put into effect, it is necessary to have a public inquiry, so that public opinion may be tested, and an opportunity given to those who wish to object to the proposed legislation to air their misgivings.

EUROPEAN COMMUNITY LAW

A completely new source of English law was created when Parliament passed the European Communities Act 1972. Section 2(1) of the Act provides that:

"All such rights, powers, liabilities, obligations and restrictions from time to time created or arising by or under the Treaties, and all such remedies and procedures from time to time provided for by or under the Treaties, as in accordance with the treaties are without further enactment to be given legal effect or used in the United Kingdom shall be recognised and available in law, and be inforced, allowed and followed accordingly...."

The effect of this section is that English courts (and all United Kingdom courts) have to recognise E.C. law, whether it comes directly from treaties or other Community legislation.

As soon as the 1972 Act became law, some aspects of English law were changed to bring them into line with European Community law. For example, certain principles of our company law were immediately amended, and certain sections of the Companies Act 1980 were the direct result of an E.C. directive (see below).

There are several institutions to implement the work of the European Community, the main institutions being:

(a) The European Parliament

The Parliament consists of representatives (Members of the European Parliament) from all the Member States, but the number of M.E.P.s from each State varies; for example, Germany, France, Italy and the United Kingdom have more M.E.P.s than some of the smaller countries. Elections for the Parliament are held simultaneously every five years in the individual States to appoint their representatives.

The Parliament has some control over the Community's budget and some administrative powers, but mainly it has an advisory function. It may, for example, advise the Commission (see below) on important policy matters. It does, however, have the power to demand the resignation of the Commission.

(b) The Council of Ministers

It consists of one member from each Member State, although again the voting rights are not equal for each State. The political interests of the Member States are represented in the Council. Many of the laws produced by the Commission may only be executed with the consent of the Council.

(c) The Commission

It has 17 members representing all Member States, who are appointed by the Council for their independence and competence. A President of the Commission is elected by the Member States.

The Commissioners work full-time to ensure the provisions of the Community are carried out and to exercise powers given to it by the Council.

It is the Commission alone which instigates and proposes Community legislation.

(d) The European Court of Justice

The Court consists of one judge from each State and a second judge from another State on a rotating basis.

The main functions of the Court are:

(a) to ensure that the law of the Treaty is followed;
(b) to decide cases which allege breaches of the Treaty by Member States. For example, the U.K. in breach of a Directive on equal pay;
(c) to rule on the interpretation of Community law, when asked to do so by a Member State.

Community legislation is enacted in the form of regulations, decisions and directives.

1. Regulations

A regulation is of general application in all Member States and, in theory, it is binding in this country without reference to Parliament. It is usual, however, for there to be some legislative action, if only to repeal law which is contrary to the regulation.

Re Tachographs: E.C. Commission v. United Kingdom (1979)

A Council Regulation provided that tachography (mechanical recording equipment) should be installed in all road vehicles used for the carriage of goods. The United Kingdom Government decided not to implement the regulation but left the road haulage industry to introduce the equipment on a voluntary basis only. The Commission referred the matter to the European Court of Justice and it was held that:

(a) the Regulation provided that the Member States shall adopt the law, and
(b) the Treaty provides that a regulation shall be binding in its entirety on the Member States.

2. Decisions

A decision has a more specific application, in that it may be addressed to a State or corporation, and is binding only on that State or corporation. It comes into effect immediately, but may need legislative action by the Member State.

3. Directives

A directive is binding on all Member States, but the States must bring it into being by whatever means they wish within a set time limit. In the United Kingdom it is usually issued by statutory instrument.

A 1975 Directive prescribed that States define how equal pay for equal work could be achieved. The U.K. omitted to do this within the time limit and the European Court of Justice held the U.K. Government to be in breach of the Treaty, *European Commission* v. *United Kingdom* (1982).

The Consumer Protection Act 1987 implemented an E.C. Directive of July 1985 (see p. 172).

European Community law has also had an effect on the courts and on case law. Any court from which there is no appeal (House of Lords) dealing with a case requiring an interpretation of a European treaty must suspend the case and submit it to the European Court for a ruling. Decisions of the European Court must be accepted, but it is the Member States' courts which must enforce them.

It is also probable that European law affects precedent, in that if the law is contrary to a binding precedent of English law, a lower court may ignore precedent and give a decision based on the Community law. In a Court of Appeal case Lord Denning discussed the effect of the Treaty of Rome upon English law.

> "The Treaty does not touch any of the matters which concern solely England and the people in it. They are not affected by the Treaty. But when we come to matters with a European element the Treaty is like an incoming tide. It flows into the estuaries and up the rivers. It cannot be held back. Parliament has declared that the Treaty is henceforward to be part of our law. It is equal in force to any statute...."

SUBSIDIARY SOURCES OF LAW

As was explained earlier, the following sources have little impact in modern times, but are still, technically, sources of law.

Local Customs

Custom is the origin of common law. From the earliest days of William the Conqueror's reign, judges have tried to discover existing customs and absorb them into the common system of law. Although custom has now become part of the formal legal system, in certain areas of England customs are still recognised and enforced by the courts. These exceptional cases only apply to the particular area in which the custom exists, and a person claiming the right of custom (usually the defendant) will have to prove that the following conditions apply:

1. The custom existed since "time immemorial"
"Time Immemorial" is fixed at 1189, which is the end of Henry II's reign. It is only necessary to claim that the custom existed beyond living memory, but if the other party can show that the custom was first used after 1189, or could not have reasonably existed at that date, the claim will not be upheld. In *Bryant* v. *Foot* (1868) a clergyman claimed that by custom he should be paid 13 shillings (65p) for every marriage he performed. He proved that the fee had been paid for nearly 50 years, but the court held that the fee would obviously have been unreasonable in 1189, and would not have existed.

2. It must be reasonable

3. It only applies to the particular locality
Fishermen in Grimsby could not claim a custom established for the fishermen of Walmer, in Kent.

4. It must not be contrary to a statute, or any basic principle of common law

5. It must have been exercised continuously
The custom does not have to have been exercised at all times, but it must have been possible to exercise the custom had the inhabitants of the locality wished to do so.

6. It must be exercised as a right
The custom must be used peaceably and openly. This means it must not be exercised with force, or in secret, or by permission.

Books of Authority

If a precedent cannot be found to cover an aspect of law, judges may refer to legal textbooks for help. In the past, only works of dead writers carried the requisite authority but in recent years judges have taken notice of the opinions of living writers.

Examples of old works which have been accepted as books of authority are:

> Glanvill, *Tractatus de legibus et consuetudinibus regni Angliae*;
> Coke, *Institutes of the Laws of England*;
> Blackstone, *Commentaries on the Laws of England*.

Works of modern authors which have been quoted or discussed in court include:

> Cheshire, *Modern Law of Real Property*;
> Cheshire and Fifoot, *Law of Contract*.

REVISION TEST

1. Name the two main sources of English law.

2. Is the House of Lords bound by its own previous decisions?

3. What is the *ratio decidendi* of a judge's decision?

4. Name three advantages of judicial precedent.

5. Name three disadvantages of judicial precedent.

6. Name the stages of a Bill's passage through Parliament.

7. Name the three types of Bills.

8. Name three bodies which have the power to make delegated legislation.

9. Give three reasons for the need for delegated legislation.

10. Name three ways by which E.C. legislation is enacted.

SPECIMEN EXAMINATION QUESTIONS

1. Describe how the system of binding precedent operates, and explain the importance of an accurate system of law reporting.

2. What is delegated legislation?
    Explain who has the power to make such legislation, and how and why it is issued.
    Discuss the advantages and disadvantages of this source of law.

3. The House of Lords may overrule previous decisions of other courts and its own previous decisions.

    (a) Do any other courts have these powers within the legal system?
    (b) What is "overruling," and how does it differ from "reversing" a decision?
    (c) Are there other ways in which a precedent may be avoided?

4. Explain the ways a judge may interpret a statute, and outline the methods and materials which may, and may not, be used.

5. What are the main sources of English law and how have they been affected by membership of the European Community?

SUGGESTED COURSEWORK TITLES

Describe how the system of judicial precedent (case law) operates. Discuss the advantages and disadvantages of the system.

What is meant by delegated legislation? Discuss the advantages and disadvantages of such legislation. Do you think the controls on delegated legislation are effective?

Chapter 3
The Administration of the Law

THE COURTS

It is now necessary to examine the structure of the courts and to consider their constitution and the jurisdiction which they exercise. The civil courts will be dealt with first, followed by the criminal courts and, finally, by courts which lie outside the English system.

THE CIVIL COURTS

The House of Lords

As a court of law, the House of Lords is the highest and final court of appeal in civil cases for the whole of the United Kingdom. In theory an appeal is to the whole House, but it is only the "Law Lords" who hear appeals. The ordinary Lords or peers of the realm do not take part in this process of the law.

1. Jurisdiction
The House of Lords hears appeals from the Court of Appeal and, in certain cases, direct from the High Court. Appeals from the Court of Appeal may only be made by leave of either that court, or the House of Lords. The Administration of Justice Act 1969 provided that, if all parties agree, in cases concerning the interpretation of a statute (or on a point of law) which was subject to a binding precedent, the appeal could go direct from the High Court to the House of Lords, thereby "leap-frogging" the Court of Appeal.

2. Constitution

Appeals are heard by a committee of not less than three from the following:

- (a)   The Lord Chancellor.
- (b)   The Lords of Appeal in Ordinary—the "Law Lords." They are life peers who have been barristers for at least 15 years. They are usually appointed after sitting as Lords Justices of Appeal in the Court of Appeal.
- (c)   Peers who have held high judicial office (*e.g.* previous Lord Chancellors).

The Court of Appeal (Civil Division)

1. Jurisdiction

The court may hear appeals from the county court and the High Court on matters of law or fact. Appeals may also be heard on questions of law from the many administrative tribunals, such as the Restrictive Practices Court and the Lands Tribunal.

Appeals may be allowed or dismissed, or the court may order a new trial. The majority of appeals are on points of law, but appeals may dispute the judges' awards of damages or costs.

2. Constitution

Appeals are heard by a court consisting of not less than three of the following:

- (a)   The Lord Chancellor.
- (b)   The Lord Chief Justice.
- (c)   The President of the Family Division of the High Court.
- (d)   The Lords of Appeal in Ordinary (the Law Lords).
- (e)   The Master of the Rolls.
- (f)   The Lords Justices of Appeal.

As a general rule the appeals are only heard by a court consisting of the Master of the Rolls and the Lords Justices of Appeal. The usual number of judges for each case is three, but several divisions of the court may sit at the same time. In cases of great legal importance, five or more judges may sit in what is called a full court.

A Lord Justice of Appeal is appointed by the Queen on the advice of the Prime Minister. He must have been a barrister for 15 years, and usually a High Court judge for many years.

High Court of Justice

This court has unlimited civil jurisdiction and hears appeals from inferior courts (civil and criminal) and tribunals. The work of the High Court is divided amongst the following three divisions:

- (a) The Queen's Bench Division.
- (b) The Chancery Division.
- (c) The Family Division.

Each division has jurisdiction to hear any High Court action, but for administrative convenience the divisions specialise in specific areas of work.

Constitution

The divisions consist of a head or president and High Court judges or puisne judges (pronounced pewny). In addition, cases may be heard before a judge or former judge of the Court of Appeal, a circuit judge, a recorder or a former High Court judge. The judges are appointed by the Queen on the recommendation of the Lord Chancellor, and must have been barristers for at least 10 years. The judges usually sit alone but in the divisional courts there must be at least two judges. The usual or ordinary High Court cases have original jurisdiction, which means that it is the first time the case has appeared before the courts. The divisional courts, in the main, have appellate jurisdiction and hear appeals from inferior or lower courts.

The Queen's Bench Division

1. Jurisdiction

(a) Ordinary court

This division hears more cases than either of the other divisions, and it has the widest jurisdiction, dealing with all matters not covered by the other divisions, the majority of them being actions in tort and contract.

The Administration of Justice Act 1970 created two courts as part of the Queen's Bench Division.

- (a) The Admiralty Court hears cases concerned with the Admiralty, and acts as a Prize Court.
- (b) The Commercial Court hears cases on commercial matters, such as banking and insurance.

(b) *Appellate court*

Appeals are heard by the Divisional Court from certain administrative tribunals, and from solicitors on appeal from the Disciplinary Committee of the Law Society.

The Queen's Bench Divisional Court also has jurisdiction to hear applications for the writ of habeas corpus, and the orders of *certiorari*, *mandamus* and prohibition (see p. 117).

2. Constitution

The head of the Queen's Bench Division is the Lord Chief Justice, although his work is mostly concerned with hearing criminal appeals. The majority of the work is heard by approximately 50 puisne judges.

The Chancery Division

1. Jurisdiction

(a) *Ordinary court*

It hears cases concerning trusts, property, company law, partnerships, winding up of companies and bankruptcy, mortgages, taxation, administration of estates of deceased persons and contentious probate cases.

(b) *Appellate court*

Appeals from the Commissioners of Inland Revenue are heard by a single judge.

The Divisional Court may hear appeals from the county court on certain bankruptcy and land registration matters.

2. Constitution

The nominal head of the Chancery Division is the Lord Chancellor, but he never sits. The Vice-Chancellor is the working head of the division and there are usually 12 puisne judges.

The Family Division

1. Jurisdiction

(a) *Ordinary court*

It hears cases dealing with:

    (a)   the validity and the breakdown of marriage and all relevant matters, such as the custody of children and the distribution of property.

(b) non-contentious probate matters.
(c) applications in respect of guardianship and wardship of minors, legitimation, adoption and disputes between spouses over title to property.

(b) Appellate court
The divisional court of the Family Division hears appeals on matrimonial and family matters from the county court and the magistrates' courts.

2. Constitution
The Family Division is headed by a president, and there are approximately 16 puisne judges.

The County Court

The county courts were set up in 1846 to provide an opportunity for claims to be settled cheaply, although it is still likely to prove expensive if a person engages the help of lawyers. It is not expensive to start an action if you conduct your own case and, with straightforward matters for small amounts, the ordinary lay person is encouraged to do so, particularly where consumer goods are involved. For small claims under £1000 the court fees are not excessive and the person winning the case is allowed to add these fees to the amount claimed. An excellent booklet and pamphlets are available from the offices of the county courts which explain the necessary steps which must be taken to sue and defend actions without a solicitor (see p. 47).

There are about 270 county courts in England and Wales in which approximately three-quarters of all civil actions start. These figures give some indication of the courts' importance within the administration of civil cases.

Each court has a district judge responsible for the administration and day-to-day running of the court and its office. In addition to this administrative function, the district judge may hear small claims for less than £1,000 (see below) and may also try any action in the county court for claims which do not exceed £5,000.

The district judge usually acts as arbitrator in the small claims court, although it may be a circuit judge, and procedure in these cases is very informal. The judge will wear normal dress (not in robes or wig) and the hearing may be in private. If one party fails to appear the arbitrator may make an award upon hearing the other party.

1. Jurisdiction

The county courts deal with most civil disputes, but their jurisdiction is governed by two factors:

(a) Locality

Actions should be started in the county court for the district in which the defendant lives or carries on business.

(b) Finance

The jurisdiction of the court, in many matters, is limited to the size of the claim. The amounts may change, particularly in times of inflation, so check for the current amounts if you intend going to court, or before taking an examination in law.

The court deals with the same sort of claims and disputes as the High Court, depending on the amount claimed, with the majority of its work in the following areas:

    (a)   Actions for claims in contract and tort may commence in a county court or the High Court, subject to the following:

        (i) Actions for claims arising from personal injury for less than £50,000 must start in a county court;

       (ii) Actions for claims other than personal injury may start in the High Court or a county court, subject to the following general rules:

Actions for claims which seem likely to be less than £25,000 shall be tried in a county court;

Actions where the claim is £50,000 or more shall be tried in the High Court.

Actions for claims between these amounts may be tried in either court depending on the following criteria.

        (i) The case raises matters of importance of general public interest.

       (ii) The complexity of the legal issues, facts or procedures.

      (iii) Which court is likely to produce a more speedy trial of action.

    (b)   Equity matters such as trusts and mortgages.

    (c)   Actions concerning the title to land or possession of land.

(d) Winding up of companies.
(e) Bankruptcy matters. This jurisdiction only applies to certain courts outside London.
(f) Admiralty matters.
(g) Probate disputes where the estate is not very large.
(h) Undefended divorce cases.
(i) Matters concerning the adoption, guardianship and legitimacy of children.
(j) Actions in respect of extortionate credit agreements under section 139 of the Consumer Credit Act 1974.

The above list is not complete, but covers the principal areas of the court's work. The court may hear claims in excess of the stipulated amounts, if both parties agree.

2. Constitution

County court judges are appointed by the Queen on the recommendations of the Lord Chancellor. The country is divided into circuits in which there are approximately 270 county courts. Each circuit has one or more judges. The circuit judge, as he is designated, travels around hearing cases in the county courts in the circuit or district.

In addition to the circuit judges, recorders, district judges and judges of the High Court and Court of Appeal, if they agree, may sit in any circuit as directed by the Lord Chancellor.

A circuit judge may also hear criminal cases in the Crown Court. As was stated earlier, each circuit has a district judge who acts as clerk to the court. The district judge must have a seven year "general qualification" (which is a right of audience in relation to any class of proceedings in any part of the Supreme Court or all proceedings in a county court or magistrates' court).

Magistrates' courts and the Crown Court also have civil jurisdiction as will be shown when these courts are discussed later.

3. Starting an action for a small claim in the county court

All actions must start by the plaintiff (the person making the claim) going to the county court office and filling in a form called a "request," (see p. 48) for the court to prepare the summons, which is the document served on the defendant giving notice of the claim.

At the same time the plaintiff must supply written details of the claim. It need not be in great detail, but should be sufficient

Request for Issue of Default Summons

Case Number

- Please read the notes over the page before filling in this form

Summons in form: N1 ☐

N2 ☐

Service by: Post ☐

Plaintiff('s solr) ☐

1 Plaintiff's full name address

2 Name and address for service and payment
(if different from above)
Ref/Tel No.

- Please be careful when filling in the request form. Do not write outside the boxes.

- Type or write in BLOCK CAPITALS using **black ink**.

- If the details of the claim are on a separate sheet you must also give the court a copy for each defendant.

3 Defendant's Name address

- You can get help to complete this form and information about court procedures at any county court office or citizens' advice bureau.

4 What the claim is for

Give brief description of the type of claim

5 Particulars of the plaintiff's claim

6

Plaintiff's claim

Court fee

Solicitor's costs

Total amount

for court use Issued on

8 Arbitration (small claims procedure)

Any defended claim for £1000 or less will be automatically dealt with by arbitration. If you do not want the claim to be dealt with by arbitration, you will have to apply to the court. The court office can give you more details.

If the claim is for more than £1000 and you would like it to be dealt with by arbitration, please tick this box ☐

7 Signed

Plaintiff('s solicitor)
(or see enclosed particulars of claim)

N201 Request for default summons (Order 3, rule 3(1))

Printed in the U.K for H.M.S.O. 10/91 Dd.8252348 C8000 38806 G4340

Notes

1 Plaintiff *the person making the claim*
Fill in the plaintiff's full name and address or place of business. If the plaintiff is:
- **a company registered under the Companies Act 1985,** give the address of the registered office and describe it as such.
- **a person trading in a name other than his own,** give his own name followed by the words 'trading as' and the name under which he trades.
- **two or more co-partners suing in the name of their firm,** 'A Firm'.
- **an assignee,** say so and give the name, address and occupation of the assignor.
- **a minor required to sue by next friend,** state this, and give the full names, address or place of business, and occupation of next friend. You will also need to complete and send in Form N235 (which you can get from the court office).
- **suing in a representative capacity,** say in what capacity.

2 Address for service and payment
If this request is completed by a solicitor or by your legal department, the name, address and reference of the solicitor or legal department should be in Box 2. The court will use this address for sending documents to you (service). (If the address is the same as shown at Box 1, please write 'as above' in Box 2).
- A plaintiff who is not represented by a solicitor or legal **department must not use Box 2** except for an address to which payment may be made. In this case you must delete the word 'service' in the title to Box (2).

3 Defendant *the person against whom the claim is made*
Fill in the defendant's surname and (where known) his or her initials or names in full. **It is essential that the defendant should be identified as fully and as accurately as possible.** Also give the defendant's address or place of business (if the owner of a business). Say whether defendant is male or female and, if under 18, state 'minor'. If the defendant is:
- **a company registered under the Companies Act 1985,** the address given can be the registered office of the company (you must describe it as such) or its place of business. If the summons is not sent to the registered office, there is a risk that it will not come to the notice of an appropriate person in the company. As a result, the court may be asked to set aside any judgment or order that has been made. **For fixed amount cases only** - Bear in mind that if the company you are suing defends the case, the case will automatically be transferred to his local court. If the registered office and place of business are not in the same court area, you may decide to choose the address which is most convenient to you.
- **a person trading in a name other than his own** who is sued under that name, add 'A Trading Name'.
- **two or more co-partners** sued in the name of their firm, add 'A Firm'.
- **sued in a representative capacity,** say in what capacity.

4 What the claim is for
Put a brief description of your claim in the box (eg price of goods sold and delivered, work done, money due under an agreement).

5 Particulars of your claim
Give a brief statement of the facts of your claim and the amount for which you are suing. Include any relevant dates and sufficient details so that the defendant understands what your claim is for. He is entitled to ask for further details. If there is not enough space or the details of your claim are too complicated, you should enclose a separate sheet for the court and a copy for each defendant. The court can help you in setting out your particulars of claim.

6 Amount claimed
Fill in the total amount you are claiming. The court fee and solicitor's costs are based on this and you should enter these too. A leaflet setting out the current fees is available from the court

7 Signature
The person filling in the form should sign and date it, unless enclosing separate details of claim (in which case the enclosed sheets should be signed).

8 Arbitration (small claims procedure)
Any defended claim for £1000 or less will be automatically dealt with by arbitration (small claims procedure). If the claim is for more than £1000 and you would like it to be dealt with by arbitration, you may include such a request in your particulars of claim. (Solicitor's costs and the grounds for setting aside an arbitrator's award are strictly limited.)

9 Personal injury claims
In these cases you must include a medical report for the court and for each defendant. If you are also claiming special damages (eg loss of income, medical expenses etc) an up to date statement, to include details of loss of any future expenses or losses, must also be included for the court and for each defendant. If you cannot provide these you should apply to the court for directions.

10 Unliquidated claims for more than £5000
If your claim is not for a fixed amount and you expect to recover more than £5000 (excluding interest and costs), you must state this in your particulars of claim.

11 Where to send the summons
- **If the summons is for a fixed amount,**
  you can ask any county court in England and Wales to issue the summons but you will usually choose your local court or the court for the area where the defendant lives or carries on business. Bear in mind that if the person you are suing defends the case, the case will automatically be transferred to the defendant's local court.
- **For a personal injury or other unliquidated claim,** you may prefer to choose the court where the cause of action arose. The case will not be automatically transferred if a defence is filed.

To be completed by the court	
Served on:	
By posting on:	
Officer:	

Further information on how to issue a default summons and what happens after issue can be obtained from any county court office.

to enable the defendant (the person being sued) to know the reason for the claim and for how much.

The defendant has 14 days from the time of serving the summons to either:

(a)   pay the claim, or
(b)   make an admission with an offer to pay, or
(c)   make a defence or counterclaim.

If the defendant does none of these within the 14-day period, the plaintiff is entitled to have judgment entered for the claim.

Should a defence be made, details are sent to the plaintiff with a date for a preliminary hearing, or the date of the trial or arbitration.

A defended money claim for £1,000 or less is automatically referred to arbitration, (see below) and no solicitors' costs are allowed. In such cases a pre-trial review is fixed by the district judge. Its purpose is to settle the matter privately, and in many cases the district judge is able to settle matters without arbitration. Should the defendant not attend the pre-trial the plaintiff may obtain judgment after proving the claim, (*e.g.* showing documents or invoices).

If the claim is over £1,000 and the plaintiff has asked for arbitration, the application is normally dealt with by the district judge at the pre-trial, unless the defendant asks that a judge should decide the case.

4. Arbitration

If both parties agree to arbitration, or it is a small claim for £1,000 or less, a judge or district judge usually acts as arbitrator, and no fees are payable. If special knowledge is required the parties may nominate any suitable person as arbitrator.

Unless the court decides otherwise the following rules apply:

(a)   The hearings are informal and strict rules of evidence do not apply.
(b)   The arbitrator may use any method to allow both parties to present their case.
(c)   If one party is absent the arbitrator may make an award to the other party present.
(d)   The arbitrator may call for an expert to report on the matter in dispute.
(e)   Costs of the action are at the discretion of the arbitrator. No solicitors' costs are allowed in disputes of £1,000 or less, except for:

    (i)   costs shown on the summons,
    (ii) costs to enforce the award,
    (iii) costs incurred by the unreasonable conduct of the
          opposite party with regard to the proceedings or
          the claim.

Changes to the rules have come into force in 1992 which are designed to encourage more claimants to use the small claims procedure in the county courts. The changes include simplifying the wording of the rules used in the court; allowing the district judge to help the parties by putting questions to them; explaining legal terms and stating the reasons for the decision. In addition, there is the right for a claimant to be represented by non-lawyers, such as friends, relatives or voluntary advice workers. Previously a non-lawyer could only present a claimant's case if the district judge gave permission.

System of Appeal through the Civil Courts

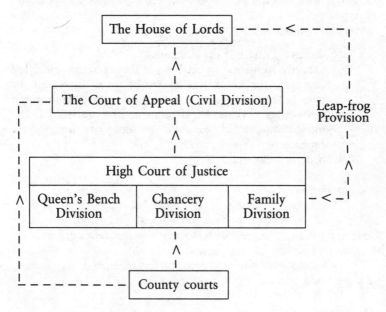

THE CRIMINAL COURTS
The House of Lords

The court hears appeals from the Court of Appeal (Criminal Division) and the Divisional Court of the Queen's Bench provided that these courts certify that a point of law of general public importance is involved, and leave to appeal has been granted by these courts or by the House of Lords.

The Court of Appeal (Criminal Division)

1. Jurisdiction

The Court hears appeals against decisions of the Crown Court by persons convicted on indictment, or by persons convicted by a magistrates' court but sentenced by the Crown Court. Appeals against conviction on matters of law may be made as of right, but only with leave of the court for other reasons.

Appeals against sentence may only be made by leave of the court. Should the Court of Appeal refuse to grant leave to hear an appeal, the convicted person may appeal to the Home Secretary, who has the power to refer the case back to the Court of Appeal.

The Court has the power to:

(a) dismiss ("quash") the decision,
(b) vary the sentence by making it longer or shorter (for example, the court has in recent years increased an over-lenient sentence in a case of incest from three years to six years imprisonment, and varied an 18-month suspended sentence to one of three years probation),
(c) order a new trial.

2. Constitution

The Lord Chief Justice is the head of this court, and in addition to the Lords Justices of Appeal, judges of the High Court (in practice, judges of the Queen's Bench Division) may sit if asked by the Lord Chief Justice.

The court must consist of at least three judges, but may consist of higher odd numbers (*e.g.* five or seven).

The Crown Court

The Courts Act 1971 abolished the courts of assize and quarter sessions, the Crown Courts at Liverpool and Manchester, and the Central Criminal Court in London, and established the Crown Court as a single court to carry out the work previously administered by these courts. The Act, however, provided that when the Crown Court sits in London, it shall be named the Central Criminal Court, or as it is traditionally called, "The Old Bailey."

The old courts, in the main, heard cases which were committed in the towns or districts in which the courts were situated, but the jurisdiction of the Crown Court is not so limited and its business may be carried out anywhere.

1. Jurisdiction

The Courts Act 1971, which created the Crown Court, provided that it shall be a superior court of record and will deal with:

- (a) all cases on indictment, wherever committed,
- (b) hear appeals from the magistrates' court against conviction or sentence,
- (c) pass sentence on cases where the accused has been found guilty by the magistrates but the lower court considers that they do not have the jurisdiction to pass the appropriate sentence,
- (d) conduct certain civil work, previously carried out by the quarter sessions, such as dealing with appeals over licensing.

2. Constitution

Judges of the Crown Court are as follows:

(a) All judges of the High Court

The Lord Chancellor may request a judge of the Court of Appeal to sit in the court, when he shall be regarded as a judge of the High Court.

(b) Circuit judges

They are appointed by the Queen, on the recommendation of the Lord Chancellor. The latter may remove them from office on grounds of incapacity or misbehaviour. Circuit judges are appointed from recorders of at least five years' standing, or from barristers of at least 10 years' standing. It should be noted that solicitors may be appointed as recorders and therefore this Act provides for the appointment of solicitors as High Court judges.

In addition to the above appointments, many persons holding judicial offices, such as all county court judges, recorders and chairmen of certain quarter sessions, became circuit judges when the Act came into operation on January 1, 1972. Circuit judges are full-time appointees, but they must retire at the age of 72, although the Lord Chancellor may allow them to continue in office until the age of 75. The jurisdiction of circuit judges is both criminal and civil (see the county courts, p. 47).

(c) Recorders

They are appointed by the Queen on the recommendation of the Lord Chancellor, who may remove them from office on grounds of incapacity, misbehaviour or failure to satisfy the requirements of the terms of appointment. Recorders must retire at the age of 72.

Recorders, who are part-time judges, must be barristers or solicitors of 10 years' standing. Their appointment, which is on a temporary basis, states the period and frequency of their duties. Although recorders are primarily concerned with criminal cases, they have authority to sit as county court judges.

(d) Justices of the peace

Not less than two, and not more than four justices of the peace must sit with the judge when hearing appeals, or when a convicted person has been committed to the Crown Court for sentence. The same constitution of judge and justices has jurisdiction to hear any case before the Crown Court.

3. The distribution of crown court business

Cities and towns (known as court centres) in which the High Court and Crown Court sit are divided into three tiers.

(a) First tier

There are 24 court centres which deal with criminal and civil work, and the cases are tried by High Court judges and circuit judges.

(b) Second tier

There are 19 court centres which deal with criminal work only, and the cases are tried by High Court judges and circuit judges.

The Crown Court. *From left to right*, the judge, clerk of the court, jury, senior counsel, junior counsel, solicitors, defendant, public gallery. *Foreground*, the Press.

(c) Third tier

There are 46 court centres which deal with criminal work only, and the cases are tried by circuit judges.

The work of the Court has been distributed amongst the various judges on the basis of the class of offence. For the purpose of the trial, offences have been divided into four classes.

Class 1 contains serious offences, tried by a High Court judge, and includes offences which carry the death sentence, treason, murder, genocide, and offences against the Official Secrets Act 1911, s.1. Murder may be tried before a circuit judge.

Class 2 offences are tried by a High Court judge, unless the case is released by the authority of a presiding judge for trial by a circuit judge. A presiding judge is a High Court judge who has the responsibility for the distribution of the judges in a given circuit. The offences in this class include manslaughter, rape, sexual intercourse with a girl under 13, sedition, mutiny and piracy.

Class 3 offences may be tried by a High Court judge, a circuit judge or recorder. The class includes all indictable offences, other than those allocated as Class 1, 2 or 4. (An indictment is a written accusation that a person has committed a crime. Indictable offences are generally the more serious crimes.)

Class 4 offences may be tried by a High Court judge, circuit judge or a recorder, but cases are usually listed for trial by a recorder. Offences in this class include causing death by dangerous driving, causing grievous bodily harm, robbery and burglary, as well as all offences which may be tried either summarily or on indictment.

All cases, with the exception of appeals and persons committed for sentence, are tried by a judge sitting alone, and before a jury.

The Magistrates' Court

The magistrates' courts deal with about 99 per cent. of all criminal cases. This percentage gives an indication of the volume of work of the court and its importance in the legal system. There is a magistrates' court in every county and in most boroughs.

1. Jurisdiction

The court has three main criminal functions:

(a) A court of petty sessions

This deals with minor offences that may be tried summarily, and carry a maximum penalty of not more than six months' imprisonment and/or a fine. With offences that may be triable either way (summarily or on indictment) the limit is £5,000. A summary offence means that the magistrates have power to hear the case without sending it for trial to the Crown Court. Examples of summary offences are drunkenness, minor motoring offences such as speeding, not obeying road signs and unauthorised parking, and riding a bicycle without lights after dark. A defendant in such cases may plead guilty by post, and need not attend the court.

(b) A court of preliminary hearing or examination

Persons accused of indictable offences are subject to an inquiry by the court to see if there is a case to be sent to the Crown Court for trial by jury. The court does not try or prejudge the case, but considers if the prosecution's evidence is sufficient for the court to decide that there is, on the face of it, a case to answer. If the court decides there is no evidence to support the prosecution's claim, the defendant is dismissed, but if the court considers otherwise, the defendant is committed for trial to the Crown Court.

(c) The youth court

When children (10–14 years) and young persons (14–17 years) are charged with a crime (other than homicide) they are brought before this special magistrates' court. The procedure is not as formal as in the usual court, and the purpose is to keep the young offender away from ordinary criminal proceedings. A youth court must not take place in a court where other sittings have taken place, or will take place within one hour. The court is not open to the public and the press may not publish the names of the charged persons.

Magistrates may fine or place a juvenile on probation: issue a care order, in which the offender is committed to secure local authority accommodation, and the parental duties are transferred to the local authority: make a hospital or guardianship order: impose an attendance centre order, whereby the youth attends on Saturday afternoons for training: order the payment of fines or compensation by the offender's parents.

The Criminal Justice Act 1991 directs magistrates to consider "binding over" parents or guardians for the crimes of their children. This means that, if the magistrates decide on this course of action, parents of a young offender under the age of 16 have to attend court and promise that their child will not commit another crime within a set period of time. Binding over orders cannot exceed £1,000 or be for a period exceeding three years.

If the child offends again within the period the parents would have to pay the set amount of money to the court. For example, if the parents are bound over for two years for £200 and the child offended again within two years, the parents would have to pay £200 into the court.

Parents are not compelled to be bound over, but could be fined up to £1,000 if they refuse to do so.

A custodial sentence is only ordered if no other punishment is justified or it is necessary to protect the public. Magistrates may only impose a sentence of detention in a young offenders institution. (Criminal Justice Act 1988) (see p. 78).

(d) Civil jurisdiction

It should be noted that the magistrates' court does have civil jurisdiction, which may be summarised as follows:

(a) recovery of civil debts, such as income tax, rates, gas and electricity charges.

(b) family and matrimonial matters, such as applications for separation and custody of a child, maintenance and affiliation orders, and adoption.

(c) granting licences for premises for showing films, for the sale of alcohol or for gambling.

2. Constitution

A magistrates' court is presided over by at least two and not more than seven justices of the peace (magistrates). In England and Wales there are about 20,000 lay magistrates and 50 stipendiary magistrates.

Stipendiary magistrates are full-time paid magistrates. They have to be barristers or solicitors of seven years' standing.

Justices of the peace are appointed by the Lord Chancellor, using a document called the "Commission of the peace." There are committees in counties and boroughs to advise the Lord Chancellor on appointments. Justices may be removed from the Commission by the Lord Chancellor, without him giving the reason for this action. Usually, removal from office is caused by the justices' refusal to recognise and enforce certain laws. Generally a magistrate retires at 70.

A single magistrate may sit alone:

(a) in minor cases involving very small fines or periods of imprisonment, or

(b) when conducting a preliminary hearing, or

(c) when appointed as a stipendiary magistrate,

but generally, there must be two or more magistrates.

There is no jury in a magistrates' court. When a youth court is in session there must be a quorum of at least three magistrates, comprising women and men (*i.e.* there must be at least one woman or one man in the quorum).

Every magistrates' court has a justices' clerk, who is paid, usually legally qualified, and helps the justices on matters of law and procedure. Although they may only preside in the magistrates' court in the area of their commission, justices may sit in any Crown Court when required (see p. 54). Appeals from the magistrates' court go to:

(*a*) *Crown Court*
The defendant may appeal against the sentence.

(*b*) *Divisional Court of the Queen's Bench Division*
The prosecutor or defendant may appeal on points of law by means of "a case stated."

System of Appeal through the Criminal Courts

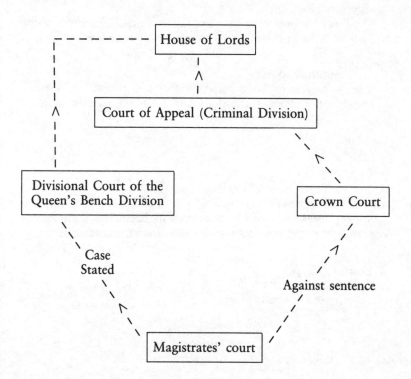

OTHER COURTS

The Judicial Committee of The Privy Council

The Committee does not make a decision but advises the Queen of its opinion, which is then implemented by an Order in Council. This Committee is outside the court system and its findings are not binding precedent on a lower court (see p. 19), but because of the constitution of the Committee, it has immense persuasive authority.

1. Jurisdiction

The main work of the Committee is to hear appeals as set out below, but it is sometimes required to advise on other matters of law, such as the validity of certain legislation.

The Committee hears appeals from:

(a) Outside the United Kingdom

The Privy Council may hear appeals from the Channel Islands, the Isle of Man and certain Commonwealth countries.

(b) Ecclesiastical courts

It is the final court of appeal on ecclesiastical matters. Appeals are heard on matters concerning church buildings or the clergy.

(c) Queen's Bench Division of the High Court

Appeals are heard from the Admiralty Court when acting as a Prize Court.

(d) Medical tribunals

Appeals are heard from doctors who have had their names removed from the medical register for disciplinary reasons.

2. Constitution

The Committee consists of not less than three, but usually five members from the following:

    (a)   The Lord Chancellor;
    (b)   The present and previous Lord President of the Council;

(c) Privy Councillors who hold or have held a high judicial office;
(d) The Lords of Appeal in Ordinary (the Law Lords);
(e) Persons who hold high judicial office in Commonwealth countries.

The Committee is usually formed from the Law Lords and, therefore, the constitution in practice is similar to the House of Lords.

Coroners' Courts

1. Jurisdiction
The main work of the court is concerned with inquests on persons who died a violent or unnatural death, or died from an unknown cause, or died in prison. A coroner may only inquire into deaths that occur in the district for which he is appointed.

If the verdict of the court is murder by a named person, the coroner may commit that person for trial. In this respect the court is similar to the preliminary hearing of the magistrates' court.

The court also has jurisdiction for disputes over treasure trove. Treasure trove is gold, silver or coins, etc., which have been deliberately hidden and the owner of which is unknown. If the coroner finds that the property was not hidden, but lost or misplaced for some reason, the finder acquires a good title, next to the real owner.

In 1992, an inquest jury decided that 14 silver coins, dating back from 1296 to 1582, and other items found in a field near Chester were not treasure trove but that they were probably lost or misplaced and were not hidden as a hoard. The coroner ordered the items to be returned to the finders.

Treasure trove belongs to the Crown, but it is often the practice for the Crown to pay a reward, based on the value of the property, to those who have not concealed the find.

2. Constitution
A coroner must be either a barrister, solicitor or medical practitioner of five years' standing, and is appointed by county, and certain borough councils to act within the district of the county or borough, but may be removed from office by the Lord Chancellor for misbehaviour. The coroner may, and sometimes must, summon a jury of between seven to 11 members. The jury's verdict need not be unanimous.

The Court of Justice of the European Communities

The Court of Justice of the European Communities which sits in Luxembourg ensures the observance and recognition of Community rules with regard to legal interpretation and application. It is concerned with disputes between Member States over Community matters. It hears appeals from Member States, individuals and the Community institutions on matters relating to the treaties, and its rulings are binding. The court is the final arbiter in all matters of law that lie within the scope of the treaties. It has an important function in creating Community case law and its decisions can have an effect on case law in the English courts (see p. 35).

There are nine judges and four advocates-general appointed for six years. One judge and one advocate-general are from the United Kingdom. Decisions are made by a majority vote but dissenting opinions are not made public.

TRIBUNALS

Administrative Tribunals

For a long period of time Parliament has delegated a judicial function to bodies or boards outside the usual system of the courts. Since 1945 this practice has grown, in the main due to the advent of nationalisation and the increase in social and welfare services provided by the state.

Instead of disputes being settled in court, certain Acts of Parliament have provided for the creation of tribunals to decide problems that have arisen within the particular scope of those Acts. In 1957, the Franks Committee (which reported on tribunals) estimated that there were over 2,000 tribunals, and it can be expected that this has increased. It is therefore impossible to give a complete list of the tribunals in existence, but the following will give some indication of their nature:

    (a) National Insurance Tribunals which hear disputes on such matters as claims for unemployment and sickness benefits;

    (b) Rent Tribunals which hear disputes between landlords and tenants;

* (c) Industrial Tribunals which hear matters concerning unfair dismissal, redundancy payments and the like;
* (d) Land Tribunals which hear disputes over the amount of compensation to be paid when land is compulsorily purchased by the local authority.

The main benefit of tribunals is that they help in administering Acts quickly and inexpensively. Procedure is less formal than in court and in many instances there is no need for the parties to be legally represented, and in some tribunals, lawyers are not allowed. The constitutions of tribunals vary, but certain tribunals must have members who are lawyers, and the chairman of some tribunals may only be appointed by the Minister of the department concerned, from a list of persons nominated by the Lord Chancellor. Generally, a tribunal will have several members, usually a lawyer will be chairman, with the other members representing organisations likely to be affected by the dispute.

Domestic Tribunals

Certain professional organisations have their own tribunals to settle disputes between members of their organisations. Conditions of membership will usually stipulate that disputes between members, and between members and the organisation, will be governed by a tribunal, and therefore members have mutually agreed beforehand how their differences will be settled.

In some cases Parliament has created a tribunal for a particular organisation. For example, the Medical Act 1956 created the Disciplinary Committee of the General Medical Council. Tribunals set up by statute are usually subject to a right of appeal, and provided that the tribunals do not go beyond the agreed powers, and follow the rules of natural justice, the courts have no jurisdiction.

Means of Control

1. By the courts

* (a) Making prerogative orders of mandamus, certiorari or prohibition (see p. 117). This method of control only applies against tribunals created by statute.
* (b) By awarding an injunction to prevent a tribunal (statutory or domestic) performing against the rules of

natural justice, or acting *"ultra vires"* (beyond its powers).

(c) Decisions from tribunals created by statute may be subject to appeals as provided by the statute.

2. By the Council of Tribunals

The Council was established by the Tribunals and Inquiries Act 1958.

It has an advisory function to review the working of statutory tribunals and makes reports when necessary to the Lord Chancellor who has the responsibility of appointing the members of the Council.

ARBITRATION

It is often the practice in commercial contracts to refer disputes to arbitration, instead of starting court actions. If you look at the booking conditions in some holiday brochures, you will find that disputes are referred to arbitration. Therefore, if there is a dispute between a holidaymaker and the travel company, the parties will not go to court, but to arbitration.

Arbitration means that the two parties agree to allow a third party to decide the dispute. The arbitrator does this by making an "award," and giving the reasons for doing so. When an award has been made, neither party may start a court action in relation to the same dispute. The courts will not interfere with the decision unless the arbitrator acted improperly, or unless fresh evidence is introduced.

A different form of arbitration was established when the Advisory Conciliation and Arbitration Service (ACAS) was created by the Employment Protection Act 1975, to help in trade disputes and to improve industrial relations.

Arbitration is also available in the county court, under the small claims procedure (see p. 50).

THE JUDICIARY AND THE LEGAL PROFESSION

Judges are appointed by the Queen and, except for the newly created circuit judges and recorders, may only be removed on an address from both Houses of Parliament. Circuit judges and recorders may be removed by the Lord Chancellor for misconduct.

When assuming office all judges take an oath, "...to do right to all manner of people after the laws and usages of this realm without fear or favour, affection or ill-will."

Judicial Officers

The qualifications and functions of most judges have been detailed in the section discussing the constitution of the courts. This section will deal with the senior judicial appointments. Students should make themselves aware of the names of the present holders of these offices.

1. The Lord Chancellor

The Lord Chancellor is appointed by the Queen on the advice of the Prime Minister. The office is the highest in the legal profession, but, strange as it may seem, it is a political appointment. The Lord Chancellor is a member of the Cabinet, and as with any other Minister, may be removed at any time, or when there is a change of Government. In the role of politician, the Lord Chancellor is speaker of the House of Lords, where he sits on the Woolsack. He does not, as one examination candidate stated, "sit on a sack of wool."

As a judge, he is head of the House of Lords, the Court of Appeal and the Chancery Division of the High Court.

2. The Lord Chief Justice

This appointment is also made by the Queen on the advice of the Prime Minister. The Lord Chief Justice is head of the Queen's Bench Division of the High Court, but his principal duties are as head of the Court of Appeal (Criminal Division) and the Queen's Bench Divisional Court. On appointment he is made a peer, but, although entitled to hear House of Lords cases, in practice he rarely does.

3. The Master of the Rolls

The Master of the Rolls is appointed by the Queen, on the advice of the Prime Minister, and is made a peer on appointment. The holder of this office is the virtual head of the Court of Appeal (Civil Division); organising the work of the court, and deciding the composition of the divisions to hear appeals. As Master of the Rolls he supervises the admission of qualified solicitors to the rolls of the court, which then allows them to practise.

4. President of the Family Division of the High Court
This appointment is made by the Queen on the advice of the Prime Minister. The president is head of the Family Division and, in addition to organising the work of the Division, sits in the High Court and in the Divisional Court.

The Law Officers

The Attorney-General and Solicitor-General are usually members of the House of Commons, and their appointment, by the Queen on the advice of the Prime Minister, is political. In addition to being Members of Parliament, they are also experienced barristers.

1. The Attorney-General
The Attorney-General has the following duties:

(a) Advising the Government on legal matters;
(b) Representing the Crown in civil cases and acting as prosecutor in important criminal cases;
(c) Certain prosecutions may only take place with the authority of the Attorney-General. The House of Lords recently upheld this right, after a private person had sought an injunction against postal workers;
(d) Is head of the English Bar;
(e) Supervises the work of the Director of Public Prosecutions.

2. The Solicitor-General
The Solicitor-General is the deputy of the Attorney-General, and has similar duties. Any act or function that may be discharged by the Attorney-General may also be carried out by the Solicitor-General, when the former has so authorised, or is ill or absent, or the office of Attorney-General is vacant.

3. The Director of Public Prosecutions
The holder of this post is appointed by the Attorney-General, but is a civil servant, not a politician. The D.P.P., who must be a barrister or solicitor of 10 years' standing, is head of a

department responsible for starting most criminal prosecutions, although mostly through the Crown Prosecution Service (see below).

The Crown Prosecution Service

The Prosecution of Offences Act 1985 established a new Crown Prosecution Service for England and Wales, which is responsible for all criminal proceedings instituted on behalf of the police. The effect of the Act is to separate the prosecution of offenders from the investigation and detection of offences by the police.

The service is headed by the Director of Public Prosecutions who is responsible for appointing prosecuting officers, who must be either solicitors or barristers.

The Legal Profession

Unlike most countries, the legal profession in England and Wales has two bodies of lawyers that have different functions in the legal system. Barristers are mainly concerned with advocacy before the courts, while solicitors carry out many aspects of legal work. Most countries have one legal profession that has the right to deal with all legal work, although lawyers in these countries may tend to specialise in one aspect of the law.

Not all lawyers publicly practise law. Many are employed by companies or the Civil Service as legal advisers, while others lecture or teach law. A large number of Members of Parliament are either barristers or solicitors.

1. Solicitors

The functions and duties of solicitors are very wide and varied. They deal with most aspects of legal work, such as giving advice, making wills, conveyancing (transferring) the ownership of houses, drafting partnership agreements and forming companies, preparing litigation, interviewing witnesses and so on. It should be noted that solicitors have lost their monopoly on conveyancing. Licensed conveyancers, who must hold certain legal qualifications and be experienced in the work of conveyancing, are allowed to practise in this field of law. Solicitors have the right to appear before the magistrates' courts, county courts,

Crown Court (on appeal or sentencing from the inferior court) and have a limited right of audience before the High Court. They may, however, concentrate on drafting documents such as wills, conveyances, etc., and never appear in court.

Solicitors may work by themselves or in partnership with other solicitors. In January 1988 the Law Society agreed that a firm of solicitors should be able to incorporate the business with limited or unlimited liability, provided that all the directors and shareholders are solicitors holding practising certificates. Although solicitors do practise in all aspects of law, it is probable that in large partnerships individual partners will specialise in certain branches of the law. Solicitors may now, subject to certain rules, advertise their practice.

Clients may sue solicitors for negligence in carrying out their professional functions, and solicitors may sue clients for non-payment of fees. In *County Personnel Ltd.* v. *Pulver & Co.* (1987), the Court of Appeal held a firm of solicitors to be negligent and liable for damages, for failing to ascertain the rent payable on a headlease and for failing to explain the effect of a rent review clause to the client before entering into the underlease agreement.

In *Smith* v. *Claremont Haynes & Co.* (1991), it was held that a solicitor was negligent when failing to act promptly in preparing a will. The testator died before the will was completed for signing, with the result that the intended beneficiaries did not inherit the gifts as expected.

Training
There are three routes by which a person may qualify as a solicitor:

(a) As a law graduate
This is the quickest route and about 75 per cent. of solicitors qualify this way. A law graduate has to proceed to the Legal Practice Course, which gives the practical skills required to become a solicitor. After successfully completing this course it is usual to undertake a two year training contract usually with a firm of solicitors in private practice, but training may also take place in other organisations such as The Crown Prosecution Service and local and central government. Within the training contract a Professional Skills Course, which covers areas such as accounts, management and advocacy, must be successfully completed. At the end of the training contract, application may be made for admission as a solicitor.

(b) As a non-law graduate

After completion of a degree it is necessary to take a course leading to the Common Professional Examination. After success in this examination the process of training generally follows a similar pattern to that of a law graduate trainee.

(c) As a non-graduate

Trainee legal executives with a firm of solicitors or similar organisations, who have successfully completed the examinations of the Institute of Legal Executives and become a Fellow of the Institute, may enrol as a student member of the Law Society and attend and complete the Legal Practice Course and, finally, the Professional Skills Course.

When a person is qualified as above, his or her name will be entered on the Roll of Solicitors (maintained by the Master of the Rolls) and the Law Society, the solicitors' governing body, will issue a certificate to practise, which certifies that the requirements of training and examinations have been satisfied and the solicitor is morally fit to be an officer of the Supreme Court.

2. Legal Executives

The Institute of Legal Executives holds examinations for staff who work in a solicitor's office but do not hold a legal qualification. A Fellow of the Institute may later qualify as a solicitor, and the Law Society makes provision for this category of entrant, similar to the requirements for a non-law graduate.

3. Barristers

A barrister's main function is to conduct a case in court. Barristers may appear before all courts and have exclusive right before superior courts, with certain exceptions (see p. 67). Besides their advocacy work, barristers will also draft legal documents, such as pleadings and "counsel's opinion" on legal problems submitted by solicitors.

Clients cannot approach a barrister directly. A meeting has to be arranged by a solicitor and this means that, to a certain extent, barristers rely on solicitors for their work. It also means a client pays two fees. The possibility of clients having a right of direct approach to a barrister is under consideration.

Barristers tend to specialise in one branch of law. They cannot enter a partnership, but must act alone, although in practice they share chambers with other barristers and the "barristers' clerk," who acts as secretary and arranges meetings between the clients, solicitors and the barristers, and also settles the amount of the fees.

Barristers are not liable in negligence for their advocacy in court and for matters which occur beforehand which are intimately connected with how the case will be conducted and managed in court. This principle is based on public policy (*Rondel* v. *Worsley* (1969)). The House of Lords, however, in *Saif Ali* v. *Sydney Mitchell & Co.* (1978) held that in certain circumstances a barrister could be liable in negligence for matters not within the area of work mentioned above. Barristers may not sue for their fees.

A barrister of 10 years' standing may apply to become a Queen's Counsel. A Queen's Counsel wears a different gown from other barristers. Originally it was made of silk, hence the expression when a barrister becomes a Q.C. that he "takes silk." It has been the practice that in cases conducted by a Q.C., a junior barrister also had to be engaged. As a result of discussions between the Director General of Fair Trading and the Bar Council, all existing provisions that restricted the freedom of Queen's Counsel to appear alone have been abrogated, and the Bar Counsel permits Q.C.s to appear alone if they wish to do so. It must be noted that the change gives a Q.C. the option to decide in the client's best interests whether or not a junior should also be instructed.

With the exception of circuit judges, all judges of the superior courts are appointed solely from the ranks of barristers.

Training

Barristers qualify by joining one of the four Inns of Court. Lincoln's Inn, Gray's Inn, Inner Temple and Middle Temple, are the Inns of Court. Students, who generally must be graduates with an upper second-class honours degree or better, must keep "terms," which means attending the Inn and dining a required number of times. They must also pass the vocational examinations set by the Council of Legal Education.

(a) Academic Training

In order to obtain a place on the Vocational Course of the Council of Legal Education, students intending to qualify as a barrister are generally required to have either:

(a) a first or upper second class honours law degree, or its equivalent;

(b)   a first or upper second class honours non-law degree and passed the Common Professional Examination;

(c)   passed the Common Professional Examination with distinction.

Students with a lower second class law degree or who have passed the Common Professional Examination may be accepted if there are places available on the Bar Vocational Course.

(b) Vocational Training

Students wishing to practise as a barrister must take the vocational course which aims to provide:

(a)   practical training in specialist skills such as legal research, opinion writing, drafting and advocacy; and

(b)   knowledge of legal principles of evidence, litigation and the rules of professional conduct.

(c) Professional Training

Following the vocational examinations, successful students are "Called to the Bar," but before they may practise it is necessary to spend an additional year in pupillage under a barrister of five years' standing. Pupillage is a form of practical training under the guidance of an experienced barrister. In the last six months of training the pupil may represent clients in court and earn fees.

Students who do not wish to practise as a barrister do not attend the Vocational course, but sit a Bar Examination. After success in this examination the student is Called to the Bar and does not undertake pupillage.

4. Complaints against the legal profession

As shown above, solicitors may be sued for negligence when their conduct is not of a reasonable minimum standard. This may be difficult, however, as other solicitors, particularly those practising in the same locality, are often reluctant to take such an action.

In 1986, the High Court held that a Welsh businessman had been overcharged by his solicitors, and reduced the solicitor's fees by nearly 50 per cent., and the solicitor was struck off. The businessman also claimed that the Law Society had failed in its duty to investigate his complaint against the solicitor.

As a result of this case the Law Society set up the Solicitors Complaints Bureau. The bureau deals with such matters as negligence, delay, unprofessional conduct, unanswered letters, breakdown in communication, etc. In its first annual report, there were 13,852 complaints from members of the public. Most complaints received by the bureau were settled by conciliation between its staff and the solicitors concerned.

If conciliation is not possible, and the complainant is still unhappy, an "investigation committee" may decide no further action is needed, or may recommend a report be prepared for the "adjudication committee." If this second committee considers the complaint to be justified, its powers include the order for remission of fees and to take action against the solicitor at the Disciplinary Tribunal. Lay persons are members of both committees. The address of the bureau is, The Solicitors Complaints Bureau, Portland House, Stag Place, London SW1E 5BL.

If all else fails the complainant may go to the Lay Observer (appointed by the Lord Chancellor) who has the power to recommend further inquiries.

In matters concerning barristers, where negligence is not alleged, clients may complain about the conduct of the barrister by writing to the General Council of the Bar. Generally, such complaints do not help the client directly, because if the complaint is upheld, disciplinary action is taken against the barrister concerned.

5. A single legal profession?

In the previous pages the different legal functions of barristers and solicitors have been set out. Many countries, however, do not have two professional bodies; America, for example, has a single legal profession (usually called lawyers or attorneys), who may deal with all legal matters. There are no restrictions to the legal tasks they may perform.

6. The disadvantages of two professions

Our system of two legal bodies with distinct functions and rights, which may only be performed by the one profession endowed with the particular right, has many disadvantages:

(a) Should a case have to appear before the High Court, it means that the client will have to pay two fees; one to the solicitor for the initial work and one to the barrister for appearing before the court.

In 1986, following the settlement of a libel action, an agreed statement was to be read out in open court, at the request of one of the interested parties, by the solicitor who prepared the statement. The judge would not allow it and he was later supported by the Court of Appeal, who upheld that barristers have an exclusive right of audience even in such circumstances. The courts insisted that the statement be read out by a member of the Bar. That, of course, meant an additional fee for the client to pay.

(b) Employing a barrister may also cause inefficiency, because of the physical difficulty of two offices dealing with the paperwork which could lead to breakdowns in communication between the solicitor and barrister, delays and possibly the return of briefs when barristers are double booked.

(c) Solicitors, however brilliant or gifted in law, cannot become advocates or judges of the superior courts.

(d) Barristers have no right to apply for probate, it is the exclusive right of solicitors.

(e) There are two separate systems of legal education and training. Should it not be possible to be qualified in both branches at the same time?

The Marre Report in 1988 recommended that solicitors should have full rights to appear in the Crown Court; that specialist professionals should have direct access to barristers and there should be a common system of vocational training for the two branches of the legal profession. In 1989 the Lord Chancellor, Lord Mackay, published three Green Papers on the work and organisation of the legal profession, which proposed the following recommendations for discussion:

(a) Solicitors will be eligible for all judicial appointments, including the House of Lords.

(b) Solicitors will be eligible to appear before all courts as advocates.

(c) Both barristers and solicitors will require a certificate of competence to appear before the courts.

(d) Clients may approach barristers directly, and barristers may practise in partnerships.

(e) Non-lawyers, such as advice workers, may appear as advocates in cases such as small claims, in the county court.

(f) Barristers and solicitors working in the Crown Prosecution Service, local government and private companies would be able to apply for an advocacy certificate.

    (g)   Lawyers should be able to take cases on a "no win, no fee" arrangement.

    (h)   Solicitors would lose their monopoly on conveyancing. House buyers will be able to have the bank or building society responsible for providing the mortgage to do this work.

Some of these proposals have been implemented, but not all. It is important, therefore, that you follow the news for any such changes.

SANCTIONS AND REMEDIES

Sanctions is the word used to indicate the sentence passed by the criminal courts, and remedies refers to awards of the civil courts to remedy the cause of complaint or compensate for an injury.

Criminal Sanctions

The purpose of criminal sanctions is, in the main, to punish the offender. As criminal offences are considered to be against the state, it is the state which provides and administers the punishment.

The Criminal Justice Act 1991 provides a statutory structure for courts to follow when deciding the appropriate sentence. The principles which the courts should consider when imposing a sentence are as follows:

    (a)   The seriousness of the offence should be reflected in the severity of the sentence.

    (b)   It is better for the public, the victim and the offender if the punishment is within the community rather than being custodial.

    (c)   Punishment should be just, in order that the victim, his family and the public at large will be satisfied that the law has been upheld.

    (d)   As imprisonment by itself does not provide an effective means of reform, a sentence of imprisonment would need to be justified in terms of protection of the public, retribution and denunciation.

    (e)   As many crimes are committed on impulse, punishment as a deterrent in such cases is generally irrelevant in the sentence.

(f) When a fine is an appropriate sentence it should be in proportion to the offender's means, whether he be rich or poor.

(g) An offender should be sentenced for the present offence and not for previous bad behaviour, which has already been punished.

1. Death

The death penalty may still be imposed on persons found guilty of treason or piracy.

2. Imprisonment

The purpose of imprisonment may be to (i) punish the offender, (ii) protect the public from further crimes (a thief in prison cannot steal from the public) and (iii) act as a deterrent (the prospect of a prison sentence may stop a would-be criminal from committing a crime).

Section 1 of the C.J.A. 1991 provides that where a person is convicted of an offence punishable with a custodial sentence (*e.g.* imprisonment), other than one fixed by law (*e.g.* life sentence for murder), the court shall not pass a custodial sentence unless:

(a) the offence is so serious that only such a sentence can be justified; or

(b) where the offence is a violent or sexual offence and only such a sentence would be adequate to protect the public from serious harm from the offender.

When passing a custodial sentence the court should explain to the offender in open court why it is passing such a sentence.

A sentence of imprisonment may vary from life to one day. Most crimes have maximum sentences, but they are rarely used. The length of the maximum sentence also varies from crime to crime and it is difficult at times to appreciate why similar crimes have different maximum sentences. For example, an indecent assault on a man or boy carries a maximum sentence of 10 years, while it is two years for an indecent assault on a woman.

A sentence of imprisonment for life or less does not mean the prisoner will spend that length of time in prison. The Criminal Justice Act 1991 provides that when a sentence is less than four years, a prisoner may be released after serving half of the sentence, but is subject to a suspended sentence for the balance of the sentence (see below).

For sentences of four years or more, prisoners will be released on licence after serving two-thirds of the sentence or may be eligible for parole when they have served half, subject to the provisions and risk of a suspended sentence. A person sentenced to life imprisonment may be released at any time on licence by the Home Secretary.

3. Suspended Sentence

A suspended sentence may be imposed. This means that the sentence is not put into effect during the period of the sentence, unless the offender commits another offence within this time. The offender would then have to serve the original sentence as well as the punishment for the second offence.

Section 5 of the C.J.A. 1991 provides that a court should not award a suspended sentence unless:

(a) the case is one where imprisonment would have been appropriate even without the power to suspend the sentence; and

(b) that the exercise of this power can be justified by the exceptional circumstances of the case.

(c) In addition to the suspended sentence the court may also impose a fine or a compensation order (see below).

4. Absolute or conditional discharge

If the court considers any punishment to be inappropriate, the offender may be discharged absolutely or conditionally. A conditional discharge means the offender must not commit an offence during a period of time between one year and not more than three years. Breach of this condition may also mean that the offender will be sentenced for the original offence. An absolute discharge means the offender leaves court without a stain on his character. It is awarded when a law has been broken, but the offender was not, in the court's opinion, at fault.

5. Fines

Any court may fine an offender for any offence other than one for which the penalty is fixed by law (*e.g.* murder). Many offences carry a fine as the punishment or as an additional punishment or as an alternative to prison, *e.g.* a £10 fine; or six months' prison and £10 fine; or six months or a £10 fine.

Where a child or young person is ordered to pay a fine, it is the duty of the court to order that the fine be paid by the parent or guardian.

As was stated in the previous section, fining should be the normal punishment (when the offence does not warrant imprisonment) and the fine should relate to the offender's ability to pay.

In order that the fines are standardised in the magistrates' courts, the C.J.A. 1991 provides a system for calculating the amount of the fine. The offender's weekly income less the weekly expenditure produces a "disposable income" which is the basis of the fine. The "disposable income" is multiplied by number of units which is related to the seriousness of the offence.

Under this system if two offenders are jointly guilty of the same offence, their fines could vary according to their incomes.

6. Community Sentences

Although community sentences are not custodial in the same sense as imprisonment, because the offender is allowed to remain in the community, he is still subject to certain restraints which restrict his liberty. A court should not pass a community sentence unless the offence committed was serious enough to warrant such a sentence.

A community sentence means any of the following orders:

(a) Probation

If the offender is over 16 and agrees to be bound over to the supervision of a probation officer, an order will be made with the aim of:

(a) securing the rehabilitation of the offender; and
(b) protecting the public from harm or preventing further offences.

The order may make conditions as to the offender's movements and it will involve regular meetings with a probation officer. An offender who breaks the conditions may receive a prison sentence for the original offence.

(b) Exclusion order

The Public Order Act 1986 provides for an exclusion order to be made to prohibit a person from entering premises to attend an Association football match, if a person uses or threatens to use violence towards another person or towards property, while at, or travelling to or from, a football match.

The exclusion order shall not be less than three months. Anyone who enters premises in breach of the order may be arrested by a police officer without a warrant, and is liable to imprisonment for one month or a fine.

(c) Community service order

This order applies to offenders over 16 and is an alternative to prison. It requires the convicted person to work unpaid for the benefit of the community for a certain number of hours, at intervals spread throughout the year. The offender, who must agree to the order, is required to carry out community tasks such as working for the elderly or handicapped.

(d) Combined Order

This order sentences the offender to both a probation order and a community service order.

(e) Curfew Order

This order may apply to offenders over 16 and requires them to remain at a specific place and for a specific time as specified in the order. The order may include the requirement for electronic monitoring (generally referred to as tagging).

7. Custodial sentences for young offenders

The Criminal Justice Act 1988, provides for detention centre orders and youth custody orders to be replaced by a single custodial sentence of "detention in a young offenders institution."

Before making the order the court must be satisfied:

(a) that the seriousness of the offence would lead to a sentence of imprisonment if committed by a person of 21 or over, and;

(b) that the offender;

  (i) has a history of not responding to non-custodial penalties, and;

  (ii) only a custodial sentence would be adequate to protect the public, or;

  (iii) the offence is so serious that only a custodial sentence is justified.

Detention in a young offenders institution will be passed on a male offender under 21, but not less than 14, and a female offender under 21 but not less than 15.

The maximum term of detention is the maximum term of imprisonment for the offence, but for male offenders under 15 the maximum sentence is four months, and for male and female offenders aged 15 and 16 the maximum sentence is 12 months. Generally, the court cannot pass a sentence of detention at a young offenders institution for less than 21 days.

8. Attendance centres

Instead of being sentenced to detention in a young offenders institution, a person under 21 may have to attend an attendance centre on several occasions, totalling between 12 and 36 hours. This sentence, often ordered for a person convicted of violence or hooliganism at football matches, usually takes place on Saturday afternoons.

9. Compensation

The court may, in addition to other sanctions, order a convicted person to pay compensation to the victim for loss or damage resulting from the offence.

In addition to compensation paid under an order from a criminal court, a victim of a crime of violence may apply to the Criminal Injuries Compensation Board for a payment. Widows and other close relatives of a person who received fatal injuries may also apply. Compensation from the Board will be reduced by any damages received in a civil claim and by any compensation awarded by a criminal court.

10. Rehabilitation of offenders

The Rehabilitation of Offenders Act 1974 aims to restore the reputation of convicted persons who have not committed another crime for a specified period afterwards. Any convicted person who received a sentence of not more than two-and-a-half years in prison and has not offended again within the "rehabilitation period," has the advantage of not having to reveal the conviction when applying for jobs; an employer cannot refuse to employ a person because of the conviction; and the conviction may not be mentioned in civil court proceedings. There are some exceptions to the above, and if a person commits another serious offence the benefit may be lost.

As an example of how the Act works, a sentence of six months to two-and-a-half years would require a rehabilitation period of 10 years free of trouble and, for sentences of under six months, the period would be seven years before the offender could benefit from the Act.

Civil Remedies

The purpose of civil remedies is not to punish but, generally, to compensate.

1. Damages (payment of money)

This is the common law remedy, and is available for all civil actions as of right. In the law of contract the aim of damages is to place the injured party in the same financial position as if the contract had been completed. In tort, the aim may be to place the injured party in the financial position enjoyed prior to being wronged.

Damages may be nominal (*e.g.* 1p), substantial or aggravated. Nominal damages may be awarded when a person has a legal right, but has suffered no financial loss. Substantial damages are the actual amount needed to compensate the injured. Aggravated damages are more than the actual loss, and are awarded where the injury suffered was aggravated by the malice or wrong conduct of the defendant.

2. Specific performance

This is an equitable order, granted at the discretion of the judge. Its purpose is to force a party to perform the contract (see p. 153). It is usually awarded in contracts for sale of land.

3. Injunction

This is also an equitable order, granted at the discretion of the judge. It has the effect of making a party perform an act (a mandatory injunction, *e.g.* an order to knock down a wall), or preventing a person from acting in a certain way (a prohibitory injunction, *e.g.* stopping an actress under contract from making a film for another company). Sometimes an injunction is granted to stop a person doing an act pending a court action (an interlocutory injunction).

For other civil remedies see the section on the law of contract (p. 152).

LEGAL AID AND ADVICE

Legal Aid is a scheme administered by the Legal Aid Board, which pays or contributes to the cost of legal fees. It has often been said "the law is for the rich," meaning that people with low incomes could not afford to pay the cost of taking legal action. The aim of the scheme is to help people to obtain their legal rights without the worry of the possible financial burden.

The financial aid available depends on the income and capital of the client, and the maximum amounts of income and capital vary with the different types of legal aid required. For the latest amounts you are advised to obtain booklets issued by the Legal Aid Office, which are available at public libraries, Citizens Advice Centres and other similar organisations, because the prescribed amounts are changed annually.

The types of legal aid available are as follows:

1. Legal advice and assistance (the Green Form scheme)
A person needing legal help may go to a solicitor for advice. The solicitor may help by writing what is known as "a solicitor's letter," which informs another party of the legal rights of the client, and that legal action will be taken if the third party does not recognise them.

Help may also be given in writing or made orally by advising clients of their rights on legal problems, such as unfair dismissal from work; or the right to redundancy pay; disputes with landlords; dissatisfaction with goods and the shopkeeper's reluctance to help; obtaining a barrister's opinion and matrimonial problems concerning divorce, claiming and collecting maintenance, and custody of children. Many solicitors are in the scheme and it is common to see the legal aid sign outside solicitors' offices.

Application for legal advice and assistance is made to a solicitor, who will help with the application form (the Green Form).

To be eligible for this form of help or advice, a client's disposable income or capital (*e.g.* savings) must not exceed the prescribed amount. The disposable income is calculated by taking a person's weekly income and deducting from it such items as income tax, national insurance contributions, allowances for dependants, housing costs and other relevant costs.

In early 1993 the Lord Chancellor announced measures to bring the assessment of legal aid in line with other ways of assessing means-tested benefits.

As from April 1993 it is proposed that the prescribed lower income limit of disposable income, below which an applicant for legal aid pays no contribution, will be reduced to the equivalent income support limit. Applicants granted civil legal aid will be required to pay one third of their disposable income above the lower income. Equivalent changes are to be made for assessing criminal legal aid and advice and assistance (see below).

A client receiving income support or family credit will be eligible to receive this service free of charge, unless the disposable capital exceeds the prescribed amount.

Disposable capital is calculated on the total amount of savings and investments, and possessions of value (such as jewellery). The value of a house is usually not included, nor are items of furniture, clothes and tools of trade. In addition, allowance is made for dependants. To qualify for legal advice and assistance, the disposable capital must not exceed the prescribed amount.

2. Civil court proceedings

Legal Aid is provided for most civil court actions, although it is not generally available in litigation for defamation or tribunals, with the exception of the Land Tribunal and the Employment Appeal Tribunal. In addition to the services of a solicitor to help with a case, it may also include the services of a barrister if necessary for the case to go to court. Application is made, usually through a solicitor, on a prescribed form to the Legal Aid office.

In order to qualify for legal aid a person has to show:

(a)   That the amounts of both disposable income and capital do not exceed the figures allowed by the scheme.
The solicitor will send the application to the assessment officer of the Department of Social Security, who will calculate whether or not a person qualifies financially.

(b)   That it is reasonable to bring or defend the action.
A local Legal Aid Office will decide if it is reasonable to grant legal aid. All matters of fact and law arising out of the application will be considered before the

decision is made whether or not to grant a legal aid certificate.

Disposable income is the amount expected to be received during the year after application. From this yearly income, deductions may be made for mortgage or rent, rates, income tax, national insurance, pension contributions, allowances for dependants and other payments deemed necessary.

Disposable capital for legal aid is calculated on the same basis as legal advice but there is no deduction for dependants.

A person with a disposable yearly income of more than the prescribed limit will not qualify for legal aid for civil proceedings.

A disposable capital in excess of the prescribed amounts does not usually qualify a person for legal aid. When a certificate for legal aid is granted, it specifies the contribution to be made (if any).

3. Criminal court proceedings

A person charged with a criminal offence may obtain legal aid which may include the services of a solicitor to help with the case, and a barrister if the case goes to the Crown Court. Application is usually made to the magistrates' court, who will decide if it is in the "interests of justice" that legal aid be granted, and that the applicant requires financial help. It is generally considered to be in the "interest of justice" if the accused is in danger of losing his liberty or job, or is mentally ill, or if there is a substantial question of law to be discussed.

As with civil cases an assessment of disposable income and capital is made and the basis of assessment is similar. Legal aid would be free if the weekly disposable income was less than the prescribed amount. If it was more, an accused would have to contribute.

In addition to legal aid, there is a right of every person at any stage of an investigation at a police station to communicate and to consult privately with a solicitor. This means that a person in custody should be allowed to telephone a solicitor or friends or have letters sent by post with the least possible delay.

4. A fixed fee interview

Although not technically legal aid, many solicitors give legal advice for a period of 30 minutes for a fee of £5. This service is available regardless of income or capital.

5. Duty solicitor schemes

A person questioned by the police about an offence has the right to have free legal advice whether or not he or she has been arrested. There is often a 24-hour duty solicitor at a police station to give advice. If the duty solicitor is not available another solicitor may be chosen.

A duty solicitor is also available to give advice and represent the accused at the first appearance before the magistrates' court. The service is free and there is no means test.

It should be noted that the figures shown above apply as at March 1993 and that they are likely to change year by year. A pamphlet "Financial Conditions for Legal Aid" gives details of current rates and contributions, and is available with other pamphlets from Citizens Advice Bureaux, Consumers Advice Centres, and other places which distribute public information. Students are advised to obtain the latest copy of the pamphlet. Free legal advice may also be available from these centres as well as Law Centres or Legal Advice Centres which operate on a voluntary basis in certain areas.

6. Recovery of legal aid costs

The cost of legal aid may be deducted from the damages and/or costs received by a successful applicant. In criminal cases, it is likely that any contribution would be returned if the accused were acquitted.

JURY

A jury is a group of men and women legally chosen to hear a case and to decide the facts from the evidence presented.

Juries are used in civil and criminal cases. Trial by jury in civil cases is not common and is usually restricted to actions involving defamation, malicious prosecution, fraud, and false imprisonment. Any party to one of these actions has the right to trial by jury. A jury will be ordered for other cases when the court considers it necessary, which it rarely does. A county court jury consists of eight jurors and a High Court jury has 12.

In criminal cases, juries of 12 persons are used in all trials in the Crown Court. There are seven to 11 jurors in a coroner's court. It is the duty of the judge to decide all matters of law, while the duty of the jury is to decide matters of fact.

Qualifications of Jurors

It is the responsibility of the Lord Chancellor to prepare the panels of jurors and issue the summonses. Most people aged 18 to 70 are eligible to serve on a jury. The only qualifications are that persons:

(a)   must be on the electoral register, which means aged 18 or older, and
(b)   have been resident in the United Kingdom for the last five years or more.

The Juries Act 1974 and the Juries (Disqualification) Act 1984 provide that certain persons are **disqualified** from jury service.
A person will be disqualified:

(a)   if, at any time in the last 10 years he has served any part of a prison sentence, youth custody or detention, Borstal detention, or has been given a suspended sentence of imprisonment, or
(b)   if, at any time in the last five years, he has been placed on probation.

A person sentenced to prison for five years or more is disqualified for life.

The following persons are **ineligible** for jury service: judges, persons concerned with the administration of justice, the clergy and persons who have, or are still suffering from, a mental illness.

Certain classes of persons such as persons over 65, doctors, full-time members of H.M. Forces and Members of Parliament, may be excused from duty by claiming "**excusal as of right.**" Other persons may be excused service if they show good reason, or if they have a physical disability, or their knowledge of English is not good enough for them to act as competent jurors. It is possible to request a temporary deferment if a person can show good cause. A student, for example, would be justified in making such a request if summoned for duty on, or for a reasonable period before, the day of an examination.

Unless a person is disqualified, ineligible or excused from duty, he or she must attend or risk a penalty, usually a fine (see p. 86). Summons to jury duty does not mean that a person will automatically serve on a jury. It is possible to turn up every day for a week or more and never actually be called upon. In addition, either party may challenge any juror and request a

In the Crown Court at

Jury Service

	Your juror's number
	You must go to

You have been chosen for jury service.
Your name was chosen, at random, from the list of
people who are registered to vote in elections.

This form is your **jury summons.** It tells you when and
where to start your jury service.

Warning
You may have to pay a fine if you
    do not attend for jury service without a good reason
or you are not available to be a juror when
    your name is called
or you are not fit to be a juror because of drink
    or drugs

There are rules about who may be a juror. Some
people whose names have been chosen cannot be jurors.
These rules are explained on pages 2 and 3. When you
have read them you must decide if you can be a juror.

If you need more advice about the rules, the **jury
summoning officer** will be pleased to help you.

You **must** fill in the Reply to the Summons on page 4
and 5, and send it to the court **within 7 days.**

*The Jury Summoning Officer
(with the authority of the Lord Chancellor)*

Issued on

on

at   am

During your jury service you may be asked
to go to another court nearby.

 **To contact the
jury summoning officer**
please get in touch with

☎ **Tel.**
*(When you write or telephone please give your
juror's number which is at the top of this page).*

please turn to page 2 >

Rules about jury service

Some people cannot be jurors by law.
These people are **not qualified** for jury service.
Other people may, **by law, have the right to
be excused** from jury service.

• Are you qualified for jury service?

> **Warning**
> **You may have to pay a fine if
> you serve on a jury knowing that
> you are not qualified for jury service.**

You are qualified for jury service if
   you will be at least 18 years old
   and under 70 years old
   on the day you start your jury service

and your name is on the Register of
   Electors for Parliamentary or Local
   Government elections

and you have lived in
      the United Kingdom,
   or the Channel Islands
   or the Isle of Man
   for a period of at least 5 years
   since you were 13 years old

But you are not qualified for jury service if
   you are someone listed in
      Box A
   or Box B
   or Box C (on page 3)

• Do you have the right to be excused from jury service?

The law gives some people **the right to be
excused** from jury service if they want to be
excused.
**You may ask the jury summoning officer to
excuse you from jury service if**
   you are more than 65 years old

or you have been on jury service during the
   past 2 years. **This does not apply if you
   were a juror at a coroner's court.**

or you have been a juror and the court
   excused you for a period that has not
   yet ended.

or you are someone listed in
   Box D (on page 3).

please turn to page 4 ⟩

Box A   Convictions

You are not qualified for jury service
- if you have **ever** been sentenced
      to imprisonment for life

   or to imprisonment or youth custody
      for five years or more

   or to be detained during Her Majesty's pleasure

   or during the pleasure of the Secretary of State for
      Northern Ireland.

- if you have **in the last 10 years**
      served any part of a sentence of imprisonment,
      youth custody or detention

   or received a suspended sentence of imprisonment
      or an order for detention

   or been subject to a community service order.

- if you have **in the past 5 years** been placed on
      probation.

This list relates to sentences passed in the
United Kingdom, the Channel Islands or the
Isle of Man.

Box B   Mental disorders

You are not qualified for jury service
- if you suffer or have suffered from a mental
   disorder and, because of that condition,
      you are resident in a hospital or other similar
      institution
   or you regularly attend for treatment by a medical
      practitioner.

- if you are in guardianship under section 37 of the
   Mental Health Act 1983.

- if a judge has decided that you are not capable of
   managing and administering your property or
   affairs because of mental disorder.

**If you are in any doubt whether this list applies to you
please talk to your doctor or ask someone to explain
it to you.**

Box C   The Clergy and those concerned with the Administration of Justice

The Clergy
You are not qualified if you are
- in holy orders
- a regular minister of any religious denomination.
- a vowed member of any religious order living in a monastery, convent or other religious community

Others concerned with the Administration of Justice

You are not qualified if you have at any time within the last 10 years been

- an authorised advocate or authorised litigator
- a barrister, a barrister's clerk or assistant
- a solicitor or articled clerk
- a legal executive employed by solicitors
- a Public Notary
- a member of the staff of the Director of Public Prosecutions
- an officer employed under the Lord Chancellor and concerned with the day to day administration of the legal system
- an officer or member of the staff of any court whose work is concerned with the day to day administration of the court
- a coroner, deputy coroner or assistant coroner
- a justices' clerk, deputy clerk or assistant clerk
- One of the Active Elder Brethren of the Corporation of Trinity House of Deptford Strond
- a shorthand writer in any court
- a court security officer

The Judiciary
You are not qualified if you are or ever have been
- a judge
- a stipendiary magistrate
- a justice of the peace
- the Chairman or President; the Vice-Chairman or President; the registrar or assistant registrar of any Tribunal.

- a governor, chaplain, medical officer or other officer of a penal establishment
- a member of the board of visitors of a penal establishment
- a prisoner custody officer
- the warden or a member of the staff of a probation home, probation hostel or a bail hostel
- a probation officer or someone appointed to help them
- a member of a Parole Board or of a local review committee
- a member of any police force (this includes a person on central service, a special constable or anyone with the powers and privileges of a constable)
- a member of a police authority or of any body with responsibility for appointing members of a constabulary
- an Inspector or Assistant Inspector of Constabulary
- a civilian employed for police purposes or a member of the metropolitan civil staffs
- someone employed in a forensic science laboratory

Box D   Other people who have the right to be excused

You have the right to be excused if you are one of the following people

Parliament
- a Peer or Peeress entitled to receive a writ of summons to attend the House of Lords
- a Member of the House of Commons
- an Officer of the House of Lords.
- an Officer of the House of Commons.

Medical and other professions
- a dentist
- a medical practitioner
- a midwife
- a nurse
- a veterinary surgeon or a veterinary practitioner
- a pharmaceutical chemist

if you are practising the profession and you are registered, enrolled or certificated under the law which relates to your profession.

European Assembly
A representative to the assembly of the European Communities.

The Forces
You may be excused if you are a full-time member of
- the army, navy or air force
- the Queen Alexandra's Royal Naval Nursing Service
- any Voluntary Aid Detachment serving with the Royal Navy

and your commanding officer certifies to the jury summoning officer that your absence would be "prejudicial to the efficiency of the service".

Reply to the jury summons

| What to do | • Read pages 1, 2 and 3 of the summons. |
| | • Fill in this Reply and send it to the court within 7 days of the day you got it. |

| Warning | You may have to pay a fine if | you refuse to give the information which is necessary to decide if you are qualified to be a juror |
| | or | you deliberately give false information, or cause, or permit, someone to give false information. |

Part 1   About you

Your jury number
This number is given on page 1.

Title Mr ☐ Mrs ☐ Miss ☐ Ms ☐ Other (say here)

Surname

Other names
Please put all your names.

Date of birth
Please give the date in numbers.   Day   Month   Year

Address

Telephone number
Please give a number where the court may leave a message during the day.   Home   Work

Part 2   Your qualification for jury service

• Read 'Are you qualified for jury service' on page 2.
• If you have any doubts about whether you are qualified please contact the jury summoning officer

Are you qualified for jury service? Yes ☐ Go to Part 3 (on page 5).

No ☐ Say why you are not qualified in the box below.

I am not qualified for jury service because

Go to Part 5

please turn to page 5 >

Part 3 Deferral and excusal

Please read the Notes on page 6 ➤

A. Do you want to have your jury service **deferred**?

No ☐ Go to B.   Yes ☐ Say why in **Box A** below.

Box A *I would like my jury service to be deferred because*

Say **when** you will **not** be available for jury service and **why** not.

Go to Part 4

B. Do you want to be **excused** from jury service?

No ☐ Go to Part 4   Yes ☐ Say why in **Box B** below.

Box B *I would like to be excused because*

Go to Part 5

Part 4 Disability ♿

Please read the Notes on page 6 ➤

Do you have a disability for which the court will need to make special arrangements?   No ☐ Go to Part 5.

Yes ☐ Say what special arrangements in the box below.

The special arrangements are

Go to Part 5

Part 5 Declaration

Please read the Warning on page 6 ➤

- I have read the jury summons and the warnings on pages 1, 2, 4 and 6.
- The information I have given is true to the best of my knowledge.

Signed

Date

What to do next

- Tear off this sheet. Send it to the court in the envelope which was sent with this summons.

- Keep the other pages carefully and take them with you when you go to the court.

(tear here)

➤ Notes about deferral and excusal

A list of those who have the **right to be excused** is given in Box D on page 3. Please read the list carefully before you fill in Part 3.

Jury service may be inconvenient for many people. However, some people have special problems which make it very difficult for them to do jury service.
If this applies to you, you may ask the jury summoning officer to

> **put your jury service off to a later date.**
> This is called 'deferral'. Jury service may only be deferred once.

or **to excuse you from jury service on this occasion.**
You will only be excused if the jury summoning officer is satisfied that it would not be reasonable to expect you to do jury service during the next year.

How long will jury service last? Usually for 10 working days.
If a trial is likely to last longer you will be asked **at the court** if this would be difficult for you.

➤ Notes about disability

There is a **local information leaflet** with this summons.
The leaflet will tell you about the court's facilities for disabled people.

The court will try to meet your special needs but you may be discharged if there is doubt about your capacity to be a juror.

➤ Warning

You may be discharged from jury service if there is doubt about your capacity to be a juror because of

• disability

• insufficient understanding of English.

Printed in the UK for HMSO 3/93 Dd. K60759 C .

replacement provided that an explanation is offered in each case. The C.J.A. 1988 abolished the right of peremptory challenge.

In *R.* v. *Ford* (1989), the Court of Appeal held that, in the absence of specific bias, ethnic origin cannot be a valid ground for challenging any juror, because juries are selected at random.

Verdicts

The verdict of a jury in criminal cases does not have to be unanimous. The J.A. 1974 provides that majority verdicts are acceptable:

- (a) (i) where the jury consists of 11 or 12 jurors and a majority of 10 jurors are in agreement.
  - (ii) Where the jury consists of 10 jurors, nine must agree, and
- (b) The jury have deliberated for what the court considers to be a reasonable length of time. In the Crown Court, the period must be at least two hours.
- (c) The foreman of the jury in the Crown Court states the number of the jurors who agreed and disagreed with the verdict.

In *R.* v. *Pigg* (1983), the foreman only stated the number of jurors agreeing with the verdict, and did not state the number dissenting. The House of Lords held that it was sufficient if the words used by the foreman of the jury made it clear to ordinary persons how the jury was divided.

Advantages and Disadvantages of Trial by Jury

1. Advantages

- (a) A verdict from a jury of ordinary lay persons appears to be more acceptable to the public than if it came from a single judge.
- (b) Ordinary lay people take part in the administration of law.
- (c) A jury is impartial and has no direct interest in the result. In *R.* v. *Gough* (1992), after the jury's verdict of guilty, it was discovered that a juror knew a close relative of the defendant, who later appealed on the grounds that this constituted a serious irregularity in

the conduct of the trial. The Court of Appeal held that it would not interfere with a jury's verdict unless it could be shown that the defendant (a) did not have a fair trial or (b) was likely to have been prejudiced. In this case the Court considered that if there was any bias it was likely to be in favour of the defendant.

(d) There is an impression that not only has justice been done, it has been seen to be done.

(e) A jury will sometimes come to a verdict which is *just* rather than legally correct. In recent years juries, in cases with exceptional circumstances, have refused to follow the letter of the law and considered that only an acquittal would be a just verdict. Clive Ponting was acquitted of a charge under the Official Secrets Act, although the judge informed the jury that the accused had no defence in law. In 1992, Stephen Owen shot a man who, by reckless driving, had killed his son. The jury acquitted Mr. Owen, while it was almost certain that a judge sitting alone would have held him to be guilty. The juries in these cases must have considered that justice was best served with an acquittal.

2. Disadvantages

(a) Jurors may not be competent to understand the evidence presented and the issues involved. Cases involving fraud, which may last for many months, may involve the use of technical terms beyond the grasp of many jurors. In libel cases, for example, an average juror may not be able to appreciate the subtle meanings of the offending words – are they statements of fact or merely comments? In addition to reaching a decision, a libel jury has to decide the amount of damages which a successful plaintiff should receive, although they have no training in this aspect and the judge is only allowed to give advice or guidance in general terms.

(b) Jurors may be easily convinced by the manner and presentation of the barristers during the trial, or be persuaded by a forceful or belligerent foreman when locked in the jury room.

(c) In some trials, for example motoring offences, juries have a sympathy with the accused. They may be fellow motorists and think, "There, but for the grace of God, go I."

(d) Although jurors receive payment for travelling expenses, etc., and an allowance for loss of earnings, it is probable that many people suffer financial loss.

(e) The period of jury service may take many weeks and this may place a strain on certain jurors, such as mothers with very young children or the more elderly. There is a danger that jurors may "agree" with a verdict to bring a quicker end to the trial.

(f) Jurors may experience frustration in having to wait in a court building for many days before being called to serve, and possibly never being called during the period of their service.

(g) Cover by television and newspapers of important or controversial trials may influence jurors. Although jurors should not discuss the case during the course of the trial, it is practically impossible to avoid the opinions of reporters and newsreaders.

(h) Jurors may suffer from post-traumatic stress disorder in the period after trials which involve horrific crimes, such as murder and rape, and in which the jury is exposed to graphic, gruesome details and photographs of the crime. In America jurors can receive psychiatric counselling directly after the trial is over, but in Britain this facility is not available and disturbed jurors have to cope as best as they can.

There is a suggestion that trials by judges alone would probably produce more correct decisions than trials before juries. This would eliminate any fear that members of the jury are in the pay or under the influence of the accused, and it may also solve many of the disadvantages mentioned above.

Trials by judges sitting alone without a jury (the Diplock Courts) exist in Northern Ireland, but it is doubtful if abolition of the jury system would be introduced in England and Wales, because of the advantages of the system mentioned on p. 92 and public opinion.

Lay Assessors

Lay assessors are qualified persons with expert knowledge, who are called to help or assist a judge in a case which needs special technical knowledge or expertise. They are mainly employed in the Admiralty Court and are known as nautical assessors.

REVISION TEST

1. What is the title of the judges who may hear appeals in the House of Lords? *Law Lords*

2. Who is head of the Queen's Bench Division of the High Court? *Lord Chief Justice*

3. May a justice of the peace hear a case before the Crown Court?

4. Name the three main functions of the magistrates' courts.

5. State the titles of the two Law Officers.

6. Name two civil remedies.

7. What are the two qualifications to serve on a jury?

8. Name the persons who are ineligible for jury service. *Mirors, Criminal record, Judges, mentals, Clergy*

SPECIMEN EXAMINATION QUESTIONS

1. (a) Explain the financial requirements for deciding whether a civil dispute goes to the High Court or a county court.
   (b) Outline the procedure, and the financial restrictions, when a person wishes to sue another person in the small claims court.

2. (a) Describe the work of lay magistrates in both criminal and civil matters.
   (b) Discuss the advantages and disadvantages of using lay persons instead of employing professional lawyers.

3. (a) The C.J.A. 1991 provides a statutory structure for courts to follow when deciding an appropriate sentence. Discuss the provisions with respect to imprisonment and fines.
   (b) Outline other sentences which the courts may impose.

4. (a) Explain the differences between legal aid and legal advice and assistance.
   (b) What is the purpose of a legal aid scheme? Do you think the present system is achieving these aims?

5. Describe the jurisdiction and purpose of the youth courts.

6. Why have administrative tribunals been established? What are the advantages over the other courts of law?

7. How is a jury formed? State the qualifications required to be called for jury service and name the class of people who are ineligible, disqualified or excused as of right.

8. Compare the training and work of solicitors and barristers.

SUGGESTED COURSEWORK TITLES

Describe the work of the magistrates' court and explain how magistrates are chosen for appointment. Could you suggest other ways of appointing magistrates that would improve the system?

Describe the training and work of barristers and solicitors. Discuss the arguments for, and against, the legal profession being fused into a single profession.

Explain how a jury is formed and describe its function in relation to the judge. Discuss the advantages and disadvantages of the jury system, and consider the effects of trial by a judge alone.

Describe the legal aid and advice available in civil and criminal cases. Discuss the purpose of the system and consider whether or not the present scheme fulfils its purpose.

Chapter 4

Legal Personality

A legal system exists for the subjects or persons within the State; in English law, there are two classes of persons; human or natural beings, and corporate beings. The latter, called corporations, are artificial persons but they are recognised as having a legal status within the legal system. A corporation is comprised of human persons but has a legal existence separate from them.

Although all persons in Britain have a legal status, not all persons within the community have the same status. As will be explained later in greater detail, in many aspects of law, children are treated differently from adults, and the mentally ill are treated differently from normal, sane persons. Generally, the legal status of a human person starts at birth and ends at death, but an unborn child has certain rights, and certain intentions and rights of a person are protected after death (*e.g.* ensuring that provisions in a will or trust are carried out).

CHILDREN

The age of majority is 18 when, generally, full legal status is acquired. Below 18 the age limit for legal responsibility and rights varies according to the particular section of law in question. The reason that young people do not have full legal status is not to prevent or curb their activities, but to protect them. Students will come across many names used to describe persons under 18, infants, minors, young persons, juveniles, children, etc., but in the main they all mean the same thing, a person who does not have full legal capacity.

1. Crime
A child under 10 is deemed to be incapable of committing a crime. Between 10 and 14 a child is presumed incapable of forming the intention (*mens rea*) of committing a crime. This

presumption may be rebutted if it can be clearly shown that the child knew that the offending act was seriously wrong and criminal. Over the age of 14, a young person is fully liable for criminal prosecution, but as previously shown (p. 57) special procedures are taken with regard to the trial and punishment.

2. Legality

(a) Legitimate children
A child is legitimate if the parents were married at the time of conception or birth, even if the marriage was later declared void, provided that either of the parents reasonably believed the marriage to be valid.

(b) Illegitimate children
A child born of parents who were not married to each other at the times stated above is illegitimate. If the mother is married, there is a presumption that her husband is the father, but this may be rebutted by evidence, such as the husband being out of the country for more than a year before the birth. An illegitimate child has the same rights as a legitimate child to an intestacy of either parents, and may claim as a dependant within the provisions of the Inheritance (Provision for Family and Dependants) Act 1975. Furthermore, if a will makes a bequest to "my children," illegitimate children are included. A legal disadvantage for illegitimate children is that they cannot succeed to a title or any property attached to the title.

(c) Legitimation
An illegitimate child may be legitimated by the subsequent marriage of the parents and is then considered to be a legitimate child with the same rights.

(d) Adoption
Children who have been legally adopted have all the legal rights as if the adopters were the natural parents.

3. Contract
A contract between an adult and a minor is binding on the adult, but it is not binding on the minor, unless it is for necessaries (food, clothes, etc.) or for the minor's benefit (training, education, etc.). A minor may make contracts to own

moveable personal property (records, cars, etc.), but a minor cannot legally own land.

4. Tort

Minors are not so well protected in tort and the age of the person is not as important as the mental understanding of the specific individual. Obviously a young child cannot be expected to show the same standard of care in negligence as an adult, and conversely, an adult may have to show greater care with respect to children than with other adults.

5. Marriage

Minors cannot marry under 16, and may only do so when aged 16 and 17 if they have the written consent of their parents or a magistrate.

6. Litigation

A minor may not personally bring a civil action, but must do so through a "next friend" (usually a parent) and defend an action through a "*guardian ad litem*." Minors under 17 may not apply for legal aid, although their parents or guardians may do so on their behalf.

7. Other restrictions on the rights of minors

(a) Voting and jury service

Young persons cannot vote at a local or parliamentary election, or be selected for jury service until they are 18 and their names appear on the electoral role.

(b) Wills

Generally, persons under 18 cannot make a valid formal will, although they may be competent to sign as a witness to a will.

(c) Passports

A British passport may be obtained at the age of 16, although children under this age are usually included on their parents' passports.

(d) Driving

A person must be 17 to obtain a licence to drive a car or motorcycle, although a person of 16 may obtain a licence to drive a moped.

(e) Drinking

Persons under 14 are not allowed in bars of licensed premises, and persons over 14 and under 18, although allowed to enter a bar may not be served with, or drink, alcohol. Persons over 16 may consume certain drinks if served with a meal.

(f) Gambling

Persons under 18 are not allowed in betting shops, gambling clubs or casinos, and they may not gamble in bars of licensed premises. A person under 18 may attend a club licensed to play "bingo" only, although they may not play or take part in the activity.

(g) Cigarettes

Although it is not an offence for persons under 16 to smoke, shopkeepers may not sell cigarettes or tobacco to persons apparently under this age, whether or not they are for their own use.

(h) Fireworks

A shopkeeper may not sell fireworks to persons under 16.

(i) Tattooing

Persons under 18 may not be tattooed.

(j) Films

Persons under 18 may not see films certified as "18" and persons aged 14 and under may not see films certified as "15" (see p. 113).

It is interesting to note that with many of the above restrictions the law has placed a duty on other persons not to help with, or to provide the activity.

BANKRUPTS

The Insolvency Act 1986 provides that an individual may be bankrupt if he cannot pay the debt on which the creditor's bankruptcy petition is based. If the debt cannot be paid the courts will make a bankruptcy order, by which an outsider (a trustee in bankruptcy) or the official receiver will find out the total amount of the bankrupt's debts and the total amount of assets. The assets, nearly everything owned privately or in business, are then distributed to the creditors in a laid down order of preference. The first to claim are any employees for wages, etc., then the Inland Revenue, then the Department of Health and Social Security for any national insurance contributions, followed by the local council for rates, any creditors who secured their loans against a particular asset (*e.g.* the house) and lastly, the unsecured creditors. When there is sufficient cash to settle all but the unsecured creditors, the latter receive a share of what is left, which is usually 10p to 15p for every pound owed. If, for example, it was 10p in the pound, a creditor for £500 would only receive £50. If there are no assets left for the unsecured creditors, they receive nothing.

When adjudicated bankrupt, bankrupts are disqualified from certain rights which were previously exercised:

(a) They cannot sit or vote in Parliament, either the House of Commons or House of Lords.

(b) They cannot become a member of a local council or become a justice of the peace.

(c) They may not be a director of a limited company or take part in its management.

(d) They may not obtain a loan over a certain figure or make a contract without declaring their bankruptcy. It is a criminal offence to ignore this requirement.

Previously, some of these restrictions could last during a bankrupt's entire lifetime, but, the Insolvency Acts 1985 and 1986 provided that anyone who has been a bankrupt for 10 years is automatically discharged. The bankruptcy courts may later review a bankrupt's position periodically, and make suggestions with the aim of restoring the bankrupt to full constitutional rights.

PERSONS OF UNSOUND MIND

The legal capacity of the mentally ill varies with the different branches of law and, in many ways, it is similar to the capacity of children.

1. Crime

A person who can show that he did not understand, or did not know that he was doing wrong may plead insanity, and the court will find that he is "not guilty by reason of insanity" (see p. 244

for the M'Naghten Rules and the defence of diminished responsibility).

2. Contract
A person of unsound mind will be liable on contracts for necessaries but other contracts may be avoided, if it can be shown that the other party was aware of the mental illness.

3. Tort
Unless mental intent is necessary, a person of unsound mind would be liable in tort because the aim of tort is to compensate the injured person, not to punish the person who committed the tort.

4. Litigation
Actions on behalf of a person of unsound mind must be brought in the name of the next friend, and defended by a *guardian ad litem*.

THE CROWN

Monarchy exists when the power of government rests in one person. The United Kingdom is a Monarchy but the Queen is a constitutional Monarch, which means that the powers and duties conferred on her may only be exercised on the advice of her ministers.

The Queen has two distinct legal personalities. She is a natural person in her personal capacity, and she is a corporation sole in her public capacity.

(a) The Queen in a personal capacity "can do no wrong." This means that the Queen cannot be brought before a British court, because technically the courts are the Queen's courts and the judges are appointed by her.

(b) The Queen in her public capacity is usually referred to as the Crown. The legal person is the corporation sole, which evolves to each person wearing the Crown. When there is a change of Monarch all Crown property is vested in the new Monarch. Although the Queen in her personal capacity may not be sued in court, the Crown and its agents may be sued. The

Crown Proceedings Act 1947 permits the Crown to be sued for breach of contract, and for torts caused by Crown agents and servants in the course of their employment.

CORPORATIONS

Corporations are artificial persons that have a corporate legal existence completely separate from the human beings that created and administer them. There are two types of corporations, (a) corporation sole and (b) corporation aggregate.

(a) A corporation sole consists of one human person at any one time, but when the human member loses office the title passes on to a successor. It is, therefore, the title or office which is the legal person, and the human holds the property and carries out the duties while in office. When the holder dies, resigns or retires from office, the corporation sole continues and the property and powers are vested in the new holder of the office.

(b) A corporation aggregate consists of more than one person, who are usually called members. As with a corporation sole, it is the corporation which has the legal existence separate from the membership. The human membership may change from day to day, but the corporation is unaffected. The Institute of Chartered Secretaries and Administrators, local councils, British Rail and all limited companies are examples of corporations aggregate.

Ways by which Corporations are Created

1. By Royal Charter

The Monarch has the power to create corporations by Royal Charter, and in the past, trading companies such as the Hudson Bay Company and the East India Company were formed in this way. The British Broadcasting Corporation was granted its Charter in 1926. The power is used mostly these days to create professional bodies, which usually have the word "Chartered" in their title. For example, the Institute of Chartered Accountants, and the Chartered Insurance Institute.

2. By special statute

A specific Act of Parliament creates a specific or particular corporation. Most of the early railway companies were created in this way and it is now used to create the nationalised industries, such as the National Coal Board and local government councils.

Corporations sole are now created by special statute, as are corporations aggregate which in the past would have been created by Royal Charter.

Unlike the B.B.C. the Independent Television Authority was established in 1964 by the Television Act.

3. By registration under the Companies Acts

The Companies Acts provide the means for a group of persons to create a corporation. This method is used as an alternative to the ways mentioned above. Most registered corporations are trading companies wishing to acquire the advantages of limited liability, and they are easily recognised by the last word of their name being "Limited." For example, "Smith & Jones Limited." The Companies Act 1985, s.25 requires all new public companies and existing public companies to include at the end of their names "public limited company" or the abbreviation p.l.c. If a public company has its registered office in Wales, the ending will be "cwmni cyfyngedig cyhoeddus," or the initials c.c.c. A public company must have a share capital of at least £50,000.

It is not only trading companies which take advantage of this method of incorporation, many charitable organisations and professional bodies, not created by Charter, are registered under the Companies Acts to acquire perpetual existence. An example of this kind of body is the Associated Examining Board which is a company limited by guarantee.

Effect of Incorporation

(a) A corporation has a distinct existence separate from the persons who are its members.
In *Salomon* v. *Salomon & Co. Ltd.* (1897) Salomon had for many years been in business as a boot manufacturer and leather merchant. The firm was solvent and he formed a limited company; the memorandum of association was signed by Salomon, his wife and five children, each holding one share. The boot business was sold to the company for £30,000;

20,000 £1 fully paid-up shares, which were allotted to Salomon, and £10,000 secured by a debenture.

The company failed and went into liquidation. The company's assets of £6,000 were insufficient to repay the debentures and the unsecured creditors, who were owed £8,000. The liquidator claimed that the company and Salomon were the same person and that the debenture held by Salomon should be set aside.

It was held that the company was a separate legal entity, different altogether from the members, and although after incorporation the business was exactly the same as before, the company in law was not the agent of the members. Therefore, as the company was properly registered, Salomon, as the debenture holder, was entitled to the available assets.

(b) A corporation may carry on business as an ordinary person, but its activities may be limited by the Charter or statute.

   (i) Chartered corporations have the rights and duties of ordinary persons and may carry on any activities that are not specifically forbidden, or are against the spirit of the Charter.

  (ii) Statutory corporations must limit their activities to the powers expressed in the creating statute. Any act outside the scope, or beyond the powers of the statute is said to be *ultra vires*, and void.

 (iii) Registered companies' activities are regulated by two documents; The Memorandum of Association, and the Articles of Association.

The Memorandum of Association governs the company's external activities and its main clauses provide information on the name and address of the registered office of the company, the objects of the company, the members' limited liability and the company's share or capital structure.

The objects clause states the purposes for which the company was formed and lays down its powers to attain them. The C.A. 1989, s.110, provides that a company does not have to state the specific trade or business it intends to carry on, but may state in the objects clause that the company may carry on "any" trade or business whatsoever, and the company has the power to do all such things as are incidental or conducive to the carrying on of the trade or business. A company may also amend its objects clause for any purpose.

The Articles of Association govern the internal administration of the company, on such matters as procedures of meetings, the appointment of directors, etc.

(c) Although a corporation cannot physically commit a crime or act in a tortious manner, it may be liable for the wrongs of its human agents. Therefore, a corporation may be prosecuted for breach of duty under the Health and Safety at Work, etc., Act 1974, or for defective motor vehicles on the highway. A company may be vicariously liable for the tortious wrongs of its agents and employees in the ordinary course of their employment (see p. 216). A company could be liable if its van driver was negligent while on company business and caused damage to another person's motor vehicle. A corporation may sue and be sued in its own name.

(d) A corporation has perpetual succession, which means that it continues to function until definite steps are taken to end its existence. The changing membership does not affect its existence, and the corporation will remain although a member or members have died, resigned, retired or transferred their interest to other persons.

UNINCORPORATED ASSOCIATIONS

There are many forms of unincorporated bodies, *e.g.* cricket clubs, darts clubs, chess clubs. All sports and pastimes will probably have a club of some size, small or large. They consist of groups of people joined together to follow their common interest. Unincorporated associations differ from corporations in that they do not have a legal entity separate from their members, and the law regards the associations as a group of individuals who all share the legal responsibility.

When a member of a club makes a contract on behalf of the club, that individual is personally liable to the other party, although the whole committee who authorised the contract may be jointly liable. Generally, a member who commits a tort is personally liable, but a committee who authorised an act which leads to a tort may be liable.

In addition to sporting and social clubs, there are large professional associations which are treated legally in a similar way.

PARTNERSHIPS

The Partnership Act 1890, defines a partnership as a "relationship which subsists between persons carrying on a business in common with a view of profit." It is the aim of making a profit which is important, and it is this which distinguishes a partnership from the clubs and societies just mentioned.

A partnership has no separate legal entity and although the courts do allow a firm to sue and be sued in the name of the partnership, all partners are liable, both individually and collectively, for the legal liabilities of the firm.

Principal Differences Between Partnerships and Registered Companies

1. Profit

A partnership must have the intention of making a profit. This is not necessary with a company, and many charitable organisations are registered companies.

2. Perpetual succession

A company, being a legal person, continues to exist regardless of its changing membership. A partnership may end with the death or resignation of a partner.

3. Membership

A partnership may not have more than 20 members (banking partnerships, only 10), although certain professions, such as accountants, solicitors and members of the Stock Exchange, may apply to the Department of Trade to have more than 20. A limited company must have a minimum of two members, but there is no maximum number.

4. Transfer of shares

Generally, shares in a company may be easily transferred to another person, but a partner may not introduce another partner in his place without permission of the other partner or partners.

5. Limited liability

A member of a company is liable for company debts only to the extent of the unpaid amount of the shares. If the shares are fully paid, the member has no further liability. A partner is personally liable for all partnership debts, and any private assets outside the partnership may be used to settle the partnership's liability.

6. Termination or dissolution

A company is wound up either compulsorily, when creditors ask the courts to end the existence of the company because it may be the only way of recovering the debts; or voluntarily, when the company decides to discontinue its existence. A partnership may end by death or bankruptcy of a member, or by agreement, or at the end of an agreed period of time for which the partnership was created. The court may also terminate a partnership if it considers it "just and equitable" to do so.

Trade Unions

A trade union is a group of persons who join together to better their working conditions by collective bargaining. Originally, trade unions were considered unlawful organisations in restraint of trade. In modern times they have legal recognition and are a very necessary and powerful part of the country's labour force.

A union may be sued for contract in its own name, but the liability rests with the members, similar to other unincorporated associations. The Trade Union and Labour Relations Act 1974 provides that collective agreements are presumed not to be legally binding unless they are in writing and expressly provide for such an intention.

Nationality

British nationality gives a person the right to vote; to be a Member of Parliament; to travel to and from the country and all other rights bestowed on a citizen. The British Nationality Act 1981 provided that United Kingdom citizenship may be acquired:

1. Acquisition by birth or adoption

A person born or adopted in the United Kingdom after the commencement of the Act shall be a British citizen if at the time of the birth or adoption the father or mother is:

(a) a British citizen, or

(b) settled in the United Kingdom.

2. Acquisition by descent

A person born outside the United Kingdom shall be a British citizen if at the time of the birth the father or mother is a British citizen (other than by descent).

3. Acquisition by registration

The following persons may apply to the Secretary of State to be registered as a British citizen:

(a) a minor whose mother or father was a British citizen by descent and that parent's mother or father was a British citizen other than by descent.

(b) a British Dependent Territories citizen or British Overseas citizen who has been in the United Kingdom for five years prior to the application for registration.

(c) Acquisition by naturalisation. The Secretary of State may grant British citizenship to a person of full age and capacity if he is satisfied that he is of good character, has a sufficient knowledge of the English or Welsh or Scottish Gaelic language, has lived in the United Kingdom for more than five years and his home, after being granted British citizenship, will be in the United Kingdom.

Section 11 of the Act provides that a person who immediately before commencement of the Act was:

(a) a citizen of the United Kingdom and colonies, and

(b) had a right of abode in the United Kingdom under the Immigration Act 1971, as then in force,

shall at commencement of the Act become a British citizen.

It is normally the domicile (where a person permanently lives) that decides the jurisdiction of the civil law, regardless of nationality. Therefore, the laws of marriage, contract, tort, taxation, etc., depend, not on citizenship, but on domicile.

REVISION TEST

1. Name the two contracts which are binding on a minor. *Necessary. Benefits*
2. May a child under 10 be found guilty of committing a crime? *No.*
3. Name two ways by which citizenship of the United Kingdom may be acquired.
4. Which letters or words must end the name of a registered public company? *Ltd.*
5. Name three ways by which a corporation may be created.

SPECIMEN EXAMINATION QUESTIONS

1. (a) Name the two types of contracts that are binding on minors (persons under 18 years of age).
    (b) Explain how the age of minors affects their criminal liability. What is meant by "rebuttable presumption"?
    (c) How does the law affect minors aged 16 and over, who wish to get married?

2. "The Queen can do no wrong." Explain the meaning of this statement. Are there any occasions when the Queen or the Crown may be subject to the law?

3. The names of many businesses end with the abbreviations Ltd. or p.l.c. What do these initials mean and what legal effect do they have?

SUGGESTED COURSEWORK TITLES

Explain the law generally with respect to minors, and discuss the reasons why they are treated in law differently from adults. Do you agree with the present situation?

How may British nationality be acquired? Do you think the current law meets the needs of the present day?

Chapter 5

Civil Liberties

RIGHTS AND DUTIES OF THE INDIVIDUAL

It is often said that we live in a free society and, therefore, individuals in the United Kingdom have freedom of speech; are free to choose where to live; may vote for whom they wish and associate with whom they wish. These freedoms are denied to citizens of some countries. It must be noted, however, that they are not absolute rights in this country, because most freedoms of the individual are subject to some restriction, large or small.

It is also contended that all rights of the individual have a corresponding duty. You have the right of freedom of speech, and the rest of the community has a duty not to prevent you from speaking.

On occasions the freedoms or liberties of the individual may conflict with the needs of the community as a whole, and in such cases the right will be restricted by Parliament or the courts.

FREEDOM OF THE PERSON

The liberty of an individual is presumed to exist in this country unless a specific law dictates otherwise. This means that a person is entitled to be free from arrest or detention unless there are justifiable reasons, or the individual agrees to the loss of freedom.

Reasons justifying loss of liberty would include (a) arrest by warrant, (b) imprisonment following conviction in court, or (c) detention of a person in need of care (a child, or person of unsound mind).

It is also possible to arrest a person without a warrant where it is reasonable to suspect the person has commited an arrestable offence (see p. 241).

Sometimes the police or armed forces are given special powers by Parliament to intern people, as happened during the recent troubles in Northern Ireland. Subject to such provision, however, a person is arrested with the intention of being brought before a court, and if this does not happen the prisoner has the right to apply for a writ of *habeas corpus*. The effect of this writ is that the prisoner must be brought before a court or judge immediately in order to see if the detention is justified, or whether the prisoner should be released.

FREEDOM OF SPEECH

This freedom is probably the best known and most frequently quoted. The right covers all forms of communication, speech and writing. In many cities and towns, there are areas set apart for individuals to talk about matters of public interest; the most famous is "Speakers' Corner" in Hyde Park, London.

Although we are chiefly concerned with the individual's rights, the importance of freedom of speech in newspapers and broadcasting must not be forgotten. In certain countries the news media are controlled by the government, and therefore, these countries do not have a "free press."

In this country the press has freedom of speech and may even be politically biased, but broadcasting must have no political bias and programmes should give a balanced argument.

Like other rights, freedom of speech is restricted. An individual may say or write what he wishes provided he does not break the civil or criminal law. Examples of the restrictions are as follows:

1. Defamation

An individual has the right to protect his reputation and the tort of defamation provides the legal means of stopping another individual from making false statements to third parties (see p. 211). Defamation may be a crime (criminal libel) if the statement is likely to cause, or lead to, a breach of the peace. Slander, which is the spoken word, may also be a crime if the statement would create an offence such as treason or sedition.

2. Censorship

Certain Acts of Parliament restrict the absolute right to perform plays and films. There is no censorship of plays, but the Theatre Act 1968 makes it a criminal offence to present an obscene play which is likely to corrupt or deprave any individual in the audience. The Attorney-General must consent to the prosecution, and defendants may claim as a defence that the play has artistic or literary merit.

There is no such protection for the showing of films, and at present anyone may start an action in respect of an alleged obscenity. Many people consider that the film industry should have the same rights as the theatre in this matter. Local authorities decide if a film is suitable for showing to the public, and they also have the responsibility of granting licences for premises used for showing films. A local authority may (but is not bound to) rely on the grading given by the British Board of Film Censors. You will have noticed at the start of every film that a form of certificate is shown with the name of the film and one of the following grades:

"*U*" Permits admission of any child of not less than 5 years, accompanied or not.
"*P.G.*" The same conditions apply, but with parental guidance as to the possibility that some scenes may be unsuitable for young children.
"*15*" Permits admission of children not less than 15 years, accompanied or not.
"*18*" Denies admission to persons less than 18 years of age.
"*Restricted 18*" Films that may only be shown to adults in licensed cinemas or film clubs.

3. National security

Certain persons (mostly civil servants) who by the nature of their employment have acquired knowledge which if made public would jeopardise the safety of the State, are forbidden by the Official Secrets Acts from disclosing this information, and are subject to prosecution if such information is disclosed.

The mass media (broadcasting and the press) are similarly liable for prosecution for publication of information in breach of the Official Secrets Acts. Although there is no direct censorship of the press, the issue of a "D" notice informs the press that the information in the notice should not be published.

In recent years the Government obtained an injunction to restrain the publication of "The Spy Catcher," a book written by Peter Wright, formerly of MI5. An injunction was also granted restraining certain newspapers from publishing extracts from the book.

4. Obscenity

It is an offence to publish any obscene material which is likely to deprave or corrupt persons who have read, seen or heard the material. It is a good defence to show that the publication was for the public benefit, in the interests of science, literature, art or some other area of public interest.

5. Horror comics

The Children and Young Persons (Harmful Publications) Act 1955 makes it an offence to publish stories (in words or pictures) which show violence, crimes, cruelty, etc., which would be harmful to the minds of young readers.

6. Indecent photographs of children

The Protection of Children Act 1978 makes it an offence to take or show indecent photographs of children. The aim of the Act is to protect children against exploitation by the taking of indecent photographs or making indecent films.

FREEDOM OF ASSOCIATION

As a general rule an individual in the United Kingdom is free to associate with other individuals for any reason, whether it be social, political, business or concerning trade unions. It is the right of individuals to form an association in direct opposition to another association. For example, employers in a particular industry or trade may join together for their common good, and their employees may form a trade union for the collective strength to bargain with the employers' organisation.

Similar to the other rights, this freedom only exists if an association's objectives and aims, and methods of achieving them, do not break the law. Examples of illegalities are:

(a)   It is the right of employees to withhold their labour (go on strike) but certain workers are subject to Acts of Parliament which make it an offence to strike. The police may not strike and workers in certain nationalised industries are similarly affected if their action would cause danger to the public.

(b)   It would be a breach of contract to strike without giving the proper period of notice. Although technically an employer could sue employees for such a breach, in reality it is very unlikely.

(c) An association which is a secret society and has illegal objectives and administers unlawful oaths is not permitted.

It is possible that there may be a change of law, so that, although membership of a certain association was legal, a later change of law could make membership illegal. For example, in 1984 the Government decreed that civil servants at the Government Communications Headquarters at Cheltenham had to resign from their union. The purpose was to stop strikes which, it was contended, could jeopardise national security.

FREEDOM TO WORSHIP

An individual in the United Kingdom may follow any religious creed, and it is generally illegal to discriminate against a person because of a religious belief. It is possible for some aspects of a religion to be opposed to the law. In some countries a Moslem man may have four wives (polygamy) but in this country a man, regardless of his religion, may only marry one (monogamy). A sikh is required by his religion to wear a turban, and the law of the United Kingdom requires a motorcyclist to wear a safety helmet; therefore it can be seen that a conflict between religion and law arose whenever a Sikh rode a motorcycle. After many protests by the Sikh community in this country the law was changed to grant an exception from wearing a helmet to drivers who object on this religious ground.

It may appear strange, but an exception to the principle of freedom of worship is the Monarch, who must be a member of the Church of England.

FREEDOM OF MEETING AND PROCESSION

Members of the public are free to demonstrate, unless in doing so they break the law. The following are examples of illegal meetings:

(a) If two or more persons meet to perform an illegal act, this is known as *conspiracy to commit a crime.*
(b) *Riot* is committed when 12 or more persons present together use or threaten to use unlawful violence for a common purpose and cause a person of reasonable

firmness present at the scene to fear for his personal safety.

(c) *Violent Disorder.* This offence is committed when three or more persons present together use or threaten to use unlawful violence and their joint conduct would cause a person of reasonable firmness to fear for his personal safety.

(d) *Affray.* One or more persons are guilty of affray if they use or threaten unlawful violence towards another and the conduct is such that would cause a person of reasonable firmness present at the scene to fear for his safety.

(e) It is unlawful for 50 or more persons to meet within one mile of Westminster when Parliament is in session.

(f) The Public Order Act 1986 provides that seven days' written notice must be given to hold a public procession, unless it is not practicable to give the advanced notice. The police may, if it is believed the procession may result in serious public disorder or cause serious damage to property, give directions to prevent the disorders, such as changing the route or prohibiting entry to any public place.

A chief officer of police may apply to the council of the district for an order prohibiting the holding of a public procession in the district for a period up to three months.

(g) Unlawful meetings exist when torts are committed. If a meeting obstructed the highway it would be the tort of nuisance. Similarly a meeting on another person's land may be the tort of trespass.

PROTECTION OF RIGHTS AND FREEDOMS

The protection of an individual's rights is provided by many Acts of Parliament and by the courts. In addition, there are societies and agencies whose aims are to ensure that the individual's rights are maintained and preserved.

Protection by Parliament

In the United Kingdom there is no guaranteed protection from Parliament, as any Act of Parliament can be repealed, and there is no safeguard that a law will not be changed. Some countries, such as the United States of America, have a written constitution where a Bill of Rights lays down the individual's rights, and which is difficult to change. Parliament is not bound by any such restriction and may legally change the law by passing an Act. In practice, however, it is very unlikely that any British government would repeal any law which protected an individual's rights if it did not have the support of the majority of the country. The writ of *habeas corpus* was created by Parliament in 1679, and it is inconceivable that this safeguard would be repealed unless replaced by another Act protecting the liberty of the individual.

While there is no Bill of Rights in the United Kingdom, the European Convention on Human Rights was signed by the United Kingdom in 1950, and, to a certain extent, this country is bound by the rights provided in the Convention. (see p. 121).

Protection by the Courts

The decisions of judges in court have created precedents on constitutional matters, and unless they are overruled by a superior court or by Parliament, they are binding and protect the rights of individuals.

A person's rights may also be protected by application to the High Court for a prerogative order.

The prerogative orders control courts and tribunals by compelling them to exercise their powers according to the law, or by restraining them from over-reaching their jurisdiction. The orders are:

(a) Mandamus

This orders or commands a court or public body to carry out its duty. The order could, therefore, be to a court, a local council or Minister of the Crown. It should be noted that this order, unlike the following two, is not confined to judicial proceedings.

(b) Certiorari

This requires the proceedings of an inferior court to be brought before the High Court, to consider whether the decision of the lower court should be quashed (made invalid). In *R. v. Bolton Justices* (1990), defendants who had pleaded guilty before magistrates on evidence which later was discovered to be faulty, successfully applied for a judicial review to the Divisional Court to quash by *certiorari* their convictions.

(c) Prohibition

This is an order to an inferior court or tribunal to stop proceedings which would be in excess of its jurisdiction.

1. Rule of Law

In addition to judicial precedent and the prerogative orders, a subject's rights are protected in the courts by the Rule of Law, which has been defined as "A principle or rule of conduct so established as to justify a prediction with reasonable certainty that it will be enforced by the courts if its authority is challenged."

The Rule of Law was first explained by A. V. Dicey in 1885. The phrase implies the following concepts which are essential and basic to the constitution of a free society.

(a)   No man shall be punished unless he has been convicted in an ordinary court of law for a definite breach of law. This concept eliminates arbitrary arrest and conviction.

(b)   All men and women are equal before the law, whatever their rank or station, and are subject to the ordinary law and procedures of the courts. For example, in 1977 the Princess Royal was fined for a motoring offence.

(c)   If there has been a breach of law, there is a certainty of enforcement of justice.

(d)   The constitution concerning the private rights of the individual exists as the result of judicial decisions made in the ordinary courts. It is the fact that every subject has a right to appear before the courts, which safeguards the liberties and freedoms of the individual.

2. Natural justice

In addition to the Rule of Law, the courts, tribunals and public authorities have a duty to act in a judicial way to ensure justice for all parties. This is achieved by following the rules of natural justice, which are basically, that the judicial body shall not be biased, and that each party must have an opportunity to be heard.

(a) Bias

The Latin maxim "*nemo judex in causa sua*" (no one can judge his own cause) means that a person in a judicial role must not have an interest in the result. In *R. v. Sussex Justices* (1812), the following phrase was first used and has since been quoted over and over again, "...that justice should not only be done, but be manifestly and undoubtedly seen to be done." If only one member of a board or tribunal is "interested" the decision will be invalid, even if the financial interest is very small. In *Dimes* v. *Grand Junction Canal Co.* (1852), the Lord Chancellor awarded the decision to the company. He was a shareholder in the company, and the House of Lords later set aside his judgment.

However, in *R.* v. *Mulvihill* (1990), M. was charged with conspiracy to rob a bank. The trial judge owned a small number of shares in the bank and did not disclose his shareholding during the trial. M. appealed on the grounds of bias. The Court of Appeal held that the trial proceedings were valid because the judge did not have a direct financial interest in the outcome of the case, which would have lead to a presumption of bias.

In local government, councillors and committee members must declare their financial interest on any item of an agenda, and will not take part in the discussion on the item.

(b) *Audi alteram partem*

The principle of *audi alteram partem* (hear the other side) ensures that when a body is exercising a judicial function both parties must be allowed to explain their point of view.

THE OMBUDSMAN

In 1967 the Parliamentary Commissioner Act created the post of Parliamentary Commissioner for Administration (the Ombudsman). His responsibility is to investigate grievances, referred to him by members of the House of Commons, from the general public who claim to have suffered injustice through maladministration by central government departments and agencies. In 1973, the Commissioner was given the additional responsibility of Health Service Commissioner, and complaints against all sections of the health service (hospitals, doctors, dentists, chemists, etc.) could also be investigated. Examples of complaints made to the Commissioner are:

(a)   A teacher from overseas, complaining that the Department of Education and Science refused to award him qualified teaching status.

(b)   A boy hurt at school, admitted to hospital, and not examined by a senior doctor for four days.

(c)   A man who had to wait four-and-a-half years to have his tax problem solved.

(d)   A 60-year-old invalid whose request for a supplementary heating allowance was dealt with by the Department of Health and Social Services in a manner "... far short of an acceptable standard."

In addition to the Parliamentary Commissioner, there is a local "Ombudsman." The Local Government Act 1974 established a Commission for Local Administration in England, and another for Wales, to investigate complaints about injustices suffered as a result of maladministration in local government, or by a police or water authority.

The complaints of maladministration by local authorities are similar to the complaints that the Parliamentary Commissioner has to investigate, concerning such matters as neglect, bias, prejudice and delay. The Commissioner looks into the manner in which the authority has carried out its functions, not into the actual merits of the decision. It must be stressed that complaints must concern the maladministration of the authorities and not action taken by the authorities.

If a Commissioner decides to investigate a complaint, a report is presented to the authority which then opens it to inspection by the press and public. If the report indicates that a person has suffered an injustice, the authority must inform the Commissioner of the action it intends to take.

The Commissioner may not investigate complaints into:

(a)   court proceedings,
(b)   investigation or prevention of crime,
(c)   matters dealing with the appointment, dismissal, etc., of personnel,
(d)   certain educational matters.

England is divided into three areas with a local commissioner in charge of a particular area. Wales has a separate commissioner.

It is interesting to note that in recent years the commercial sector has followed along similar lines.

In January 1966, 19 banks, including all the big companies, established the Office of the Banking Ombudsman to investigate customers' complaints.

The Insurance Ombudsman was appointed in March 1986 to look into disputes where clients considered that the settlement of an insurance claim was too small or the claim was turned down completely, or where there has been undue delay in settling the claim. It should be noted that the ombudsman may only look into claims on companies within the scheme, and not all insurance companies are in the scheme.

A year later, in June 1987, the Building Societies Ombudsman was set up to delve into complaints from borrowers and savers. (The addresses of these officers are given in the appendix at p. 287).

INTERNATIONAL CONVENTIONS AND COURTS

There are organisations outside British jurisdiction which endeavour to attain human rights for all subjects regardless of a country's own laws. The United Nations has a Declaration of Human Rights which aims at a common standard of achievement for all peoples and all nations and lays down that,

"...every individual and every organ of society...shall strive by teaching and education to promote respect for these rights and freedoms and by progressive measures, national and international, to secure their universal and effective recognition and observance."

The European Convention on Human Rights was signed in Rome in 1950, and the document followed the pattern of the United Nations, in declaring the individual rights and freedoms which should be protected in all the European countries. Many countries have incorporated the convention into their own law, but although Britain has not done so, other nations and nationals as well as British subjects may bring a complaint against her before the European Court of Human Rights. For example:

(a)   The Irish government complained of British torture on prisoners in Northern Ireland.

(b)   A prisoner in an English gaol was prevented by prison rules from bringing an action against a prison officer. He complained to the court that it was in contravention of his human rights, and when his claim was upheld the Home Office changed the prison rules to bring them in line with the Convention (*Golder's Case* (1975)).

As a result, or in anticipation, of the findings of the Court, in these and other cases, our law has been changed accordingly.

The Court of Justice of the European Communities, in the main, deals with actions concerning the Community or its institutions, but recently the issue of protection of human rights was discussed and, while there is nothing in the Treaty of Rome on the matter, the court declared that "Fundamental rights form an integral part of the general principles of law the observance of which it ensures..."

REVISION TEST

Defamation, obscenity, National Security

1. Name three restrictions on free speech.

2. What is another name for the Parliamentary Commissioner for Administration? *Ombudsman*

3. Name the European court which hears complaints when an individual's rights or freedoms have been violated.

4. Name the two basic principals of natural justice.

5. Name the three prerogative orders.

SPECIMEN EXAMINATION QUESTIONS

1. Give four examples of specific freedoms which one has under the law.

2. There is no such thing in the United Kingdom as total freedom of speech. Explain why a person may be brought before a court if he makes a public speech in which he makes false statements about another person.

3. To what extent is a subject ot the United Kingdom protected by the "rule of law" and "natural justice?"

4. It is often said that we live in a free society and therefore individuals in the United Kingdom have certain rights and freedoms. However, these freedoms are not absolute. In some situations they must be restricted to protect the rights of the community as a whole.

   In each of the following situations, state which right or freedom is involved, and explain how, if at all, it has been restricted.

   (a) Brian is a lecturer in law in a further education college. One of his GCSE students tells a group of her friends in the 5th year at the local school that he is a hopeless lecturer and doesn't know his subject. In fact, he is a good lecturer and frequently gains the best examination results in the college.

   (b) Malcolm is walking down the street when he is arrested by a police officer on suspicion of theft. Malcolm had been picked out from photographs at the police station by a witness to the crime. The witness was mistaken.

(c) Katrina is the leader of a pressure group which campaigns for the re-introduction of capital punishment. She knows Parliament is voting on the issue next week. She intends organising a rally to finish outside the Houses of Parliament on the day of the vote.

S.E.G. 1991

SUGGESTED COURSEWORK TITLES

How far is the United Kingdom "a free country?" Do you consider that the subjects of the United Kingdom need a Bill of Rights or other similar convention?

Describe the main "freedoms" for the subjects in the country. Discuss the necessity of the restrictions which are attached to these freedoms. Do you agree that they are all necessary?

Chapter 6

Contract

A contract is an agreement between two or more parties, who promise to give and receive something from each other (legally known as consideration) and who intend the agreement to be legally binding.

All contracts are agreements but there are many agreements which are not contracts. If a friend promised to pay for the petrol in return for a lift home from college on your motorbike, and later refused to do as promised, you would not expect to take the matter to court. This is because there probably was no intention by you or your friend that there should be a legal relationship. There was an agreement between you, but it was not a contract.

As a general rule the law which governs the terms of a contract is the law where the contract is carried out. The Contracts (Applicable Law) Act 1990 is intended to make it easier for business within the European Community, by providing that:

(a) the parties are free to choose the law to govern the contract; and
(b) if no choice is made, the contract will be governed by the law of the country with which it is most closely connected.

ESSENTIALS OF A CONTRACT

The following elements are considered to be essential to the formation of a legally binding contract:
A. (1) Offer and (2) Acceptance.
B. Consideration.

C. Capacity.
D. Legal Relations.
E. Legality.
F. *Consensus ad idem* (agreement).

A. Offer

Every contract must start with an offer by one person to another. An offer is a declaration by which the maker (offeror) intends to be legally bound by the terms stated, if accepted by the offeree.

I may offer to sell my car to you for £1,000 and if the offer is accepted, I am legally bound by the terms of my offer. I may not later increase the price, nor change the agreed terms.

The following points must be considered when making an offer.

1. It may be made to an individual or to a large number of people

Carlill v. *Carbolic Smoke Ball Co.* (1892). In an advertisement, the company promised to give £100 to anyone who purchased their smokeball remedy for influenza, and caught the illness within 14 days. To show good faith, the company deposited £1,000 with a bank to meet any claims. Mrs. Carlill bought the remedy, caught influenza and claimed £100. The court awarded Mrs. Carlill £100 and held that:

   (a) an offer may be made to the world, it does not have to be to a specific person.

   (b) although the general rule is that advertisements are not offers, the fact that £1,000 had been deposited with a bank showed it was a firm offer and legal relations were intended (see p. 140).

   (c) communication of acceptance may be implied by the conduct of the acceptor (see below p. 130).

This is an important case and students are advised to study the different legal implications which arise later in the chapter.

2. It may be made in writing, by words or by conduct

Many people think of a contract as a written document, because they read and hear of footballers or T.V. stars "signing a two-year contract." Although it is sometimes desirable to have written evidence of what was agreed, it is not essential for most contracts, and an oral contract is just as legal. On occasions the parties may not contract verbally, but may communicate their intentions by conduct. For example, a taxi may be hired by raising a hand; or a nod at an auction may make a bid for the item on sale.

Certain contracts, however, are required by statute to be in writing, in a particular form, to be enforceable. For example:

(a) consumer credit agreements;
(b) sale or disposition of land or interests in land;
(c) contracts of guarantee (see p. 155).

3. It must be communicated to the acceptor

A person who performs the terms of the offer but who is unaware that an offer exists, cannot later claim that the performance was the acceptance of the offer. It is of no avail to claim that he would have conducted himself in the same way, had he known at the time that the offer had been made. Such situations arise in reward cases. Suppose, for example, a reward was offered for returning a lost dog and a person unaware of the offer returned the dog to the owner. The finder could not later claim the reward, because at the time of returning the dog he did not know that there was an offer to be accepted.

4. Revocation

An offer may be withdrawn at any time before acceptance, but the revocation of the offer must be communicated to the offeree. In *Dickenson* v. *Dodds* (1876), the offeree was informed by a reliable third party that the property, which was the subject of the offer, had been sold. It was held that this communication, although by an outside party, was good notice of the revocation of the offer. An offer may not be revoked if consideration (see p. 133) was given to keep the offer open for a certain period of time.

5. An offer must be distinguished from an invitation to treat

It is important to know which party makes the offer and which accepts. In the case of goods on display in a shop, it has long been decided that it is the customer who makes the offer and the shopkeeper who accepts. The price displayed on goods is not the offer, it is only an invitation for the customer to make an offer and the amount shown is an indication of the acceptable price.

After the Second World War, many self-service shops were opened in this country for the first time and there was doubt whether this law would apply. The goods were individually priced and the customer took them off the shelf and placed them into a basket. When was the offer made, when was it accepted? In *Pharmaceutical Society of Great Britain* v. *Boots Cash Chemists Ltd.* (1953), it was held by the Court of Appeal that the customer makes the offer when the goods are presented for payment at the cash desk, and acceptance takes place when the cashier accepts the money. The law gives a cashier the right to accept or reject a customer's offer.

In a more recent criminal case, *Fisher* v. *Bell* (1961), the defendant was charged with offering for sale an offensive weapon. He had displayed a flick knife with a price in his shop window. The court followed the law of contract and held that a priced article in a shop window is an invitation to treat and is not an offer for sale. The defendant, therefore, was not guilty of "offering for sale" the flick knife.

The above rule has been applied to some advertisements. In *Harris* v. *Nickerson* (1873) it was held that an advertisement giving details of an auction to take place was not an offer but an invitation to come and make an offer. In *Partridge* v. *Crittenden* (1968), Partridge was charged with illegally offering for sale wild live birds. He had placed an advertisement in a paper offering birds for sale but the court held that he had not made an offer for sale, as the advertisement was only an invitation to treat.

These cases should be contrasted with *Carlill's* Case (see p. 126), where the court considered that the advertisement was intended to be an offer by the deposit of the £1,000 into a bank. The wording of an advertisement is important in order to decide if it is an offer or an invitation to treat.

An offer must also be distinguished from an intention to make an offer. An interesting point of law was made in *Harvey* v. *Facey* (1893), in which Harvey sent a telegram asking Facey if he wished to sell Bumper Hall Pen, and asked him to state his lowest price. Facey replied by telegram that the lowest price would be £900. Harvey accepted at that price but Facey refused to sell. The court held that there was no contract. Facey's telegram was not an offer but a mere invitation to treat, and £900 was the lowest price he would consider if he decided to sell in the future.

The law stated above has been decided by cases but there are many similar "offers" which have still to be decided by the courts.

For example, is the wording on a slot machine the offer or is it an invitation to treat so that the customer makes an offer when he places the coin in the slot? Is a bus making an offer when it stops, or is it inviting the passengers to make an offer which the conductor accepts when he takes the money? It is my opinion that the customer in each case makes the offer, but until such a case is decided by the courts the law is not certain.

ACCEPTANCE

Once a valid acceptance of an offer has been made and all the other factors are present, a contract is in existence and neither party may escape from the terms expressed, unless both parties agree. As it is important to know when an offer is made, it is equally important to know the exact time an acceptance is made, because from that moment all the duties, obligations and liabilities of the contract are binding on the parties. The following rules of acceptance have been decided by the courts over many years, but are still subject to change by the introduction of new techniques of communication.

1. Acceptance may only be made by the person to whom the offer was made

An offer made to a specific person may be accepted by that person only (*Boulton* v. *Jones* (1857)). Otherwise there could be some odd situations, such as A offering C, a famous painter, £1,000 for a portrait, and D, a housepainter who was standing nearby, accepting the offer. The rule only applies when the offer is made to a specific person and not to the world at large, as in *Carlill's* Case.

2. Acceptance must be absolute and unqualified

The offeree must accept the offer as made, and not add any conditions or terms. If a counter-offer is made the offer is terminated and the offeror is under no obligation to honour the offer, even if at a later date the acceptor wishes to accept the original terms. In effect, when a counter-offer is made the acceptor is saying "I do not accept your offer, will you accept my offer?" In *Hyde* v. *Wrench* (1840), the defendant offered to sell his land for £1,000. Hyde counter-offered to buy at £950 but after Wrench had refused this offer, Hyde "accepted" the original offer and sued for the land. It was held by the court that the counter-offer terminated the original offer.

Generally a seller would probably be prepared to sell at the price in the original offer but circumstances may change, for example another party may wish to buy at a higher price.

It must be noted, however, that a request for further information (*e.g.* an inquiry as to whether or not credit would be granted) is not a counter-offer. *Stevenson* v. *McLean* (1880).

3. Acceptance must be communicated to the offeror

Generally, this must be actual communication, either orally or in writing, but in *Carlill* v. *Carbolic Smokeball Co.* (see p. 126) the Court of Appeal considered that acceptance may be implied from the conduct of the acceptor. In this case, Mrs. Carlill's action in buying the remedy implied her acceptance of the terms of the offer, and it was not necessary to actually communicate her acceptance.

A person making an offer may not stipulate in the offer that no communication will be deemed an acceptance. In *Felthouse* v. *Bindley* (1862), the plaintiff wrote to his nephew offering to buy a horse for £30, and "if I hear no more I consider the horse to be mine." The nephew did not reply but ordered Bindley, the auctioneer, to withdraw the horse from sale. In error the horse was auctioned and Felthouse sued for his loss. The court held that, as the nephew had not communicated his acceptance of the offer, no contract existed and Felthouse had no right of action.

4. Acceptance must generally be in the mode specified in the offer

If a particular method of acceptance is not specified in the offer, any reasonable method of communication may be used, but if the offeror stipulates a specific mode of acceptance, it must be carried out in this manner. In *Eliason* v. *Henshaw* (1819), the plaintiff offered to buy flour from Henshaw. The offer stipulated that acceptance must be given to the waggoner who delivered the offer. The acceptance was sent by post and arrived after the return of the waggoner. It was held that as the specific mode of acceptance was not followed there was no contract.

This rule may be relaxed if it is shown that a different method of acceptance places the offeror in a no less advantageous position. (*Manchester Diocesan Council of Education* v. *Commercial & General Investments Ltd.* (1970).)

This is particularly relevant with modern means of instantaneous communication. For example, if acceptance was specified to be by return of post and the offeree replied by fax.

Termination of an Offer

An offer is terminated by the following events, and is no longer capable of being accepted:

1. Refusal
The other party refuses to accept the offer.

2. Counter-offer
The offeree does not accept the offer as made, but changes the terms or conditions. (See *Hyde* v. *Wrench* above.)

3. Revocation
The offeror may revoke or withdraw the offer at any time before acceptance, unless consideration to keep the offer open has been given (see p. 127). (*Dickenson* v. *Dodds* (1876).)

4. Lapse of time
If no fixed time is allowed for acceptance, the offer is only effective for a reasonable time. What is a reasonable time depends on the circumstances of each case. Therefore, if a person made an offer to buy perishable goods, such as fresh tomatoes, it would be reasonable to expect an immediate or fairly prompt acceptance, but when more durable goods are the subject-matter of the offer, a longer period of time may be considered reasonable.

Ramsgate Victoria Hotel v. *Montefiore* (1866). M. offered to buy shares in the company. Nearly six months later the company accepted the offer but M. refused to take the shares. It was held that the period between the offer and acceptance was unreasonable and the offer had lapsed before the company's acceptance was made.

5. Death
Death by either party before acceptance terminates an offer, unless the acceptor does not know of the offeror's death and the dead person's personal representatives are capable of performing the contract. Obviously, this would not apply if the dead person's personal services were needed to perform the contract. (*Bradbury* v. *Morgan* (1862).)

Many candidates in examinations confuse "termination of an offer" with the "discharge of a contract" (see p. 148). If an offer is terminated a contract never came into existence. As both of these aspects of contract law are regularly examined, students should know the difference between the two.

Offer and Acceptance by the Postal Services

Provided that the post is considered a reasonable means of communication between the parties, the following rules apply:

1. An offer is effective when it actually arrives

An offer in a letter posted on July 1 and delivered on July 6 because of a postal delay becomes operative on July 6 and not when it would be expected to be delivered. (*Adams* v. *Lindsell* (1818).)

2. Acceptance

The general rules of acceptance apply when using the post, that is, the acceptance must actually be received by the offeror. (*Holwell Securities* v. *Hughes* (1974).) However, if it can be clearly or reasonably shown that the offeror intended that it be sufficient for acceptance to be posted, acceptance is effective as soon as it is placed in the post-box, provided the letter is correctly addressed and properly stamped (*Henthorn* v. *Fraser* (1892)). It would be considered a good acceptance if the letter was lost in the post and not delivered to the offeror. In *Household Fire Insurance Co.* v. *Grant* (1879), the defendant applied for shares in the company. The company accepted the offer and posted the letter of allotment, but it was never delivered to Grant. The Court of Appeal held that acceptance took place as soon as the letter was posted, because the post was considered the agent of the offeror. A possible reason for this reversal of the general rule is that it is easier to provide proof of posting than to prove actual receipt.

When Telex is used as a means of communication, the rule established by the Court of Appeal in *Entores Ltd.* v. *Miles Far East Corporation* (1955) is that acceptance takes place when the telex is received. Telex is considered similar to using the telephone and not the post. However, in *Brinkibon Ltd.* v. *Stahag Stahl* (1982) the House of Lords held that this is not a universal rule and would not apply in every case. For example, if the telex was sent at night and was not read until next morning when the office staff arrived at work, the acceptance would not take place until it was read, *e.g.* communicated.

3. Revocation
Revocation takes place when actually received by the offeree, not when posted. (*Byrne* v. *Van Tienhoven* (1880).)

B. CONSIDERATION

Unless it is clearly stated otherwise, all that follows in this chapter concerns the formation of a simple contract (see p. 154).

Consideration is merely the price in a bargain. The price does not have to be money, but it must have a monetary value. In a simple contract a party must promise to give consideration in return for a promise of consideration from the other party. A bookseller promises to give you sole ownership of a book, if you promise to pay him the cost of the book. The bookseller's consideration is the promise to give you the book, and your consideration is the promise to pay the price. The promise for a promise (*quid pro quo*) is essential, because in English law a promise by only one party is not enforceable (unless made by deed).

If a person promised to give you a £100 as a gift at the end of the month, the promise would not be enforceable, because it is a gratuitous gift. It has not been supported by a promise from you.

Consideration may, therefore, be defined as the price, although not necessarily a monetary one, which induces a party to enter into a contract.

Over the hundreds of years in which the doctrine of consideration has developed, the courts have ruled whether or not the following promises are sufficient to be valuable consideration:

1. The position of a third party
A plaintiff bringing an action must show the court that he made a promise of consideration. If my father and my uncle promise each other to pay me £100 if I pass an examination, I will not be able to enforce the contract if my uncle refuses to pay, because I gave no consideration for his promise. The contract was between my father and uncle, and I was not a party to the agreement. My father could sue my uncle because he gave consideration. In *Tweddle* v. *Atkinson* (1861) William Guy and John Tweddle each promised the other to pay a sum of money to

William Tweddle. Guy died before paying and William Tweddle sued Guy's executor. His action failed because he had not provided any consideration and he had not made any promise to do so.

This is known as the "doctrine of privity," which means that a person who is not a party to the contract cannot sue on it.

2. Value and adequacy

Although consideration must be valuable, it need not be adequate. The courts will not consider the merits of the bargain, provided that each party received what was promised. For example, a football fan may consider paying £100 for a £10 ticket for a cup final. In *Chappell & Co. Ltd.* v. *Nestlés Co. Ltd.* (1960) the House of Lords held that the wrappers off three bars of chocolate were good consideration.

3. The promise must be more than a duty

It would not be good consideration for a school teacher to promise a class that in return for extra money he would teach to the best of his ability, because it is his duty to teach in such a manner. It may, however, be good consideration if the teacher promised extra lessons after school hours, because this would be outside his duty. In *Stilk* v. *Myrick* (1809) two seamen deserted their ship, and the captain offered to share their wages between the rest of the crew if they brought the ship back to London. Stilk sued for his share, but the court held that he had not provided consideration as it was his duty to work the ship back to London (see *Atlas Express* v. *Kafco Ltd.* (1989), p. 147).

In a similar case, *Hartley* v. *Ponsonby* (1857) the ship was in a dangerous situation, and because of this the court held that the promise to bring the ship home was good consideration because of the new danger.

This concept of consideration was discussed more recently in *Williams* v. *Roffey Bros. & Nicholls (Contractors) Ltd.* (1990). Williams was subcontracted by the defendants to carry out refurbishing work on 27 flats for a fixed price. After completing only part of the work Williams found that he was in financial difficulties because the price was too low. The defendants were liable for a penalty clause if the work was not completed on time, so they offered to pay additional money if the plaintiff completed the work on time. The plaintiff completed the work on eight additional flats but when the defendants refused to pay the extra money he stopped work and claimed the total amount owing. The defendants argued that the plaintiff had not provided

consideration for the promise of the additional payments as he
was only carrying out work under the original agreement.

The Court of Appeal upheld the plaintiff's claim, and held that
as the defendants were receiving a benefit in offering extra
money if the work was completed on time, because they would
have suffered under the penalty clause, it was good consideration
for the promise to pay the extra money.

4. Promises involving debts

A promise to pay a smaller sum to be released from paying a
larger sum already owing, is not good consideration.

A promise to pay £50 as payment in full settlement of a debt
of £100, is not consideration, and the other party may sue for
the balance. This is known as the Rule in *Pinnel's* Case (1602),
and applies because in promising to pay £50 the debtor is doing
nothing more than he is already legally obliged to do. (*Foakes* v.
Beer (1884).)

5. Consideration must not be past

The promise must be to do something in the future. A party
may not offer an act previously carried out as consideration for a
future promise.

In *Roscorla* v. *Thomas* (1842) a horse was bought at an
auction. As the purchaser was leading the horse away, the
previous owner promised that if the horse was vicious he would
return the price. The horse was in fact vicious, but the court held
that the promise by the original owner was not supported by
consideration from the plaintiff. His action in paying the
purchase price was before the second promise of the seller, and
therefore his consideration was past.

In a more recent case, *Re McArdle* (1951), a widow had a life
interest in a house and she repaired and decorated the property
at a cost of £488. The person who would eventually become the
owner of the property after the widow's death, later promised to
pay the cost of the work. The Court of Appeal held that as the
promise to pay was made after the work was completed the
consideration was past and there was no legal obligation to pay.

If, however, a party acts at the request of another and it is
inferred that payment is intended, the consideration may be good
to support a later promise for payment. This is known as the
Rule in *Lampleigh* v. *Braithwaite* (1615). Braithwaite asked
Lampleigh to obtain a King's Pardon for him, which he
endeavoured to do, and later Braithwaite promised £100 for his
efforts. The court held that there had been consideration for

Braithwaite's promise because Lampleigh had acted on Braithwaite's request. Further exceptions to past consideration, are bills of exchange and the revival, in writing, of a statute-barred debt.

C. Capacity

Generally, any person may make a contract, but the law sometimes protects certain classes. In the main, where a person is denied full contractual capacity, the aim is to protect and not to prohibit, and difficulty in enforcing the contract is usually experienced by the party with full contractual capacity.

This section will deal with persons, both natural (minors, drunks, mental patients) and legal (corporations), who have slightly less than full capacity.

Minors

Since the Family Law Reform Act 1969, the age of majority is attained on the first moment of the eighteenth birthday. It must be understood that minors may enter into contracts and do so most days. They buy chocolate, papers, clothes, records, travel on buses and trains, pay to watch films and football, etc., etc. The law does not stop a person under 18 from making a contract, but it aims to protect the minor from certain types of contract.

Since the Minors' Contract Act 1987 came into force, minors' contracts come into two categories:

(a) binding contracts—whereby the minor must carry out the contract as agreed, and

(b) voidable contracts—which do not bind the minor, but the other party to the contract is bound. The contract is voidable at the minor's option.

1. Binding contracts

These are contracts for which the minor has full contractual capacity and may be enforced against, as well as by, the minor. There are two types:

(a) contracts for necessaries, and

(b) beneficial contracts of service.

(a) Necessaries

These may be defined as "goods suitable to the condition in life of such a minor, and his actual requirements at the time of sale and delivery."

It has been considered that a luxury cannot be a necessary, but it must be borne in mind that what might be considered a luxury for a person of small income might be a normally accepted part of life for the more wealthy.

In addition to the nature of the goods supplied, consideration must be given to the actual requirements at the time of sale. A pair of shoes would be necessaries if the minor was barefooted, but they would not be necessaries if the minor had several pairs of shoes.

In *Nash* v. *Inman* (1908), a Cambridge undergraduate, who was a minor, ordered 11 fancy waistcoats from a tailor, but refused to pay the bill. It was held by the court that the tailor's action failed because the minor already had a sufficient supply of clothing and therefore the waistcoats were not necessaries. (See p. 138.)

However, in *Chapple* v. *Cooper* (1844), an infant widow contracted with an undertaker to arrange for the funeral of her deceased husband, and later refused to pay the cost. It was held she was liable, as the funeral was for her private benefit and a necessary service.

It is the responsibility of the party supplying the goods to prove that they are necessaries, and where goods are considered necessaries, a minor need not pay the contract price, but must pay a reasonable price.

(b) Beneficial contracts of service

Included under this heading are contracts for training, education, apprenticeship and other similar contracts. They are binding if, taken as a whole, they are for the minor's benefit.

In *Doyle* v. *White City Stadium* (1935) Doyle was a professional boxer and he entered into a contract which provided a clause that if disqualified he would lose the prize money. He was disqualified, but claimed that as a minor the contract was not binding on him. It was held that although this particular clause appeared onerous, the contract taken as a whole was for his benefit.

This case must be contrasted with *De Francesco* v. *Barnum* (1890), in which a minor became apprenticed as a dancer, on the terms that she would not marry, would receive no pay and would not dance professionally without the plaintiff's consent.

When she made a contract to dance for the defendant, the plaintiff sued for damages and the court held the terms of her contract of apprenticeship to be unreasonably harsh and would not enforce the contract against the minor.

2. Voidable contracts

All other contracts which are not binding are voidable at the minor's option. This means that the minor may force an adult to perform the contract but it cannot be enforced against the minor. If, however, a minor repudiates a contract which has been partly performed by the other party, the minor will have to pay for the benefit received. For example, if a minor contracted to rent a flat for six months at £100 per month, and after three months wished to end the contract, he would be able to do so, but would have to pay £300 for the three months in which he lived in the flat. A minor who pays a deposit on goods may not, after returning the goods, claim back the deposit unless there has been a total failure of consideration (*Steinberg* v. *Scala* (*Leeds*) *Ltd.* (1923)).

When a minor refuses to complete his or her part of a voidable contract, the Minors' Contract Act 1987 gives power to the courts, when "it is just and equitable," to allow the other party to recover from the minor any property acquired under the contract or any property representing it.

For example, should a minor receive goods under a contract (obtained by fraud or otherwise) and refuse to pay for the goods, the court may order the minor to return the goods to the plaintiff. If, however, the minor had sold the goods or exchanged them for other goods, the court may order the return to the plaintiff of the proceeds of the sale, or the return of the goods bought with the proceeds of the sale or the goods received in exchange.

In the case of *Nash* v. *Inman* (p. 137), the undergraduate would now have to return the waistcoats to the supplier or pay for them, whether they were necessaries or not.

If, however, a minor sells or exchanges the property acquired under an unenforceable contract and then consumes or dissipates the proceeds of the sale or exchange, the court may not order the minor to pay over a sum equal to the price originally paid for the goods. For example, if a minor bought a sports bag on credit and then sold it, using all the proceeds of the sale to attend a Michael Jackson concert in London, the seller could not recover anything from the minor, because all the money has gone. But, if the minor had used the proceeds of the sale to buy a compact disc of the concert, instead of actually attending the concert, the plaintiff could recover the compact disc.

Long-term contracts concerning land, shares in companies and partnerships are voidable and may be repudiated by a minor before reaching 18 or within a reasonable time afterwards. If such contracts are not so repudiated they would be binding on both parties when the minor becomes 18.

Drunks and Mental Patients

Drunks and mental patients are liable on contracts for necessaries, and, similarly to minors, must pay a reasonable price. Other contracts are voidable at the option of the drunks or mental patients if they can prove that at the time of making the contract:

(a)   they were so drunk or ill that they did not know what they were doing; and

(b)   the other party knew of their condition.

In *Hart* v. *O'Connor* (1985) the Privy Council decided, in a case where the other party did not know that the plaintiff was insane, that the validity of a contract made by a lunatic who appears sane is to be judged by the same standards as a contract made by a sane person.

Mental patients will be liable on contracts made during a lucid period, and contracts made while the patient was of unsound mind may be ratified during the lucid period. A mental patient whose property is under the control of the court may not make a contract and any contracts purported to be so made are void.

Corporations

The legal position of corporations is covered in Chapter 4 (p. 103). The limitations placed upon corporations to make contracts arise from the manner in which they are created.

Chartered Corporations (*e.g.* the Institute of Chartered Secretaries and Administrators) are created by a Royal Charter, which lays down the purpose and objects of the corporation. The corporation is not restricted and may make any contract, but the Charter may be withdrawn if contracts are persistently made against the spirit of the Charter.

Statutory Corporations are usually public bodies, created by Acts of Parliament (*e.g.* British Rail). Contracts may only be made within the scope of the creating statute, and any contract outside of the Act is *"ultra vires"* (beyond the power of) and void.

Limited companies are governed by the C.A. 1985. Companies registered under the Companies Act have their powers specified in the objects clause of the Memorandum of Association, and contracts should not be made which go beyond these objects. If a person makes a contract with the company, knowing it to be outside the powers of the memorandum, the contract is *"ultra vires"* and void. The European Communities Act 1972 provides that if a person deals with the company in good faith (*i.e.* does not know the powers of the objects clause) any contract is valid, whether or not it is outside the powers of the objects clause. (See p. 105 for the provisions of the C.A. 1989, s.110, which allow companies to carry on any trade or business.)

D. LEGAL RELATIONS

As was shown when dealing with offer and acceptance, it is essential to a contract that the parties intend to create legal relations. The courts presume that with business contracts the parties intend legal relations, and if the parties intend otherwise it must be clearly expressed.

In *Rose and Frank Co.* v. *Crompton* (1925) a written agreement between the parties stipulated that it was not a formal or legal agreement and should not be subject to the legal jurisdiction of the courts. The House of Lords held that the agreement had no legal effect.

The most common case of a contract in which legal relations are excluded occurs on football pools coupons. The contract is made "binding in honour only," and several court actions have been unsuccessful because the courts have held that the intention to create legal relations was expressly excluded (*Appleson* v. *Littlewoods Pools* (1939)).

With social or domestic agreements the courts are reluctant to hold that a contract exists and will look at the relationship of the parties and facts of the agreement before declaring the intention of the parties.

In *Balfour* v. *Balfour* (1919) the husband went to work in Ceylon and agreed to pay his wife £30 per month. He did not pay the money and the wife sued. It was held that there was no contract because the parties did not intend to create a legal relationship.

However, in *Merritt* v. *Merritt* (1970) a married couple separated and the husband agreed to make over the ownership of the house to the wife when she had completed paying all the mortgage repayments. The court held that there was an intention to be legally bound, because the parties were apart and consideration had been provided.

E. Legality

There is a rule of law that no court action will arise from an illegal act. If the contract requires either party to act against the law, the courts will not help the guilty party. A contract may be illegal because it is (i) forbidden by statute, or (ii) against public policy.

The first type is easy to understand. If A made a contract with B to steal C's motorbike for £50, the court would not award A a remedy if B later refused to carry out the contract.

The second type is more difficult, because in this instance the courts consider that in the public interest the contracts should not be enforced. Examples of contracts considered to be against public policy are as follows:

1. Contracts to commit a crime

In *Alexander* v. *Rayson* (1936) the rent for a flat was reduced to avoid paying rates, but the difference was charged as "services." The contract was illegal, because one of its purposes was to defraud the local council.

2. Contracts to corrupt public life

It is considered illegal for a person to make a contract to purchase a public honour. In *Parkinson* v. *College of Ambulance* (1925), the plaintiff donated £2,000 on condition of obtaining a knighthood. When no honour was awarded Parkinson sued for the return of his money. The court held the contract was against public policy and illegal, and therefore no money was recoverable.

3. Immoral contracts

Contracts which are against public morals or against the sanctity of marriage are considered illegal.

In *Pearce* v. *Brook* (1866), a prostitute hired a coach to help her acquire clients. The coach owner sued for the hire charge when she refused to pay, but the court held that the contract was illegal, and, as the coach owner knew the purpose of the contract, he could not recover the charge.

4. Contracts where damages are claimed for the birth of a healthy child

It has previously been considered that, as a matter of public policy, damages should not be awarded when, as a result of a breach of contract (sterilisation, etc.) a healthy baby was born. In *Thake* v. *Maurice* (1986), a vasectomy operation was performed, but the operation was ineffective and a healthy child was later born to the parents. The surgeon did not warn the parents that there was a chance that a pregnancy could occur. The Court of Appeal held the defendant to be in breach of contract for not warning the plaintiff of the risk, and awarded damages for the cost of the birth, the upkeep of the child and for the discomfort of the normal pregnancy.

5. Contracts in restraint of trade

The courts are reluctant to enforce a contract which stops a person from carrying on employment or a business, even if only for a limited period of time. The courts' attitude vary according to the nature of the contract, as follows:

(a) Contracts between employer and employee (contract of employment)

An employer may make it a condition of employment that if the employee leaves his job, he will not work for a competitor for a period of time, and/or within a stated distance. Generally the courts will not enforce such agreements if contrary to public policy, unless it is protecting a proprietary interest, such as a trade secret.

In *Attwood* v. *Lamont* (1920), Attwood employed Lamont as a tailor on the condition that if he left, he would not work as a tailor within 10 miles. The court held the agreement to be illegal, because Attwood had no trade secrets to protect.

Fitch v. *Dewes* (1921) was a contrasting case in that a solicitor in Tamworth employed his managing clerk on the agreement that if the clerk left his employment he would not practise as a solicitor within seven miles. The court held that this was reasonable and legal because it protected the interests of the master's clients.

The Court of Appeal, in *Oswald Hickson Collier and Co.* v. *Carter-Ruck* (1984), held that a partnership agreement which restrained a retiring partner from advising previous clients of the firm was, as a general rule, contrary to public policy, as it denied a client the right to choose his own solicitor.

However, in *Kerr* v. *Morris* (1986) an agreement between medical practitioners provided that a partner who left the practice would not set up as a general practitioner within two miles of the partnership surgery for a period of two years. The defendant left the partnership and immediately started a practice a few doors away. The Court of Appeal granted an injunction to the plaintiff restraining the new practice, and held that it was not contrary to public policy to allow medical practitioners to be subject to reasonable covenants in restraint of trade.

In *Clarke* v. *Newland* (1991), a case with similar facts, the Court of Appeal considered the restraint, "not to practise within the practise area" not too wide because, for example, the defendant could have worked in a hospital. The plaintiff was awarded damages and an injunction.

(b) Contracts for the sale of a business

A business may be sold on condition that the seller will not carry on a similar business within a fixed time and/or distance. The courts are more likely to uphold such agreements if they are considered reasonable between the parties.

In *Nordenfelt* v. *Maxim Nordenfelt Guns & Ammunition Co.* (1894), Nordenfelt was known throughout the world as an inventor, and a maker of machine guns and similar weapons. He sold his business on condition that he would not, for 25 years, engage in similar work anywhere in the world. It was held that because of his reputation, the restriction was reasonable.

It was held in *British Reinforced Concrete* v. *Schelff* (1921) that a similar agreement was not binding on a small local company, because it was not reasonable between the parties.

(c) Solus agreements

Traders agree to be supplied by only one company. For example a garage may agree to be supplied for the next 21 years by only one particular petrol company. The courts consider such restraints as illegal unless reasonable. In *Esso Petroleum Co. Ltd.* v. *Harpers Garage Ltd.* (1967), the House of Lords held that an agreement for 21 years was too long, but an agreement for five years was reasonable. The Court of Appeal in *Alex Lobb (Garages) Ltd.* v. *Total Oil (G.B.) Ltd.* (1985), held that an agreement to purchase the defendant's petrol exclusively for 21 years, with a provision for a mutual break after seven and 14 years, was a reasonable restriction on trading.

F. CONSENSUS AD IDEM (AGREEMENT)

If a party agreed to enter into a contract because of fraud, misrepresentation or mistake, the contract may be void or voidable. What may appear to be a valid contract, may be invalid because consent was affected by one of these elements. There is no *consensus ad idem*, no real agreement, if one party enters into a contract believing that certain facts, important to the contract, are different from what actually exists.

Mistake

Mistake, as a general rule, does not avoid a contract, unless the mistake was such that there never was a real agreement between the parties.

Raffles v. *Wichelhaus* (1864). A contract was made for the sale of cotton aboard the SS. *Peerless* sailing from Bombay. Unknown to the parties, there were two ships of this name, one sailing in October and the other in December. The buyer thought he was buying cotton on the first ship, but the sale was for cotton on the second ship. The court held that there was no contract.

Mistake as to the quality of goods will not avoid the contract. A mistake of judgment which results in making a bad bargain will not avoid a contract if all relevant facts are revealed.

The courts have avoided the following contracts for mistake:

1. Mistake as to the subject-matter
Where one party sells goods, but the other party thinks he is buying something different (*Raffles* v. *Wichelhaus*).

2. Mistake as to the existence of the subject-matter
Couturier v. *Hastie* (1856). A contract was made for the sale of corn which was being shipped by sea. Unknown to the parties, the corn had begun to perish and had been sold at a port en route. The court held that at the time of making the contract the corn was not really in existence, having already been sold.

3. Mistake as to the nature of the contractual document
(*Non est factum*: not my deed.)

A contract will be avoided if it can be shown that the party who signed a document:

(a) thought the document to be of a completely different nature, and
(b) was not negligent in signing the other document.

In *Foster* v. *McKinnon* (1869). An old man of feeble sight thought he was signing a guarantee, but a bill of exchange had been substituted. It was held that he was not liable on the bill.

In *Saunders* v. *Anglia Building Society* (1971) an old lady signed a deed of gift of a house to her nephew. She had not read the document but a rogue had substituted his own name for that of her nephew, and later mortgaged the house to the building society. The House of Lords held that the contract was valid and the plea of "*non est factum*" could not be used because the lady had signed the kind of document she intended to sign: it was the contents which were different.

4. Mistake as to the identity of the other party

As a general rule, where parties are in a face-to-face position, the courts consider the identity of the parties unimportant, because it is presumed that the parties intended to contract with each other.

In *Phillips* v. *Brooks* (1919) a rogue purchased jewellery and paid by cheque. The jeweller would not allow him to take the jewellery until the cheque was cleared by the bank, but when the rogue claimed he was "Sir George Bullough," he was allowed to take a ring from the shop. The rogue pawned the ring before the bank returned the cheque. It was held by the court that the contract was not void, because the jeweller's mistake was not the customer's identity, but his financial position. The pawnbroker thereby acquired a good title.

This decision was followed by the Court of Appeal in *Lewis* v. *Averay* (1972). The facts were similar to the case above and the rogue, when buying a car, purported to be Richard Greene, a well-known film and T.V. actor (Robin Hood), and signed a cheque for the price as agreed. The court held there was a presumption that the seller intended to deal with the person in his presence, although he was mistaken as to his identity. As a third party had acquired the car in good faith, the seller could not avoid the contract.

Where the parties do not meet, but negotiate at a distance, say by using the post or telephone, identity is important, and a contract is more likely to be avoided for mistake.

Cundy v. *Lindsay* (1878). A person named Blenkarn ordered goods by post and signed his name on a letter-head so that it appeared that the order came from Blenkiron, a well-known and reputed company. The rogue also used a similar address. Goods were sent to Blenkarn and he resold them to Cundy. When the fraud was discovered, Lindsay (the supplier) sued Cundy in the tort of conversion, claiming that the goods were sent to Blenkarn by mistake. It was held that the contract was void for mistake, because the supplier never intended to deal with the rogue.

5. Unconscionable bargains

In cases where one party is able to exploit a weakness in the other party, the courts may grant an equitable relief. In *Watkin* v. *Watson-Smith* (1986) the plaintiff, a frail man of 80, agreed to sell his bungalow for £2,950. There was obviously a mistake, as a reasonable price would have been £29,500, and the court set aside the agreement as an unconscionable bargain.

Misrepresentation

A misrepresentation is a false statement of fact, which induces the other party to enter into a contract and who as a result suffers damage. The statement may be made orally, in writing or by conduct, but, generally, silence will not be considered a misrepresentation.

Misrepresentation must be a statement of fact, not opinion, so that if a salesman claims a car to be "free of rust" it would be misrepresentation if, in fact, the car was rusty. However, if he claimed he only "thought it free of rust," this would not be so. It is a general rule that "the buyer beware" (*caveat emptor*), and with the second statement it would be the buyer's responsibility to check for rust.

Misrepresentation must also be distinguished from manufacturers' boasts or "puffs." Claims such as "our butter is best" or "we give the best service" are really only the manufacturers' opinions and are not intended to be the basis of a contract.

Misrepresentation may be fraudulent, innocent or negligent.

1. Fraudulent

This is defined in *Derry* v. *Peek* as a false statement made:

    (a) knowingly, or
    (b) without belief in its truth, or
    (c) recklessly, not caring whether true or false.

2. Innocent
This is a false statement which the maker believed to be true.

3. Negligent
This is a false statement which the maker had no reasonable grounds for believing to be true.

As a result of the Misrepresentation Act 1967, remedies available to the injured party are rescission or damages. In cases of fraudulent misrepresentation the remedy may be rescission *and* damages (for the tort of deceit).

Rescission means that the parties are no longer bound by the contract and goods or money which changed hands are returned to the original owner. This is an equitable remedy, granted at the discretion of the court and will not be awarded where:

(a) The injured party was aware of the misrepresentation and carried on with the contract.
(b) The parties cannot be returned to their original position (*e.g.* the goods which changed hands have been consumed).
(c) Another party has acquired an interest in the goods.
(d) The injured party waited too long before claiming this remedy.

Duress

Originally duress meant threats of, or actual physical violence to the person, and a contract entered into by duress is voidable at the option of the threatened party. So a contract which resulted from a threat such as, "If you wish to walk again you better sign this contract," would be voidable.

In recent years the principle of duress has been extended to economic duress, where strong commercial pressure is applied.

In *Atlas Express* v. *Kafco Ltd.* (1989), the defendants were coerced into either entering a new contract or suffering serious financial loss. The plaintiffs had demanded an increased payment from that agreed in the original contract. The defendants agreed to pay the increased rate because they could not find another carrier and they were aware that if the goods were not delivered to their customer they would be sued for damages and lose the contract for future orders. When the plaintiffs presented the bill for work under the new contract the defendants refused to pay.

The court held that,

(a) economic duress may make a contract voidable if the coercion applied affects free consent, and therefore the defendants need not pay at the new rates because their agreement to do so was due to the economic duress exerted by the plaintiffs; and

(b) there had been no consideration for the promise to pay the new rate, and therefore the plaintiffs were merely performing an existing contractual duty (see p. 134).

Undue Influence

Where a party makes a contract because of undue influence by another, the contract is voidable and may be set aside by the court, at the option of the party influenced.

Undue influence can arise where a "stronger" person has some special or fiduciary relationship over another, and uses this power to gain an advantage.

In *Re Craig* (1971) an 84-year-old widower engaged a secretary until he died six years later. During this time he made gifts of large amounts of money to the secretary, which were later set aside by the court, because it was considered the relationship raised a presumption of undue influence.

This doctrine also applies to business contracts and in *Lloyds Bank Ltd.v. Bundy* (1975), the Court of Appeal set aside a guarantee which an old man had given to cover his son's bank balance. The son's business was in danger of failing and the court considered the bank had used undue influence to obtain the guarantee.

In *O'Sullivan* v. *Management Agencies Ltd.* (1984), Gilbert O'Sullivan, when young and unknown, entered into contracts to further his song-writing and singing career. He later applied to the court to have the contracts set aside. The Court of Appeal held that the contracts were unenforceable as a restraint of trade (see p. 142) and as the defendants had been in the position of a fiduciary relationship, the contracts had been obtained through undue influence.

DISCHARGE OF A CONTRACT

A contract is discharged (when it imposes no further legal responsibilities on the parties) by:

(a) Performance
(b) Agreement
(c) Breach
(d) Impossibility (or frustration)

Performance

A contract is discharged when the parties carry out their promises. If Jones Ltd. agrees to paint Mrs. Smith's house for £150, the contract is performed when the house is painted and payment made.

Generally a party must do everything promised in the contract, and part-performance is no performance. If performance is not complete, payment for work done may not be recoverable, unless the other party was responsible for non-performance or accepted the work done. Time is not of the essence (that is, the date of performance is not important) unless it is a term of the contract, or becomes a term after agreement.

Agreement

The parties may agree to discharge the contract in the following ways, even though it has not been performed:

1. Discharge by deed and accord and satisfaction
When one party has performed the contract, the other party may be released from the promise to perform, either

(a) By deed, where no consideration for the release is given, or
(b) By accord and satisfaction. The parties agree to fresh consideration, by giving and accepting something outside the original contract.

2. Discharge when neither party has performed
Where neither party has performed, they may agree to waive their rights and release each other from their obligations.

3. Discharge on occurrence of specific events
The parties may agree beforehand that the occurrence of some specific event may discharge the contract. For example, a charterparty contract for the hire of a ship may contain a term that a dock strike will discharge the contract.

Breach

If one party will not perform the contract as promised, the other party may sue in the courts for breach of contract. Breach of contract may occur when one party fails to perform or does not perform as agreed (*e.g.* a manufacturer supplying sub-standard goods.) When a party gives notice of intention not to perform the contract at a future date, there is no need for the injured party to wait until the agreed time of performance as the action may be started immediately. For example, if in January you contract to start work in six months' time as a hotel courier, and in February the employer informs you that he will not honour the agreement, you may sue for breach of contract in February; there is no need to wait until July, the agreed date of performance, before starting the action (*Hochster* v. *De La Tour* (1853)).

Impossibility or Frustration

It may be no excuse that performance is impossible because of an event which occurred after the contract was made. The old common law view was that the parties should have foreseen all eventualities, and this rule to some extent still applies, as in *Davies Contractors* v. *Fareham U.D.C.* (1956) where the plaintiffs agreed to build 76 houses for a cost of £92,000. There were difficulties with labour and supplies, and when the houses were completed, the cost was £17,000 more than the agreed price. The builders contended that because of the difficulties, the contract was frustrated, and claimed the actual cost. It was held that the contract was not frustrated, as the events could have been foreseen and provided for.

The courts, however, have recognised the following events as being sufficient to render performance impossible, thereby automatically discharging the contract and excusing the parties from further performance:

1. Subsequent statute

After a contract has been made, an Act of Parliament makes performance impossible or illegal.

Re Shipton, Anderson & Co. (1915). A contract for delivery of wheat was frustrated when, before delivery took place, an Act of Parliament was passed requisitioning all wheat for the Government.

2. Destruction of a thing necessary for performance

Taylor v. *Caldwell* (1863). A contract for the hire of a music hall was frustrated when the hall was destroyed by fire before the time of performance.

3. Personal incapacity in contracts for personal services

Robinson v. *Davison* (1871). A piano player was ill on the day of a concert and the artist could not play as had been contracted. The court held that the contract was frustrated, as it was not the artist's fault that he was unable to perform.

4. Failure of some event which is the basis of the contract

If a contract is based on the happening of a specific event, the contract is frustrated if this event does not take place. The postponed coronation of Edward VII provided several interesting cases.

In *Krell* v. *Henry* (1903), the defendant hired a room which overlooked the route of the procession of King Edward VII's coronation. The King was ill and the coronation was cancelled. It was held that the contract was frustrated because the procession was the basis of the contract.

This case must be contrasted with *Herne Bay Steamboat Co.* v. *Hutton* (1903). After the coronation the King was to travel to Spithead to review the fleet, which was assembled there. Hutton hired a boat to follow the royal barge, but because the King's illness prevented the royal review Hutton did not use the boat. It was held that the contract was not frustrated because the purpose of the contract was to review the fleet, and as it was still assembled at Spithead, the contract was possible. Hutton was liable to pay damages.

5. Effect or consequence of frustration

When a contract has been frustrated by an event, such as above, it is automatically discharged. Difficulty is sometimes experienced when money or property has been transferred beforehand, or where one party has worked on the contract before the frustrating event. The Law Reform (Frustrated Contract) Act 1943 provides that:

(a) Money or property (other than specific goods which have perished) paid or passed over beforehand may be recovered.

(b) A party who has incurred expenses on the contract may claim out of the money paid beforehand or the amount payable.

(c)   Money due to be paid before frustration is no longer payable.

(d)   Where one party has gained a benefit from work done before frustration (*e.g.* a half-built house) the other party may be awarded an amount which the court considers fair and just.

The Act does not apply to (i) charterparties, (ii) carriage of goods by sea, (iii) insurance contracts.

REMEDIES FOR BREACH OF CONTRACT

When there has been a breach of contract, the injured party, in addition to treating the contract as discharged, may claim certain remedies, the most common of which are damages, specific performance, injunction and rescission.

Damages

Damages are the common law remedy and are awarded to place the injured party in the same financial position as if the contract had been completed. If a contract was made for the sale of a car for £800, and the seller refused to transfer the car, and another similar car was purchased at the market price of £1,000, the purchaser would claim £200 damages. If this sum is deducted from the £1,000 paid for the second car, the purchaser would have paid £800, the price agreed in the original contract.

An injured party will not always receive damages for financial loss suffered as a result of a breach of contract if the court considers the damages too remote from the consequences of the breach.

The plaintiff in *Hadley* v. *Baxendale* (1854) owned a mill and ordered a crankshaft to be delivered by a certain date. The carrier (Baxendale) delayed delivery and Hadley sued for loss of profits for the period during which the crankshaft was not working. The court held that the damages were too remote and the carrier was not liable, because he was unaware that his delay caused the mill to be idle. Baron Alderson considered that damages should be awarded where:

(a)   they arise naturally from the contract, or

(b)   the damages were reasonably in the contemplation of both parties at the time they entered into the contract, as the probable result of the breach.

An excellent example of how these principles are followed came in *Victoria Laundry* v. *Newman Industries Ltd.* (1948). A boiler was ordered for the laundry to be delivered by a certain date. The boiler was delivered five months after the agreed date and the plaintiffs sued for:

(a) loss of normal profits;
(b) loss of profits from special dyeing contracts.

The court held (i) that the defendants were liable for normal profits, because they knew the laundry needed the boiler for ordinary production, (ii) the defendants were not liable for the special profits because they were unaware of the dyeing contracts and, therefore, had not contemplated the loss at the time of making the contract.

Liquidated Damages and Penalties

Damages may be either liquidated or unliquidated. The latter is not decided beforehand but left to the courts to determine. Liquidated damages are decided at the time of making the contract and are a genuine pre-estimation of the damage. The amount agreed as liquidated damages is payable, whether the actual loss caused by a breach is more or less than agreed.

Liquidated damages must be contrasted with penalties. Penalty clauses in a contract are not a pre-estimation of the likely damage, but are usually included to ensure the contract is performed properly. A penalty is void, and unliquidated damages will be awarded by the court to cover the actual financial loss. A penalty will exist:

(a) If the amount stipulated is extravagantly greater than could be reasonably expected.
(b) When the breach occurs because a sum of money has to be paid and the damages are greater than this amount.
(c) When the same amount of damages is payable on several occurrences, which would vary with regard to their effect on the financial loss.

Specific Performance

This is an equitable remedy, granted at the discretion of the court. Its effect is that the court orders one party to perform the contract as agreed. It is never awarded in the following cases:

   (a) Where damages are an adequate remedy.
   (b) Where either party is an infant (or minor).
   (c) In moneylending contracts.
   (d) Where the court would have to supervise the contract.
   (e) In contracts for personal services.
   (f) In contracts for sale of goods, unless the goods are unique.

It is usually awarded in contracts for sale of land or interests in land.

Injunction

This is an equitable remedy, granted at the discretion of the court. Its effect in contract is to stop a party from causing a breach of contract. It will not be awarded if damages are an adequate remedy, but will be awarded to restrain a breach of contract for personal services. It will, therefore, be used to stop a party under an exclusive contract from contracting with another third party. For example, a footballer under a two-year contract cannot join another football club until after the two years have elapsed, unless his club agrees to the move. In *Warner Bros.* v. *Nelson* (1937), the defendant, a film actress better known as Bette Davies, agreed to make a film for another company although she had an exclusive contract with the plaintiffs. The court granted the injunction to the plaintiff and restrained the defendant from carrying out the contract with the third party.

Rescission

This is an equitable remedy, which endeavours to place the parties in the pre-contractual position by returning goods or money to the original owners (see p. 147).

The Form of a Contract

There are two classes of contract:

   (a) Specialty (or contracts made by deed).
   (b) Simple contracts.

The important difference is that a simple contract may be formed orally, in writing or by conduct, and must be supported by consideration. (See p. 133.) Specialty contracts must be written, "signed, witnessed and delivered," and do not need consideration. (See p. 160.)

While the majority of contracts may be made informally by word of mouth or by implication, the following contracts need to be made formally to be effective:

Contracts Which Must be in Writing

Certain Acts of Parliament have laid down that the following contracts must be in writing:

Contracts of Marine Insurance.
Transfers of shares in a registered company.
Bills of exchange, cheques and promissory notes.
Hire-purchase contracts, and other regulated consumer credit agreements.

Contracts Which Must be Evidenced in Writing

The following contracts must be in writing if they are to be enforced in the courts. Technically, without writing they are good contracts but the courts will not enforce them unless the plaintiff has a memorandum in writing signed by the defendant.

1. Contracts of guarantee (Statute of Frauds 1677)

This is a promise to answer for the debt, default or miscarriage of another person. For example, a person may obtain an overdraft (a loan) from a bank on condition that his or her employer or parents give the bank a guarantee (a promise) to repay the loan if the borrower fails to do so.

2. Contracts for the sale of land (Law of Property (Miscellaneous Provisions) Act 1989)

This Act provides that any contract for the sale of land or disposition of land or any interest in land shall only be in writing and all the terms expressly agreed by the parties shall be incorporated in to one document (or two where contracts are to be exchanged) and signed by or on behalf of all parties to the contract. The details in the contract would include:

(a) the parties (their names and description),
(b) the property (the subject-matter of the contract),

No.

F.A. Copy	
League Copy	
Club Copy	
Player Copy	

F.A. PREMIER LEAGUE AND FOOTBALL LEAGUE CONTRACT

AN AGREEMENT made the.................................. day of................................ 19 ....

between (name)..

of (address)..

acting pursuant to Resolution and Authority for and on behalf of ....

.... Football Club Limited (hereinafter referred to as "the Club") of the one part and

(name) ....

of (address)..

....

a Football Player (hereinafter referred to as "the Player") of the other part.

WHEREBY it is agreed as follows:–

1.　　This Agreement shall remain in force until the 30th day of June 19.. unless it shall have previously been terminated by substitution of a revised agreement or as hereinafter provided.

2.　　The Player agrees to play to the best of his ability in all football matches in which he is selected to play for the Club and to attend at any reasonable place for the purpose of training in accordance with instructions given by any duly authorised official of the Club.

3.　　The Player agrees to attend all matches in which the Club is engaged when directed by any duly authorised official of the Club.

4.　　The Player shall play football solely for the Club or as authorised by the Club or as required under the Rules of The Football Association and either the Rules of The F.A. Premier League or the Regulations of The Football League* dependent on the League in which the Club is in membership. The Player undertakes to adhere to the Laws of the Game of Association Football in all matches in which he participates.

5.　　The Player agrees to observe the Rules of the Club at all times. The Club and the Player shall observe and be subject to the Rules of The Football Association and either the Rules of The F.A. Premier League or the Regulations of The Football League* as appropriate. In the case of conflict such Rules and Regulations shall take precedence over this Agreement and over Rules of the Club.

6.　　The Club undertakes to provide the Player at the earliest opportunity with copies of all relevant Football Association Rules and F.A. Premier League Rules or Football League* Regulations as appropriate, the Club Rules for players and any relevant insurance policy applicable to the Player and to provide him with any subsequent amendments to all the above.

7.　(a)　The Player shall not without the written consent of the Club participate professionally in any other sporting or athletic activity. The Player shall at all times have due regard for the necessity of his maintaining a high standard of physical fitness and agrees not to indulge in any sport, activity or practice that might endanger such fitness. The Player shall not infringe any provision in this regard in any policy of insurance taken out for his benefit or for the benefit of the Club.

　　(b)　The Player agrees to make himself available for community and public relations involvement as requested by the Club management, at reasonable times during the period of the contract (e.g. 2/3 hours per week).

8.　　Any incapacity or sickness shall be reported by the Player to the Club immediately and the Club shall keep a record of any incapacity. The Player shall submit promptly to such medical and dental examinations as the Club may reasonably require and shall undergo, at no expense to himself, such treatment as may be prescribed by the medical or dental advisers of the Club in order to restore the Player to fitness. The Club shall arrange promptly such prescribed treatment and shall ensure that such treatment is undertaken and completed without expense to the Player notwithstanding that this Agreement expires after such treatment has been prescribed.

9.   Subject to the provisions of clause 10, in the event that the Player shall become incapacitated by reason of sickness or injury the Club shall, unless provision for the continuation of bonus payments be set out in the Schedule to this Agreement during the period of incapacity, pay to the Player for the first twenty-eight weeks of incapacity his basic wage as specified in the Schedule plus a sum equivalent to the amount of sickness benefit which the Club is able to recoup. After twenty-eight weeks of incapacity the Club shall, unless provision for the continuation of bonus payments be set out in the Schedule to this Agreement, pay to the Player his basic wage as specified in the Schedule without reduction for any state sickness or injury benefit that he may receive. The provisions of this Clause apply only to the playing season.

The Player agrees to notify the Club of any sickness benefit received after the end of the playing season in order for the Club to deduct the amount from the Player's gross wage.

10.   In the event that the Player shall suffer permanent incapacity the Club shall be entitled to serve a notice upon the Player terminating the Agreement. The Player's minimum entitlement shall be to receive 6 month's notice where the Agreement has not more than 3 years to run with an extra month's notice for each year or part year in excess of the said 3 years, provided that the parties shall be able to negotiate a longer period of notice if they so wish.

The notice may be served at any time after:–
(a)   the date on which the Player is declared permanently totally disabled in a case where the Player suffers incapacity within the terms of the Football League and/or F.A. Premier League Personal Accident Insurance Scheme; or
(b)   in any other case, the date on which the incapacity is established by independent medical examination.

Where the player is declared permanently totally disabled under the terms of The Football League and/or F.A. Premier League Personal Accident Insurance Scheme he will be entitled to receive a lump sum disability benefit in accordance with the terms of the relevant policy.

11.   (a)   The Player shall not reside at any place which the Club deems unsuitable for the performance of his duties under this Agreement.
(b)   The Player shall not without the previous consent of the Club be engaged either directly or indirectly in any trade, business or occupation other than his employment hereunder.

12.   The Player shall be given every opportunity compatible with his obligations under this Agreement to follow courses of further education or vocational training if he so desires. The Club agrees to give the Footballers' Further Education and Vocational Training Society particulars of any such courses undertaken by the Player.

13.   The Player shall permit the Club to photograph him as a member of the squad of players and staff of the Club provided that such photographs are for use only as the official photographs of the Club. The Player may, save as otherwise mutually agreed and subject to the overriding obligation contained in the Rules of The Football Association not to bring the game of Association Football into disrepute, contribute to the public media in a responsible manner. The Player shall, whenever circumstances permit, give to the Club reasonable notice of his intention to make such contributions to the public media in order to allow representations to be made to him on behalf of the Club if it so desires.

14.   (a)   The Player shall not induce or attempt to induce any other Player employed by or registered by the Club, or by any other Club, to leave that employment or cease to be so registered for any reason whatsoever.
(b)   The Club and the Player shall arrange all contracts of service and transfers of registration to any other Football Club between themselves and shall make no payment to any other person or agent in this respect.

15.   No payment shall be made or received by either the Player or the Club to or from any person or organisation whatsoever as an inducement to win, lose or draw a match except for such payments to be made by the Club to the Player as are specifically provided for in the Schedule to this Agreement.

16.   If the Player shall be guilty of serious or persistent misconduct or serious or persistent breach of the Rules of the Club or of the terms and conditions of this Agreement the Club may on giving fourteen days' written notice to the Player terminate this Agreement in accordance with the Rules of The Football Association and either the Rules of The F.A. Premier League or the Regulations of The Football League* as appropriate and the Club shall notify the Player in writing of the full reasons for the action taken. Such action shall be subject to the Player's right of appeal (exercisable within seven days of the receipt by the Player of such notice and notification of reasons from the Club) as follows:–
(a)   he may appeal to the Board of either The F.A. Premier League or The Football League, dependent on the League in which the Club is in membership, who shall hear the appeal within fourteen days of receipt of the notice of appeal.
(b)   either the Club or the Player may appeal against the decision of the Board to The Football League* Appeals Committee and such further appeal shall be made within seven days of the receipt of the Board's decision and shall be heard within fourteen days of receipt of the notice of the further appeal.

Any such termination shall be subject to the rights of the parties provided for in the Rules of The F.A. Premier League or the Regulations of The Football League* as appropriate. The Club may at its discretion waive its rights under this Clause and take action under the provisions of Clause 18.

2

17.   If the Club is guilty of serious or persistent breach of the terms and conditions of this Agreement the Player may on giving fourteen days' written notice to the Club terminate this agreement. The Player shall forward a copy of such notice to The Football Association and either The F.A. Premier League or The Football League* dependent on the League in which the Club is in membership. The Club shall have a right of appeal as set out in Clause 16(a) mutatis mutandis (exercisable within seven days of the receipt by the Club of such notice from the Player) and the Club or the Player as the case may be shall have a further right of appeal as set out in Clause 16(b).

18.   If the Player is guilty of misconduct or a breach of any of the training or disciplinary rules or lawful instructions of the Club or any of the provisions of this Agreement the Club may either impose a fine not exceeding two weeks' basic wages or order the Player not to attend at the Club for a period not exceeding fourteen days. The Club shall inform the Player in writing of the action taken and the full reasons for it and this information shall be recorded in a register held at the Club. The Player shall have a right of appeal as set out in Clause 16(a) (exercisable within seven days of the receipt by the Player of such written notification from the Club) and the Club or the Player as the case may be shall have a further right of appeal as set out in Clause 16(b) of this Agreement. Any penalty imposed by the Club upon the Player shall not become operative until the appeals procedures have been exhausted.

19.   In the event of any grievance in connection with his employment under this Agreement the following procedures shall be available to the Player in the order set out:–

(a)   the grievance shall be brought informally to the notice of the Manager of the Club in the first instance;

(b)   formal notice of the grievance may be given in writing to the Manager of the Club;

(c)   if the grievance is not settled to the Player's satisfaction within fourteen days thereafter formal notice of the grievance may be given in writing to the Secretary of the Club so that it may be considered by the Board of Directors or Committee of the Club or by any duly authorised committee or sub-committee thereof. The matter shall thereupon be dealt with by the Board or Committee at its next convenient meeting and in any event within four weeks of receipt of the notice;

(d)   if the grievance is not settled by the Club to the Player's satisfaction the Player shall have a right of appeal as set out in Clause 16(a) (exercisable within seven days of the Club notifying the Player of the decision of the Board or Committee) and the Club or the Player as the case may be shall have a further right of appeal as set out in Clause 16(b) of this Agreement.

20.   The Player may if he so desires be represented at any personal hearing of an appeal under this Agreement by an official or member of the Professional Footballers' Association.

21.   Upon the execution of this Agreement the Club shall effect the Registration of the Player with The Football Association and The F.A. Premier League or The Football League* as appropriate in accordance with their Rules and Regulations. Such Registration may be transferred by mutual consent of the Club and the Player during the currency of this Agreement and this Agreement will be deemed to be terminated (but not so as to affect accrued rights) on the Registration by the The Football Association and by The F.A. Premier League or The Football League* as appropriate of such transfer.

22.   The Rules and Regulations of The F.A. Premier League and The Football League* as to the re-engagement and transfer of a registration shall apply to the Club and Player both during the currency and after the expiration of this Agreement.

23.   The remuneration of the Player shall be set out in a Schedule attached to this Agreement and signed by the parties. The Schedule shall include all remuneration to which the Player is or may be entitled. In the event of any dispute the remuneration set out in the Schedule shall be conclusively deemed to be the full entitlement of the Player.

24.   The Player shall be entitled to a minimum of four weeks' paid holiday per year, such holiday to be taken at a time which the Club shall determine. The Player shall not participate in professional football during his holiday.

25.   Reference herein to Rules, Regulations or Bye-laws of The Football Association; The F.A. Premier League, The Football League*, the Club and any other body shall be treated as a reference to those Rules, Regulations and Bye-laws as from time to time amended.

26.   If by the expiry of this Contract the Club has not made the Player an offer of re-engagement or the Player has been granted a Free Transfer under the provisions of The F.A. Premier League Rules or The Football League* Regulations then he shall continue to receive from his Club as severance payment his weekly basic wage for a period of one month from the expiry date of this Contract or until he signs for another Club whichever period is the shorter provided that where the Player signs for a Club within the month at a reduced basic wage then his old Club shall make up the shortfall in basic wage for the remainder of the month.

27.   The terms and conditions of this Contract shall continue to apply in the event of the Club losing Football League status to join The Football Conference except that the references to "Football League*" in Clauses 4, 5, 6, 16, 17, 21, 25 and 26 shall be deemed to read "The Football Conference" and in Clause 22 the words "The Regulations of The Football League" shall be altered to read "The Rules of The Football Association".

28.   All previous agreements between the Club and Player are hereby cancelled.

SCHEDULE

(a) The Player's employment with the Club began on the.. 19...................

(b) No employment with a previous employer shall count as part of the Player's continuous period of employment hereunder.

(c) The Player shall become or continue to be and during the continuance of his employment hereunder shall remain a member of the Football League Players' Benefit Scheme (and a member of the .... Pension Scheme) and as such (in the latter case shall be liable to make such contribution and in each case) shall be entitled to such benefits and subject to such conditions as are set out in the definitive Trust Deed or Rules of the Scheme.

(d) A contracting out certificate is not in force in respect of the Player's employment under this Agreement.

(e) Basic Wage.

£...................................per week from ....to ....

£...................................per week from ....to ....

£...................................per week from ....to ....

£...................................per week from ....to ....

(f) Any other provisions:–

Signed by the said ....

.... (Player)

and ....

in the presence of

.... (Club Signatory)

(Signature)..

(Occupation)...

.... (Position)

(Address)...

....

....

4

(c) the price (the consideration),
(d) any particular or special terms.

Contracts Which Must be Made by Deed

A deed is a document which makes it clear on its face that it is intended to be a deed, and has the following formalities:

(a) it must be signed by the person making the deed and attested by witnesses; and
(b) it must be delivered.

Deeds need only be sealed when contracts involve a corporation.

The principal contract which requires the formality of a deed is a lease of land for more than three years. Conveyances of land are made by deed, and the promise of a gift unsupported by consideration (see p. 133) would have to be made by deed to be enforceable.

LIMITATION ON BRINGING AN ACTION

The Limitation Acts provide that an action for damages in contract must be brought within a specified period of time. The Limitation Act 1980 provides that actions become "statute barred" and cannot be brought after the periods of time have expired, depending on the type of action as follows:

(a) an action based on a simple contract (see p. 154) becomes "statute barred" and cannot be brought after six years from the date on which the right of action arose;
(b) an action for a specialty contract (a deed) cannot be brought after a period of 12 years;
(c) an action where damages for personal injuries are claimed cannot generally be brought after 3 years.

With cases involving fraud, mistake, misrepresentation and the like, the period of limitation does not start until the frauds etc. have been discovered or should have reasonably been discovered. In *Lynn* v. *Bamber* (1930), the plaintiff bought plum trees in 1921, which were warranted as "Purple Pershores." In 1928, when the trees produced fruit, it was discovered that they were not that type of plum. The court held that the limitation period ran from the time that the fraudulent misrepresentation was discovered. In addition, the period may start again if a defendant acknowledges in writing that a debt exists or makes a part payment of it.

REVISION TEST

[handwritten: offer + acceptance, legality, Legal Relation Capacity. Consensus ad idem]

1. Name six essentials of a contract.
2. Name five ways by which an offer may be terminated. *[handwritten: Lapse Revocation]*
3. Which two types of contracts are binding on a minor? *[handwritten: Necessaries Benefits]*
4. Name four ways by which a contract is discharged.
5. Name four remedies for breach of contract.

SPECIMEN EXAMINATION QUESTIONS

1. Explain the two elements which are necessary to distinguish a binding contract from an agreement.

2. Discuss the legal position of the parties in the following situations:

   (a) David offers to sell his cricket bat to Nick for £50. Nick says he will buy it for £45, but David refuses to sell. Nick then agrees to accept David's original offer.

   (b) Smith Motors Ltd. have a car in their window with a £500 price ticket on the windscreen, which should read £1,500. Peter enters the garage and accepts the offer at £500. Smith Motors refuse to sell the car for this amount.

3. Every contract must start with an offer by one person to another. An offer is a declaration by which the maker (offeror) intends to be legally bound by the terms stated, if accepted by the offeree. In each of the following situations, explain whether or not a valid offer has been made which is capable of being accepted and turned into a valid contract.

   (a) Nadim sees a brand new stereo system for sale in a shop window with a £40 price ticket on it. He knows that the proper price is normally £400 but he goes into the shop and insists on buying it at the stated price.

   (b) Heidi, a health fanatic, goes every morning for a swim across the local reservoir. On her return home she sees that her local newspaper is offering a "£50 prize for the first person to swim across the reservoir this morning." She wishes to claim the prize.

S.E.G. 1991

4. Jim was rescued from the sea by Linda and he promised to pay her £50 for her action. He later refused to pay. Explain to Linda her legal rights to claim the £50.

5. Michael, aged 17, went to work away from home;

   (a) he took a one-year lease on a flat from Debby, at an annual rent of £1,000 p.a., and moved in, paying one quarter's rent in advance;
   (b) he bought five suits on credit from Lin at £100 each; and
   (c) he borrowed £2,000 from Shirley after claiming that he was 21 years old.

   Explain the legal consequences if,

   (a) after six months he wishes to terminate the lease;
   (b) he refused to pay for the suits; and
   (c) he spent all the £2,000 on a holiday.

6. There are established rules in contract. One rule states that, if a minor enters into a contract to buy goods, that contract will only be binding if those goods are necessaries. Another rule states that a contract will only be binding if the parties intended to create legal relations.

   The problem
   Bernard, aged 17, agrees to buy his father's motor bike for £200 and to pay him back at £50 per month, starting at the end of the month. Bernard intends using the bike to travel to work instead of catching the bus. Before the end of the month, Bernard decides that he cannot afford to buy the bike.

   (a) What is the legal significance of Bernard's age in this problem?
   (b) Would your answer to (a) differ if there were no local bus service? Explain why.
   (c) Will the fact that this agreement was made between father and son have any effect on whether the contract is legally binding? Give your reasons.
   (d) Explain why the law is reluctant to enforce agreements between members of a family.

(e) The aim of the law relating to minors' contracts is to protect the minor. Explain why this is so and say how well you think the law achieves this aim.

S.E.G. 1990

7. How are offers, acceptances and revocations affected when the postal services are used as a means of communication? Do they differ from the normal rules? Do you consider these rules to be suitable for modern methods of instantaneous communications?

SUGGESTED COURSEWORK TITLES

Explain the law regarding the capacity of minors to make contracts. Do you think that all minors, regardless of age, should be treated differently from adults?

Distinguish "offers" from "invitations to treat." Do you consider a trader should be able to advertise a "special offer" and not be legally bound by the terms of the offer?

Explain the importance of consideration in the law of contract. Discuss the implications of allowing unsupported promises to be binding.

Chapter 7

Consumer Law

Many statutes have been passed to give the consumer certain rights when buying goods or hiring services. In addition, many institutions and bodies have been set up to protect and inform the consumer. The aims of these bodies and statutes are to help the consumer obtain value for money and place the consumer on a more equal standing when bargaining with the more professional and experienced businessman. Previously, English law has tended to follow the doctrine of "*caveat emptor*" (let the buyer beware) and left the buyer to take the goods as he found them. Once the goods had been bought the buyer had no recourse to the courts if they proved unsuitable. To some extent *caveat emptor* still applies, but the Sale of Goods Act and other legislation has eroded this harsh doctrine.

One of the reasons for protecting the consumer is that due to the technical development of consumer goods, the ordinary consumer cannot be expected to know if the goods are fit for the purpose for which they were bought, or if they are of good or bad quality. Most companies and firms do give value for money and wish to give to a consumer goods which are serviceable and well made, but there are others who lack such fine intentions. It is to protect the consumer from the latter that the following legislation has been passed:

SALE OF GOODS ACT 1979 Now REPEALED Sale of Goods Act 1994.

This Act consolidates the law relating to the sale of goods, and it repeals the Sale of Goods Act 1893, and certain sections and Schedules of other consumer legislation such as the Misrepresentation Act 1967 and the Supply of Goods (Implied Terms) Act 1973. A contract for sale of goods is a contract whereby the seller transfers or agrees to transfer the ownership of the goods to the buyer for a money consideration (the price) (s.2).

As the name suggests this Act only deals with contracts for sale of goods and has no effect on other contracts. Goods, within the meaning of the Act, may be defined as tangible things which can be physically possessed (cars, hot-water bottles, furniture, food, etc.). Things not within the meaning of the Act include land, barter (which is the exchange of goods for goods) and legal rights such as debts, copyrights, patents or trade marks. (The latter group is sometimes referred to as intellectual property.)

Implied Terms

The Act provides that there are certain implied conditions and warranties which apply in most contracts for sale of goods.

The Act aims to protect people who purchase goods which are faulty, etc. This protection may also be available when you buy "seconds." A purchaser of faulty goods is entitled to have the goods replaced, or to return the goods and have a refund of the cost. This is why it is always wise to retain your receipt or credit card receipt, etc. as proof of purchase.

There is no right to return goods if:

(a)   they are not faulty, but you just do not like them. Some large organisations will change goods which are not faulty, but they are under no legal obligation to do so;

(b)   you hold on to the goods for more than a reasonable time, as it may be considered that you have accepted them; and

(c)   you received the goods as a present. Why do you have no rights with presents? Because you were not a party to the contract (see the controversial "doctrine of privity of contract," p. 134).

1. Conditions

A condition is a term of a contract which goes to the root of the contract. In a contract for the sale of a Rolls Royce car, the buyer would expect a car of that make to be delivered; a farmer would expect cattle food to be delivered which would not poison his cows. If this was not so, a buyer could order, say, a red Liverpool F.C. shirt, but have to accept a white Leeds United shirt. Therefore, if there is a breach of a condition there is no contract and the buyer may treat the contract as ended and return the goods. If it is impossible to return the goods (for example, if it was only after the cows had eaten the cattle food, that it was discovered the food was poisonous) the buyer may sue for damages.

(a) Implied undertakings as to title (section 12)

(1) An implied condition on the part of the seller that he has the right to sell the goods, and in the case of an agreement to sell, he will have the right to sell at the time the property (ownership) is to pass. A person who steals goods would not, generally, have the right to pass on a good title to a "buyer" of them. See p. 174 for exceptions to this general rule, *i.e.* when a person who does not own the goods may pass on a good title to a third party.

In *Rowlands* v. *Divall* (1923), the plaintiff bought a car from the defendant, who had stolen it from the true owner. The defendant did not therefore have a good title to the car. The car was later seized by the police for the true owner, and the plaintiff successfully sued the defendant for the return of the price paid.

(b) Sales by description (section 13)

(1) Where there is a sale by description, the goods must correspond with the description.

(2) Where sale is by sample as well as by description, the goods must correspond with both.

In *Nichol* v. *Godts* (1854) Nichol agreed to sell "foreign refined rape oil" as per sample. He delivered oil of similar quality, but it was not as described. It was held that Godts could refuse delivery.

(3) A sale of goods shall not be prevented from being a sale by description by reason only that, being exposed for sale or hire, the buyer selects the goods.

In *Beale* v. *Taylor* (1967) the defendant advertised a car for sale as a "Triumph Herald 1200." The plaintiff inspected the car and bought it at the sale price. He later discovered that the rear of the car was a Triumph Herald 1200, but welded to the front was a Triumph Herald 948. The car was not roadworthy and the plaintiff sued for damages under section 13. The Court of Appeal awarded damages and considered that, as the plaintiff had relied on the advertisement, it was a sale by description, even though the plaintiff had inspected the car.

This subsection was originally introduced by the Supply of Goods (Implied Terms) Act 1973 to resolve the doubt as to whether or not self-service sales could be sales by description.

(c) Undertakings as to quality or fitness (section 14)

(2) Where the seller sells goods in the course of a business, there is an implied condition that goods shall be of merchantable quality, except:

    (a)   where the defects are specifically drawn to the buyer's attention before the contract is made, or

    (b)   where the buyer examined the goods before the contract is made, then as regards defects which the examination ought to have revealed, the condition does not apply.

Subsection (6) defines goods as being of merchantable quality if they are fit for the purpose for which goods of that kind are commonly bought, as is reasonable to expect having regard to the description, price and other relevant circumstances.

(3) Where the seller sells goods in the course of a business and the buyer, expressly or by implication makes known to the seller any particular purpose for which the goods are being bought, there is an implied condition that the goods supplied are reasonably fit for that purpose, except:

    (a)   where circumstances show that the buyer did not rely, or

    (b)   that it would have been unreasonable to rely, on the seller's skill or judgment.

In *Grant* v. *Australian Knitting Mills Ltd.* (1936) a doctor bought a pair of woollen underpants and contracted dermatitis when they were worn. The wool contained a chemical which should have been removed before the sale. It was held that the sellers were liable because the buyer had made known the purpose for which the goods were required and they were neither fit for this purpose, nor of merchantable quality.

In a more recent case, *Wormell* v. *R.H.M. Agricultural Ltd.* (1986), the plaintiff discussed with the defendants a method of killing wild oats growing among his wheat crop. On the defendants' recommendation, the farmer used their spray but it had little effect on the wild oats. The court held that the goods were not reasonably fit for their purpose and the plaintiff was able to claim compensation for the cost of the goods and the cost of the labour used in spraying the wheat.

(d) Sale by sample (section 15)
(2) Where sale is by sample, there is an implied condition that:

(a)   The bulk shall correspond with the sample in quality.
(b)   The buyer shall have reasonable opportunity of comparing bulk with sample.
(c)   The goods shall be free from defects rendering them unmerchantable which would not be apparent on reasonable inspection.

Godley v. *Perry* (1960) is an interesting case in that it involved sections 14 and 15. The plaintiff, aged six, bought a catapult which broke when used and injured his eye. The rubber of the catapult had a defect which was not apparent upon reasonable examination. The shopkeeper was held liable in breach of section 14 because the catapult was not of merchantable quality (it was bought by description) and, as a boy aged six relied on the seller's skill and judgment, it was not fit for the purpose for which it was required.

The shopkeeper claimed an indemnity from the wholesaler who supplied the goods and the court held that as the goods had been bought in bulk by sample the suppliers were in breach of section 15 and liable to indemnify the shopkeeper.

2. Warranties

A warranty is not a vital term of the contract and therefore a breach of warranty does not end the contract, but it gives the buyer the right to sue for damages. An example of a breach of warranty would be if the Rolls Royce car was delivered but the cigar lighter was not working properly. This term should not be confused with a guarantee (or warranty) given by manufacturers to repair their goods, if faulty, within a fixed period.

Section 12
(2) The goods shall be free from any charge or encumbrance not disclosed or known by the buyer. The buyer will enjoy quiet possession of the goods except to a person disclosed or known at the time of making the contract.

3. Exclusion clause

Section 6 of the Unfair Contract Terms Act 1977 provides that when a person deals as a consumer the seller may not exclude any of the implied terms. "Consumer sales" means sale of goods bought for private use or consumption, where the buyer does not buy them in the ordinary course of business. With sales in the course of business (*e.g.* a sale by a manufacturer to a retailer, where the goods will be resold), sections 13, 14 and 15 may be excluded, but the exclusion clause may not be enforced, if it could be shown that it would not be fair or reasonable to rely on such a clause.

The implied condition in section 12 may not be excluded or varied in any contract.

Passing the Ownership of the Goods

It is important to know when ownership passes, because between the time of making the contract and the time fixed for delivery, the goods may be destroyed and one party will have to suffer the loss.

Unless it is agreed otherwise, ownership and responsibility for the goods (the risk) pass at the same time. If the buyer and seller do not clearly state the time they intended passing the ownership, the Act provides rules to help find the parties' intention. The rules depend on whether the goods are specific or unascertained.

Specific Goods

Specific goods are identified and agreed upon at the time of making the contract. For example, a seller offers to sell a Ford car, registration number F123 BC, which the buyer accepts.

Under the Sale of Goods Act 1979 ownership of specific goods passes as follows:

Section 18
   Rule 1. When goods are in a deliverable state, the ownership passes at the time of making the contract. It is immaterial if time of payment and/or delivery be at a later date.
   Rule 2. When goods are not in a deliverable state and the seller is bound to do something to put the goods into a deliverable state the ownership does not pass until this thing has been done and the buyer has been informed.
   Rule 3. When goods in a deliverable state have to be weighed, measured, tested or other such things by the seller to ascertain the price, the ownership does not pass until this has been done and the buyer has been informed.

Rule 4. When goods have been delivered on approval, or on a sale or return or other similar terms, the goods do not pass until:

(a) The buyer signifies his approval or keeps the goods beyond the agreed time, or beyond a reasonable time if no limit was agreed, or

(b) The buyer, by his conduct, adopts the goods (*e.g.* sells or pawns the goods, thereby acting as the owner).

Unascertained Goods

Unascertained goods or future goods are sold by description and at the time of sale have not been identified. For example, a contract for the sale of 10 gallons of oil from a lorry with 500 gallons in the tank.

Rule 5. The ownership of unascertained goods passes when goods of that description and in a deliverable state are unconditionally appropriated to the contract by the seller with the assent of the buyer, or vice versa. The assent may be expressed or implied.

In the above example, when 10 gallons of oil have been poured and separated from the bulk, it has been ascertained and appropriated to the contract.

SUPPLY OF GOODS AND SERVICES ACT 1982

The definition of a contract for sale of goods (p. 165) explains the need for a consideration of money, the price. It points out that the Sale of Goods Act 1979 does not cover transactions where money does not pass in the contract, and gives barter as an example (goods for goods).

The Supply of Goods and Services Act 1982 gives protection for contracts which relate to the supply of goods and services but were not covered by the 1979 Act. The Act gives protection, similar to the implied terms in sections 12–15 of the Sale of Goods Act.

The 1982 Act relates to the following contracts:

1. Contracts for the transfer of goods

Contracts under this heading would include barter, offer of goods for tokens or packets (*e.g.* "Send 10 chocolate wrappers for a free record") and offers of free goods in respect of a service ("anyone who introduces a new customer will receive a free kettle").

Goods received as a result of similar contracts would be covered by the implied terms.

2. Contracts of hire

Such contracts do not include hire-purchase contracts (where the goods will eventually become the property of the hirer). Contracts of hire occur when a person has the temporary possession of another's goods, for example, cars, tools, tents, etc. A fee is paid for the loan and the goods are later returned to the owner. While the goods are in his possession the hirer has the benefit of the rights similar to the implied terms of the 1973 Act.

3. Contracts for services

A contract for services (with or without the supply of goods) is subject to the following implied terms where the supplier of a service is acting in the course of a business:

(a) The service will be carried out with reasonable care and skill.

(b) Where a time for the service to be carried out is not agreed beforehand, the service will be carried out within a reasonable time.

(c) Where the consideration for the service has not been decided beforehand the supplier will receive a reasonable charge.

In these matters what is reasonable is a question of fact.

An example of how the above Act may work would be an electrician installing a new socket. The supplying of the socket would be subject to the implied terms of the Sale of Goods Act 1979, but supplying the service of installation would be covered by the Supply of Goods and Services Act 1982.

The Act does not cover the services of an advocate in court or tribunal, or the services of a director to the company for which he acts in that capacity. The Secretary of State has power to make other exceptions.

CONSUMER PROTECTION ACT 1987

This Act provides that it is the producer of defective goods who is primarily liable for damage caused by such defective goods.

1. The product and producer

The producer is strictly liable (see p. 194) for defective goods and the plaintiff need not prove negligence or fault, although the courts will consider the balance of probabilities.

The plaintiff must show that:

    (a) the product contained the defect,
    (b) the plaintiff suffered damage,
    (c) the product caused the damage, and
    (d) the defendant was the producer of the product.

The definition of the "product" is wide including goods within the Sale of Goods Act, and also growing crops and things on land such as fences, although not the land itself. Intangible products such as electricity and gas are within the Act. Producers of fresh food, such as fish or vegetables which have not been processed in any way, are exempt from liability.

The "producer" means the manufacturer, but this term covers any person who holds out as being the producer. For example, a person who puts a name or trade mark on goods supplied by another.

2. The defect

Defects are defined as:

    (a) defects in design,
    (b) defects in processing or manufacture, and
    (c) an inherent defect without a warning being given.

There is a "defect in a product" if its safety is not that which a reasonable person might generally be entitled to expect. A producer would probably not be liable if the goods were badly misused by the plaintiff.

3. Defences

A producer may have a defence if it can be shown that the defect was caused by following a statutory requirement, or that the goods were not supplied in the course of business. For example, a person who donates a home-made cake at a local "bring and buy" would not be liable if a buyer ate the cake and was sick.

The burden of proof lies with the producer, although he may claim contributory negligence if the plaintiff fails to take reasonable care with a foreseeable risk.

4. Damage
Damage means death or personal injury or any loss of or damage to property.

Nemo Dat Quod Non Habet

The rule of law that "no one can give what he has not got" when applied to sale of goods means that a seller cannot give to the purchaser a better title than he has himself. If Tom owns a pen and sells it to Dick, Dick obtains a good title of ownership. But if the pen is then stolen and the thief sells it to Harry, Harry would not own the pen because the thief did not have a good title. The pen would still be owned by Dick and he could claim it back from Harry.

Exceptions to "Nemo Dat" Rule

It can be seen from the above example that with such a sale, one innocent party will suffer; either the real owner or the purchaser. The Sale of Goods Act and other statutes provide exceptions to the general rule. In all the following cases the buyers receive a good title:

1. Estoppel (section 21)
An owner who is aware that his goods are being sold by a person without a good title and does not inform the buyer, will later be estopped from denying the seller's right to sell.

2. Market overt (section 22)
This rule affects transactions in open markets, and only relates to shops in the City of London, and markets which have been established by custom, statute or Charter. A buyer in market overt will obtain a good title if he purchased for value and without notice of the seller's defect in title. The sale must take place in a public part of a shop which usually deals with the type of goods being sold, and within the usual times of business.

Therefore a sale of a diamond ring at the back of a fish stall at midnight, would not be a sale in market overt and the buyer would not get a good title.

3. Sales by persons with voidable titles (section 23)

A sale by a person with a voidable title, will give the buyer a good title provided (a) the seller's title had not been avoided at the time of sale, and (b) the buyer had no knowledge of the seller's defect of title and acted in good faith (see p. 145).

4. Seller or buyer in possession after sale (sections 24 and 25)

If a seller allows the buyer to obtain possession of the goods or documents of title before payment, a sale by the original buyer gives the new purchaser a good title. Similarly, if the seller retains possession of the goods after the sale and sells the goods to another purchaser, the second purchaser gets a good title in preference to the original buyer. Obviously, the moral to be derived from this exception is do not part with goods until you have been paid or if you have paid for goods, take possession as soon as possible.

5. Factors (Factors Act 1889, s.2)

A factor is a mercantile agent, whose ordinary business is to sell goods in his possession. A sale by a factor, even if he has no authority to sell, gives the buyer a good title, provided the owner deposited the goods with the factor and the buyer acted in good faith.

6. Motor vehicles subject to hire-purchase agreement

A private purchaser (not a person in the motor trade) will obtain a good title to a motor vehicle which is subject to a hire-purchase agreement or conditional sale agreement provided the buyer had no knowledge of the agreement and acted in good faith.

Rights of Action by the Seller and Buyer

A seller and buyer have the usual remedies for breach of contract (see p. 152). The Sale of Goods Act 1979 lays down the following rights of action:

1. The seller

    (a) For the price.
        When the ownership in the goods has passed to a buyer who refuses to pay for the goods, the seller has a right of action for the price of the goods (s.49).

    (b) Damages for non-acceptance.
        When the buyer wrongly refuses to accept and pay for the goods, the seller has a right of action for damages for non-acceptance (s.50).

2. The buyer

    (a) When the seller does not deliver the goods, there is a right of action against the seller for:
        (i)   recovery of the price if paid beforehand.
        (ii) damages for non-delivery of goods. (s.51).
        (iii) a decree of specific performance. (s.52).
              The goods would have to be unique or for a special or specific purpose (see p. 153).

    (b) When there is a breach of warranty by the seller, there is a right of action for damages (s.53).

    (c) When there is a breach of condition by the seller, there is a right of action for rescission and/or damages.

UNFAIR CONTRACT TERMS ACT 1977

This Act affects many of the terms and exclusion clauses used in contracts between businesses and consumers, and improves (a) a consumer's protection when buying goods or services, and (b) the legal position of the consumer when entering or using business premises.

    The Act provides the following protection to consumers:

    (a) Generally, a business cannot exclude, by contract or by notice, liability for negligence resulting in a consumer's death or personal injury.

    (b) A contract may not exclude or restrict a business's liability for breach of contract or claim that it may perform the contract in a way substantially different from what was agreed. As a result of this Act for example, a holidaymaker is entitled to be booked into the hotel and resort stipulated in the contract, and the travel company may not unreasonably exclude this right.

(c) A manufacturer's guarantee may not exclude or restrict liability for negligence to a consumer which results in loss or damage.

(d) The implied conditions in the Sale of Goods Act 1979 (with the exception of condition of title) are similarly available to consumers of goods obtained under hire, rental, and similar contracts, and under contracts for work and materials. Clauses excluding these conditions are subject to a test of reasonableness.

(e) A business may exclude or restrict liability for negligence (other than death or personal injury), but the clause must be reasonable as between the parties.

The effect of this Act is that it protects consumers, when buying goods or services, from unreasonable contractual exclusion clauses or terms, and it protects consumers from injury to their person or property by the unreasonable negligence of businessmen or their employees. For example, a garage would be liable if its employees were unreasonably negligent and damaged your car. The garage may no longer exclude such liability.

CONSUMER CREDIT ACT 1974

This Act covers most aspects of buying and hiring on credit.

Any provider of credit who does not comply with the Act will not be able to enforce the debt.

The Act concerns itself with "regulated agreements," and therefore it is necessary to know what this term means, and any exemptions that are not covered by the Act. A regulated consumer credit agreement exists when credit not exceeding a prescribed amount is provided for an individual, and it is not an exempt agreement. The meaning of "credit" under the Act is very wide, and covers cash advances or loans, hire-purchase, credit sales, conditional sales, credit cards and the like.

There are five exemptions to consumer credit agreements: (i) traders who grant normal trade credit are exempt. It is normal in trade for trade customers to pay all the credit transactions of the period (usually a month) by one payment; (ii) agreements involving low-cost credit are exempt, provided that no supplier is involved and the agreement is solely between a debtor and a creditor. The charge for credit must not exceed 13 per cent., or the Bank of England Minimum Lending Rate plus 1 per cent., if this is higher than 13 per cent. An example of a debtor and creditor agreement would be between a bank and a customer, where the customer may spend the loan anywhere or anyway he chooses; (iii) finance for foreign trade; (iv) loans for land transactions which are settled in four instalments or less; (v) mortgages.

The Act requires traders to show the true cost of credit, and all advertisements, whether in shop windows or in the mass media, must show the A.P.R. This means the Annual Percentage Rate of the total charge for credit. Consumers can easily see which traders are giving the lowest terms of credit, as it includes all costs that the consumer will have to pay.

1. The agreement
The debtor must be made aware of all the regulations as required by the Act. An agreement would be unenforceable without this requirement, or if it was not made in the following way:

    (a)   in writing,
    (b)   containing all the express terms in legible form with no small print,
    (c)   complying with the provisions of the Act as to form and content,
    (d)   signed by the debtor and creditor, or their representatives.

A copy of the agreement must be given to the customer immediately if signed by the creditor, or, if not signed, it must be sent within seven days of the date of the agreement.

2. Default notice
If a debtor is in breach of the agreement, the creditor cannot exercise his rights unless a default notice has been given to the debtor. The notice gives details of the breach, the action the creditor intends to take and the time limit, which must not be less than seven days. Should the debtor not comply with the provisions of the notice, the creditor has the right to:

    (a)   end the agreement,
    (b)   demand earlier payment,
    (c)   consider that any right of the debtor is terminated,
    (d)   recover the property,
    (e)   enforce any security.

Regardless of the creditor's rights as above, a court order is needed if the goods are "protected." Protected goods are concerned with a regulated hire-purchase or conditional sale agreement, and the debtor has paid more than one-third of the price and has not terminated the agreement.

Credit card holders are liable for a charge of £50 if their cards are lost or stolen and used fraudulently. This liability ends once the credit company has been informed of the loss.

3. Termination

Section 99 provides that a debtor under a regulated hire-purchase or conditional sale agreement may terminate the agreement if he has paid:

(a)   all sums due (including arrears), and

(b)   one-half of the price, or less if the court so orders,

(c)   compensation, if the debtor has not taken reasonable care of the property.

The debtor may pay off the whole debt before the date agreed, and will be entitled to a rebate of the interest or charges due to be paid.

Section 37 provides that a debtor may cancel a regulated agreement, if notice of the cancellation is given before the end of the fifth day following the day on which he received the copy of the agreement provided that:

(a)   the agreement was signed at any place other than the place of business of the creditor or his associates;

(b)   in negotiations before the agreement was signed, oral representations were made to the debtor by a person acting as a negotiator.

The Consumer Credit Act 1974 is a very complex piece of legislation, made more difficult to understand by the way in which it was introduced, step-by-step. It has a great effect on most people as consumer credit is very much a part of modern life. The foregoing paragraphs are only an introduction to the Act, and it is suggested that before making a credit agreement (or taking an examination) advice is sought from a Citizens Advice Bureau or Consumer Advice Centre on the current situation regarding introduction of this Act. There are excellent booklets and leaflets on all aspects of the Act available at the offices mentioned above.

REVISION TEST

1. Name four implied conditions provided by the Sale of Goods Act.

2. Name the two implied warranties provided in the Act.

3. Explain the difference between a condition and a warranty.

4. Name the remedies of a buyer for breach of contract by the seller.

5. Must a credit transaction be in writing to be enforced?

SPECIMEN EXAMINATION QUESTIONS

1. Generally people are free to make whatever contracts they wish. However, in some situations, especially those involving consumers, certain terms are implied into contracts by statute.

   In a contract for the sale of goods, terms can be implied relating to the description of the goods as well as to their quality and fitness (the Sale of Goods Act 1979).

   In a contract for the provision of services, terms can be implied relating to time and price as well as to the quality of the service provided (the Supply of Goods and Services Act 1982).

   In each of the following situations, explain how this legislation may apply.

   (a) Rachel buys a coat from her local store. The coat is described as "waterproof." The first time Rachel wears the coat in the rain, it leaks.

   (b) Mandy takes her car to a local garage for a simple repair. The garage keeps the car for two weeks and then charges her double the original estimate.

   S.E.G. 1990

2. Katherine bought a raincoat for £30 from Ashley's shop. The first time she wore the coat, it let in the rain and the buttons fell off because the stitching was faulty. Ashley would not refund the cost of the coat, although he offered a credit note. Advise Katherine of her rights under the Sale of Goods Act. Should she approach the manufacturer?

3. Richard is shown a sample of some oranges at the local shop and places an order to be delivered to his home. When they are delivered they are:

   (a) a different type of orange, and
   (b) are bad and unfit for consumption.

   Explain Richard's rights under the implied conditions of the Sale of Goods Act 1979.

SUGGESTED COURSEWORK TITLES

Describe the legislation aimed at protecting the consumer against the supply of shoddy goods and services. Do you think that consumers receive adequate protection from the present law?

Explain the implied conditions in contracts for sale of goods. Are the current laws sufficient to protect consumers from badly made and dangerous goods? Can you make any suggestions to improve the law for the benefit of consumers?

Chapter 8
Contracts of Employment

A contract of employment is created when an employee starts to work for an employer. The same essentials of a contract apply to a contract of employment as to a contract for sale of goods. The usual employer/employee relationship is known as a contract of service by which a person called the employee or servant works for another called the employer or master. This form of employment should not be confused with a contract for services, which is the employment of an independent contractor. If a painter is hired to paint your house, you may say what has to be done but not how. This is because there is a contract for his services, not a contract of employment. The painter does not work for you; he either works for himself or is employed by a firm of painters. The difference between the two contracts may best be summed up to the effect that in a contract of service the employee is part of the employer's business, and certain duties are owed by each party to the other. In contracts for services, however, the independent contractor is outside the employer's business.

THE NATURE OF THE CONTRACT

With the majority of contracts there is freedom by both parties to negotiate or bargain for terms and conditions. With contracts of employment, however, there is often less freedom than would be expected.

An employer, particularly in times of high unemployment, may stipulate the wages and conditions of work, and employees have no opportunity to bargain because it may be a matter of "take it or leave it." If the terms offered are not accepted, they will not be employed.

On the other side, trade unions may have agreed conditions with employers' organisations which have to be followed by both employer and employee, and in such cases neither may be able to bargain for different conditions and wages.

A third agent has, in comparatively recent years, intervened to erode the principle of freedom of contract. There have been successive Acts of Parliament regulating contracts of employment. The Acts, in the main, aimed to protect the employee, giving new rights and greater job security and encouraging collective bargaining.

It is probable that the lack of freedom of contract in regard to contracts of employment now works to the benefit of the employee, in that the employer is not able to dictate conditions and terms, but has in many cases to accept what has previously been collectively agreed.

FORM OF CONTRACT

As with other contracts, contracts of employment may be by word of mouth, but the Employment Protection (Consolidation) Act 1978 lays a duty on an employer to give a written statement to an employee within 13 weeks of starting work on matters such as pay, hours, holidays, pensions, sick pay, notice and disciplinary rules and procedures which apply to the employee. The aim of this section is to give employees particulars of their rights and conditions of employment which can be used as evidence of the terms and conditions of an unwritten contract.

DUTIES OF EMPLOYER

The duties owed by an employer to his employees are governed by common law and statute.

The most usual duties are:

1. To pay wages as agreed

If the rate of pay was not agreed beforehand, the parties may look at external conditions to reach an agreed wage, such as union rates of pay, or the usual rate for the particular type of work.

The Employment Protection (Consolidation) Act 1978 provides that all employees, whether manual or non-manual workers and regardless of the method of payment, are entitled to receive from their employers an itemised pay statement, in writing. The statement must show:

(a)   the gross amount of wages or salary,
(b)   any fixed deductions (trade union subscriptions, savings, etc.),
(c)   variable deductions (taxes, pensions),
(d)   the net payment and the method of payment (cash, cheque or paid into bank account).

2. To indemnify against liability and loss

An employee, properly performing the duties of employment, is entitled to be indemnified by the employer for any loss or liability incurred (see vicarious liability, p. 216).

3. To provide a safe system of work

The common law and many statutes place a duty on an employer to provide a safe place to work and safe appliances to work with.

The Health and Safety at Work, etc., Act 1974, for example, places a duty on every employer to ensure, so far as is reasonably practicable, the health, safety and welfare of all employees. It is a comprehensive Act, covering all places of work and protects not only most workers, but also the public against risks arising out of the activities of people at work.

In *Dexter* v. *Tenby Electrical Accessories Ltd.* (1990), an employee of an independant contractor, while working on the defendant's roof, fell through the roof which was unsafe and suffered injuries. The Health and Safety Executive charged the defendants with a contravention under the Factories Act 1961. The Divisional Court held that an occupier of factory premises has a duty to make the premises as safe as is reasonably practical for all persons who may work there, even if they are not his employees. If a person is ordered by his employer, an independant contractor, to work on a factory roof, the occupier of the factory is therefore liable under the Act if the roof is in an unsafe condition.

There is a Health and Safety Commission and an Executive, which are responsible for the administration and implementation of the Act. Inspectors visit places of work and give advice on the requirements of the Act; failure to comply with the provisions may lead to severe penalties, including imprisonment.

4. References

There is no legal duty for an employer to give a reference to an ex-employee, but if one is given, the employer may be subject to the torts of negligence or defamation. Therefore, a false statement may be actionable, but a statement of opinion which is critical of the employee's ability would not be actionable if made without malice. This is because the employer has a duty to other employers, and provided he does not act in spite or with an improper motive (malice) the employer has qualified privilege and would not be liable.

The practice of giving references "To whom it may concern" is now declining, and being replaced by confidential references from the current employer to the prospective employer. In such circumstances, however, the previous employer owes a duty of care to the employee not to give an unfair or inaccurate reference.

In *Lawton* v. *B.O.C. Transhield Ltd.* (1987) the defendants gave an unfavourable confidential reference which became known to the plaintiff, and he sued for loss of earnings, claiming the defendants' negligence in giving an unfair reference. The court held that the defendants owed the plaintiff a duty of care when giving the reference, although in this case the court found that the defendants had not been negligent.

DUTIES OF EMPLOYEE

1. Obedience

It is the employee's duty to obey a lawful order, and refusal to do so may justify immediate dismissal without notice. Generally, a single act of disobedience would not warrant dismissal without notice. However, the facts of particular cases need to be examined, so that when a gardener refused to plant flowers, which died as a result, it was held to be grounds for instant dismissal.

2. To show good faith

An employee has a duty to work in the best interests of the employer, and the employee's interests should not conflict with those of the employer. For example, a company's buyer should purchase goods on the best terms for his employer, and any secret profit or bribe received from a salesman to persuade the buyer to purchase goods on less favourable terms is legally the property of the employer, and failure to disclose the bribe gives the employer the right to dismiss the employee.

It is also a duty of an employee not to disclose confidential information gained from the employment, which is likely to cause the employer to suffer. If, however, an employee discloses the employer's illegal activities, the courts would consider the duty to the public interest to be more important than the duty to the employer.

It is generally considered that an employee has no duty to disclose his own misconduct or breach of contract, but in *Sybron Corporation* v. *Rochem Ltd.* (1983), the Court of Appeal held that an employee, with certain standing and authority, may have a duty to disclose misconduct of other employees, whether they be of higher or lower positions in the company's staffing hierarchy.

Termination of Employment

1. With notice

If a contract of employment has provided for employment to be for a particular period, the contract is terminated at the end of that period. Contracts of professional footballers are usually for a fixed period, but often give either party the option of renewing the contract for a further period.

The usual contract of employment is terminated by either party giving notice. The length of time varies, and may be stated at the commencement of employment. For example, teachers agree to give two or three months' notice on specified dates so that replacements may be appointed in time for the start of the next term. If the period is not agreed beforehand, a reasonable period of notice has to be given, taking into consideration the nature of employment. In the past, the courts have considered that reasonable notice for a newspaper editor was one year, and for a theatrical manager, six months.

The 1978 Act as amended by the Employment Act 1982 provides that most employees are entitled to minimum periods of notice as follows:

(a)   after four weeks' continuous service—one week,
(b)   after two years' continuous service—two weeks, and
(c)   for every additional year's service—one week, up to a maximum of 12 weeks.

An employee is required to give at least one week's notice if employed continuously for one month or more. This notice is unaffected by longer service.

2. Without notice

Termination by either party without notice ends the contract of employment, and gives the injured party the right to bring an action for damages. It should be noted that this applies to employee and employer. If an employee leaves without notice, the employer may sue if it can be shown that he suffered damage as a result of the employee's illegal termination of the contract of employment. In practice this rarely happens and it is usually the employee who brings an action for dismissal without notice.

Summary dismissal without notice may be considered lawful if the employee breaks the terms of the contract of employment. The terms may be implied in respect of acts of disobedience, dishonesty, incompetence or misbehaviour. In *Denco Ltd.* v. *Joinson* (1991), the Court of Appeal held that an employee's unlawful use of a computer password was gross misconduct.

A dismissed employee who has been continuously employed for 26 weeks or more has the right to request from the employer a written statement giving particulars of the reasons for dismissal.

3. Unfair dismissal and employees' rights

Comprehensive procedures to enable employees who have been unfairly dismissed to complain to an industrial tribunal are provided by the Acts. The Acts apply to most employees who work full-time or part-time and who have worked for more than 52 weeks continuously and for not less than 16 hours per week.

The main provisions are as follows:

(a) The right to complain applies to dismissals with or without notice, and where the employee is forced to resign because of the employer's conduct.

(b) The employee must make a complaint of unfair dismissal within three months of the effective date of termination.

(c) The employee has the opportunity of choosing, should the complaint be successful, to continue working for the employer or receiving financial compensation.
Financial compensation, when unfair dismissal is proved, usually consists of a basic award of a number of weeks' pay plus a compensatory award, which the tribunal considers just and equitable. There are limits to amounts awarded.

(d) The following may be considered fair reasons for dismissal:

> (i) the lack of capacity of qualification of the employee to carry on working,
> (i) redundancy,
> (iii) the employee's conduct,
> (iv) where the continued employment of the employee would be illegal, or in breach of a statutory duty or requirement,
> (v) some other substantial reason justifying dismissal.
> (e) The following are considered unfair reasons for dismissal:
>> (i) trade union membership or activity,
>> (ii) pregnancy,
>> (iii) industrial dispute, when other employees involved are not dismissed.

4. Redundancy

The 1978 Employment Act provides for the payment of "redundancy pay" for employees who are dismissed because there is no work to do. This would occur:

(a) where the employer has ceased or intends to cease business at a particular place; or
(b) where the need for the particular work of the employee is no longer required.

An employee is entitled to redundancy pay if he/she:

(a) works under a contract of employment;
(b) has been employed continuously by this employer for at least two years for more than 16 hours per week; or employed for five years but working for less than 16 hours but more than 8 hours per week;
(c) has been actually or constructively dismissed by reason of redundancy.

The amount of redundancy pay a dismissed employee receives is calculated on the basis of continuous service, age and the gross average wage. For each year of service an employee:

aged 18–21 would receive half a week's pay,
aged 22–40 would receive one week's pay, and
aged 41–64 would receive one and a half week's pay.

The "weekly wage" for calculating redundancy pay is limited to a fixed maximum sum, which may change from year to year. This means that employees earning a wage in excess of the limit would only have their redundancy pay calculated on this lower amount, not at their actual average weekly wage. At March 1993 the limit on the weekly wage was £205. In addition, the maximum number of years which is taken into the calculation is 20 years. It should be noted that many employers give redundancy payments well in excess of the statutory requirements.

Sex Discrimination

The Equal Pay Act 1970 provided that women should receive the same pay and benefits as men for like work or for work which is rated as similar or equivalent to work done by men. A woman has a right of action to sue for breach of contract if an employer is in default of this requirement.

The Sex Discrimination Act 1975 as amended by the Sex Discrimination Act 1986 and the Employment Act 1989 makes it illegal, with certain exceptions, for employers to discriminate on the grounds of sex. The Act, which applies to most forms of employers, professions, training and employment agencies, implements the principle of equal treatment for men and women with regard to access to employment, vocational training, promotion, social benefits and working conditions. The Act also covers sex discrimination in education, housing and the like. In R. v. Birmingham City Council (1989), the House of Lords held that there was unlawful sex discrimination when the Council provided 542 grammar school places for boys and only 360 places for girls, as the number of boys and girls starting secondary education each year was roughly equal.

It should be noted that sex discrimination does not only apply to women, but is available to men who have been discriminated against on the grounds of sex. In James v. Eastleigh Borough Council (1990), the plaintiff and his wife were both aged 61. The Council provided free leisure facilities to persons who were of State pensionable age, which meant that the plaintiff had to pay but his wife did not. The House of Lords considered that as the statutory pensionable ages were discriminatory, the Council's provisions were equally discriminatory.

The Act does not apply in employment where a particular sex is necessary for the job (a man would be required to play Superman in films and conversely a woman to play Wonderwoman).

RACE DISCRIMINATION

The Race Relations Act 1976 makes it illegal for employers to discriminate on grounds of race, colour or nationality. This Act covers most forms of discrimination as shown above in sex discrimination, and relates to housing, education, training, membership of professions, trade unions and the right to public services and facilities. With relation to employment it does not apply:

(a) in private homes,
(b) when the discrimination can be shown to be a genuine occupational qualification.

The Courts and Legal Services Act 1990 amended the Race Relations Act 1976 and the Sex Discrimination Act 1975, by prohibiting discrimination in the legal profession, so that no barrister is unreasonably refused training or pupillage. The Act also prohibits discrimination in the giving or withholding instructions to a barrister or advocate.

Complaints against racial discrimination in employment are brought before certain county courts, or the industrial tribunal.

In addition, the Public Order Act 1986 makes it an offence for any person to use words, or behaviour, or display written material, or to perform a play, record, video or television, which is intended or is likely to stir up racial hatred.

Racial hatred means hatred against a group of persons in Great Britain by reference to colour, race, nationality, or ethnic or national origins.

REVISION TEST

1. State four duties owed by an employer to the employees.

2. Name two duties owed by an employee.

3. What are the minimum periods of notice to which an employee is entitled?

4. Name some reasons for dismissal which would be considered fair.

5. State three occasions when the Sex Discrimination Act would not apply.

SPECIMEN EXAMINATION QUESTIONS

1. When an employee is dismissed from employment, what are considered to be:

   (a) fair reasons; and
   (b) unfair reasons for dismissal?

2. Shirley worked as a clerk in the office of a large company. After working for a year she discovered that a male member of staff, appointed at the same time, was receiving a larger salary and had one week's holiday more than her. They were both carrying out similar duties, and Shirley asked the employers for the same conditions of service.

   (a) What law is concerned with Shirley's complaint?
   (b) Will the question of pay be dealt with differently from the holidays complaint?
   (c) If Shirley's request is turned down does she have any recourse to a legal tribunal?

3. A contract of employment consists of a range of duties, many imposed by law, between employer and employee. The employer's duties include providing the employee with a written statement of the main terms of his contract of employment, paying wages as agreed, indemnifying (compensating) against liability and providing a safe system of work.

   In each of the following situations, identify the duty involved and explain what legal consequences may arise.

(a)   Megan starts a full-time job as a dental receptionist. Four months later her employer provides her with a statement identifying her job title and rates of pay.

(b)   John is employed as a machine operator in a factory. Due to a faulty safety guard, John traps and badly injures his hand.

(c)   Helen is employed as a full-time delivery driver. During the course of her duties she negligently runs over and injures Sam.

S.E.G. 1992

SUGGESTED COURSEWORK TITLES

Describe the law relating to sex discrimination and racial discrimination in employment and education. Do you think it fair? Make some suggestions to improve the situation.

Describe the law relating to dismissal, and explain the procedure that a employee may take who considers that the dismissal was unfair. Do you consider the law to be adequate in this matter?

Chapter 9

The Law of Torts

Tort is a French word meaning a wrong. It is a civil wrong, as opposed to a crime, because it is committed by a private person against another private person. A tort has been defined as a "civil wrong, other than a breach of contract or a breach of trust." The terms of a contract or trust are agreed beforehand by the parties, and a breach of the terms by one party gives the other a right of action in a court of law. A tort, however, is a duty fixed by law which affects all persons. For example, all road users have a duty not to act negligently. They do not agree beforehand not to injure each other; the duty or liability not to be negligent is fixed by law. A pedestrian who jay-walks and causes injury to a motor-cyclist will be liable to compensate the motor-cyclist for the injury suffered, in the same way as a car driver who negligently damages another car will be liable for the cost of the damage.

The usual remedy for tort is damages, but with certain torts other remedies such as injunctions are necessary because damages would not be an adequate compensation.

It is possible for one event to be a breach of contract, a crime and a tort. For example, David hires Michael to drive Peter to the station, and Michael exceeds the speed limit, crashes and injures Peter. Michael could be liable for:

(a) an action by David for breach of contract,
(b) an action by Peter for the tort of negligence, and
(c) a criminal prosecution for dangerous driving.

Malice

The intention or motive with which an act is committed is generally unimportant when deciding whether or not the act is tortious. A wrong intention will not make a lawful act into an unlawful one. In *Bradford Corporation* v. *Pickles* (1895), the

193

Corporation obtained water from springs fed by undefined channels through Pickles' land. In order to coerce the Corporation to buy the land at a high price, Pickles sank a shaft which interfered with the flow of water. The plaintiffs sought an injunction to restrain Pickles from collecting the underground water, but the court held that the defendant had the right to draw water from his own land. The motive behind his act was irrelevant.

Malice, however, in the sense of improper motive, is an essential requirement or an important factor in the following torts:

(a) Malicious prosecution

This tort is committed when one party, out of spite, brings an unjust criminal prosecution against the other party.

(b) Injurious falsehood

This tort occurs when a party makes a deliberate false statement with the intention that the other shall suffer loss or damage.

(c) Conspiracy

When two or more persons conspire together to injure another person.

(d) Defamation

Malice can defeat certain defences (see p. 214).

(e) Nuisance

Malice may turn a reasonable use of one's own property into an illegal use (see p. 209).

STRICT LIABILITY

A person is generally liable in tort when an act is done (i) intentionally (e.g. trespass) or (ii) negligently. In some cases, however, a person may be liable when he acts neither intentionally nor negligently. In these instances the law has imposed a strict limit on a person's activities, and if this limit is exceeded the defendant is strictly or absolutely liable. The most common example of such liability is known as the Rule in *Rylands* v. *Fletcher* (1868). The Rule applies when:

(a) a person brings on to his land for his own purpose some dangerous thing, which is not naturally there (water, wild animals, gas, fire). In *Emanuel* v. *Greater London Council* (1970), a contractor for the Council lit a fire on the Council's land and negligently allowed sparks to fly on to the plaintiff's land which caused damage to buildings. The court held that the Council was strictly liable under the rule in *Rylands* v. *Fletcher* for the escape of the fire; and

(b) the dangerous thing escapes from the land, (strict liability does not apply if the injury occurs on your own land). In *Read* v. *Lyons & Co. Ltd.* (1947), Read was working in a munitions factory and was injured by an explosion in the factory. She did not claim negligence, but brought an action based on the rule in *Rylands* v. *Fletcher*. The House of Lords held that the rule did not apply because there had not been an escape from the land of the thing which caused the injury; and

(c) causes damage.

If these three events occur the occupier of land is liable for the damage caused, but the following defences may be used:

(a) The untoward event was caused by the act of a stranger.

(b) It was the plaintiff's own fault.

(c) It was an act of God.

(d) There was statutory authority.

The Consumer Protection Act 1987, is an example of a statute creating strict liability for producers of defective goods which cause damage to person or property. (See p. 172.)

NEGLIGENCE

A plaintiff must prove three things to succeed in an action for negligence.

(a) The defendant owed the plaintiff a legal duty;

(b) There was a breach of that duty;

(c) The plaintiff suffered damage.

1. Duty owed to the plaintiff

In *Donoghue* v. *Stevenson* (1932), the plaintiff drank ginger beer from an opaque bottle, in which there was a decomposed snail which caused the plaintiff to be ill. The House of Lords held that a manufacturer of goods is liable if the goods are used by a consumer without an intermediate examination, because the manufacturer owes the consumer a duty of care. See p. 172 for the Consumer Protection Act 1987, which provides strict liability for a producer of defective goods which cause damage to the consumer.

Probably the most important principle to emerge from the judgment came in the definition of Lord Atkin, of who is owed a duty of care. "You must take reasonable care to avoid acts or omissions which you can reasonably foresee would be likely to injure your neighbour." My neighbours are "...persons who are so directly affected by my act that I ought reasonably to have them in contemplation..."

The neighbour principle and "reasonable foreseeability" have been used in many different situations. For example, a duty of care has been held to be owed to:

(a) A lady locked in a public toilet (see p. 201).
(b) Wearers of underpants who caught dermatitis from a chemical in the material (see p. 168).
(c) Persons living in the neighbourhood of an open borstal.
(d) An opponent in a football game (see p. 218).
(e) A fireman attending a fire (see p. 219).

To succeed in an action for negligence a plaintiff must show that a duty of care was owed by the defendant.

In *Bourhill* v. *Young* (1943), a motor-cyclist crashed and was fatally injured. A pregnant fishwife, who was 15 yards away, later looked at the scene of the accident and the sight of the blood caused shock and, subsequently, a miscarriage. The House of Lords held that the lady was not owed a duty of care because it could not reasonably be foreseen that the accident would cause her to suffer such injuries.

In *Smith* v. *Littlewoods Organisation Ltd.* (1987), vandals started a fire on the defendant's empty, derelict property, which also caused damage to the plaintiff's property. The House of Lords considered that as a general rule there was no duty of care to prevent a third party from causing damage to the plaintiff's property.

In *King* v. *Phillips* (1953) the Court of Appeal held that a mother was not owed a duty of care, when, after hearing her child scream and seeing the child's tricycle under a taxi, she suffered shock. In fact the child was not hurt.

The defendant might be liable if aware that the plaintiff was nearby. In *Boardman* v. *Sanderson* (1964) the defendant negligently backed his car and injured the plaintiff's son. The plaintiff, who was nearby, heard his son's screams and suffered shock. It was held that the plaintiff could recover damages because the defendant was aware the plaintiff was nearby and the consequence of the accident was reasonably foreseeable.

NERVOUS SHOCK

The decision in *McLoughlin* v. *O'Brian* (1983) should be considered carefully. A mother visited a hospital to see her husband and daughters, injured in a serious road accident, and as a result of what she saw and the account she heard from witnesses, she suffered severe nervous shock. The House of Lords held that although distance and time were factors to be considered they were not legal restrictions. The plaintiff was entitled to damages for nervous shock, even though she was not present at the accident, because it was a reasonably foreseeable consequence of the defendant's negligence.

The decision in *McLoughlin* v. *O'Brian* has been followed by a spate of similar cases, particularly in the aftermath of the Hillsborough disaster where many lives were lost while attending a football match. In *Alcock* v. *Chief Constable of South Yorkshire Police* (1991), following the judgement in *McLaughlin* v. *O'Brian*, the House of Lords considered:

(a) Other than in exceptional circumstances, only those within a parent/spouse relationship may obtain damages for nervous shock sustained. The exceptional circumstances would be relationships which could show the same criteria of love, affection and care, such as a fiancée or grandparent, and which would be decided on a case by case basis.

(b) As a general rule, watching television is not generally regarded as the same as being present at the scene or its immediate aftermath, but simultaneous television may in certain circumstances be the equivalent as being within the sight and hearing of the event. In this case the House of Lords considered the position of ten claimants who had lost relatives at Hillsborough. The majority had witnessed the scenes on television. The plaintiffs' appeals were dismissed because the claimants did not have:

(i)   the close relationship required; or
(ii) had viewed the scenes on television, which did not show the suffering of any recognisable individual.

It was considered that relatives who attended the mortuary for the purpose of identification at least eight hours after the incident, were outside the immediate aftermath of the disaster.

2. A breach of duty

Defendants will be in breach of duty if they have not acted reasonably. The standard of care varies with each situation, but as a general rule, the standard of care is that of a reasonable person who uses ordinary care and skill.

The courts will consider the risk involved. In *Paris* v. *Stepney Borough Council* (1951), the plaintiff had only one eye and the defendants employed him on work that involved a certain risk to the eyes, although not sufficient to warrant ordinary workers to wear goggles. Paris was blinded as a result of his work and the court held that the defendants were in breach of their duty to that particular worker.

A professional person must use the skill expected of the profession, therefore in *Carmarthenshire C.C.* v. *Lewis* (1955) a teacher was dressing young children before taking them out, when a four-year-old under her control left the school premises and ran into the road. A lorry driver was killed when swerving to avoid the child. The court held that the teacher was not negligent, but the county council had been negligent in allowing a situation to arise in which the child could leave the school.

A duty of care is not owed as a matter of public policy by a participant to a crime to a partner in the crime. In *Ashton* v. *Turner and Another* (1980) the plaintiff and defendants had been drinking together and the second defendant allowed Turner to drive his car without insurance. Ashton and Turner later committed burglary and when driving away from the crime had an accident which injured Ashton (the passenger). Turner pleaded guilty to dangerous driving and driving while drunk. Ashton claimed damages against both defendants and the court held that as a matter of public policy the plaintiff was not owed a duty of care when injured during the commission of a crime. The court also held that Turner could successfully plead the defence of *volenti non fit injuria* (see p. 218).

In *Hill* v. *Chief Constable of West Yorkshire* (1988), the mother of the last victim of the "Yorkshire Ripper" (Peter Sutcliffe) brought an action against the plaintiffs, claiming negligence in failing to catch the killer before her daughter's murder. The House of Lords held that the police do not owe a duty of care to an individual member of the public in respect of an attack by a criminal.

However, in *Kirkham* v. *Chief Constable of Greater Manchester Police* (1990), the Court of Appeal held that the defendant was in breach of a duty of care and awarded damages when the police did not pass information to the prison authorities that the plaintiff's husband had suicidal tendencies. Her husband was consequently treated as a normal prisoner and placed in a cell alone, where he hanged himself.

3. Damage has been suffered

Although a plaintiff must prove damage, not all damage is actionable if it is too remote. The general rule is that a defendant is only liable for damages that a reasonable man should foresee.

In *The Wagon Mound* Case (1961), oil was negligently spilt from a ship and floated across Sydney Harbour to a ship repairers, where sparks ignited the oil and caused damage to the wharf and to a ship. At that time it was not foreseeable that the oil would be set alight and cause the damage, and the Judicial Committee of the Privy Council held that there was no liability.

This decision was followed in *Doughty* v. *Turner Manufacturing Co.* (1964). The plaintiff was injured when a fellow worker dropped an asbestos cement cover into molten liquid. An explosion followed and the plaintiff was injured. It was discovered later that a chemical reaction would be caused by the cement and molten liquid. The Court of Appeal held that the accident was unforeseeable and the defendants were not liable.

It must be stressed that the plaintiff must suffer damage. A person cannot be sued in negligence just because he acted negligently. The negligent act must injure the plaintiff or his property.

Res ipsa loquitur (*the facts speak for themselves*)

It is a general rule of law that a plaintiff must prove that the defendant has been negligent. In cases, however, where the act or omission obviously indicates negligence, the burden of proof moves to the defendant who must show that, in fact, he was not negligent. This rule has been applied where:

(a) Bags of sugar fell on the plaintiff from an upper floor of a warehouse. (*Scott* v. *London & St. Katherine's Dock Co.* (1865).)

(b) Swabs were left in a patient after an operation. (*Mahon* v. *Osborne* (1939).)

(c) A customer slipped on yoghurt which had spilled on to the floor of a supermarket. (*Ward* v. *Tesco Stores Ltd.* (1976).)

The application of the rule does not automatically mean that the defendant was negligent, but it is presumed that the act or omission was negligent, unless it can be shown otherwise. In *Pearson* v. *N.W. Gas Board* (1968), a gas explosion killed the plaintiff's husband and destroyed her home. The court applied the rule, but the defendants were able to show that severe frost caused the gas leak and, as there was no reasonable way in which the explosion could have been prevented, they were not negligent.

Contributory Negligence

The Law Reform (Contributory Negligence) Act 1945 provides that where a person suffers damage which is partly his own fault and partly the fault of another, the injured party will be able to claim damages, but the amount recoverable shall be reduced to the extent that the court considers just and equitable, having regard to the claimant's responsibility for the damage.

In practice the court usually awards damages and then reduces the award by the percentage the plaintiff is deemed to be responsible.

For example, suppose a motor-cyclist suffered injuries caused by the negligence of a motorist and was awarded £5,000 damages. This amount would be reduced if it could be shown that the plaintiff contributed to the damage suffered to the extent of 20 per cent. of the blame, by not wearing a crash helmet. The damages received by the motor-cyclist would be £4,000 (*i.e.* £5,000 less 20 per cent.). In *Capps* v. *Miller* (1989), the plaintiff, a motor-cyclist, received head injuries as a result of the defendant's negligent driving. The plaintiff's crash helmet, which was unfastened, fell off before his head hit the road. The Court of Appeal held that although the sole responsibility of the accident lay with the defendant, the plaintiff's failure to secure his helmet had contributed to the injury. The Court held that the plaintiff's damages be reduced by 10 per cent. It was also considered that the reduction would have been greater if a helmet had not been worn at all.

In *Sayers* v. *Harlow U.D.C.* (1958), the plaintiff entered a public toilet and, because of a faulty lock, could not open the door to get out. She was due to catch a bus, so in order to climb over the door she stepped on to the toilet-roll, slipped, and injured herself. The court held the defendants to be negligent, and although the plaintiff had acted reasonably in attempting to release herself, she had contributed to the injury by stepping on a revolving toilet-roll. The damages were reduced by 25 per cent.

It is generally considered that a young child is never guilty of contributory negligence.

Occupiers' Liability for Dangerous Premises

The Occupiers' Liability Act 1957, provides that the occupier of premises, or the landlord if responsible for repairs to the premises, has a common duty of care to see that all lawful visitors will be reasonably safe when using the premises.

Lawful visitors include persons invited expressly or impliedly (milkman, postman, paper-boy), or people who enter the premises under a contract (spectators at a football match). (See below for the 1984 Act which deals with the liability for visitors outside the scope of this Act.)

The standard of care varies according to the visitor. Obviously the care shown for a child must be greater than for an adult. A notice "danger" would be of little use to a young child who could not read. Some dangers on premises may actually allure or attract children. In the case of allurements the occupier must take greater care to protect children. Occupiers have been held responsible for injuries to children caused by a railway turntable, red berries on trees, building sites, railway trucks, and threshing machines.

An occupier may not be liable for injuries to a very young child if it could be expected that the child would be accompanied by parents or other responsible persons.

In addition to the general defences (see p. 218), the occupier may show that:

(a) adequate notices or warnings of the danger were given (*e.g.* a "wet paint" sign).

(b)   with visitors under contract, liability was excluded. For example it is usual for exclusion notices to be displayed at most sporting events, but it should be noted that the Unfair Contract Terms Act 1977 may limit exclusion clauses to a test of reasonableness (see p. 176).

(c)   the injury was caused by the negligence of a competent independent contractor. For example, the occupier would escape liability if electrical fittings, erected by a qualified electrician, fell on a visitor. The occupier would be liable, however, if the fittings had been erected by a gardener. Independent contractors may be liable if they leave premises in a dangerous state and lawful visitors are injured as a result.

A.C. Billings & Sons Ltd. v. *Riden* (1958). Building contractors had to remove a ramp from the front of a house. Mrs. Riden left the house after dark and fell into a sunken area and suffered injury. It was held that the contractors were negligent as they had not taken reasonable care to ensure that visitors were not exposed to dangerous premises.

(d)   the person injured was a trespasser and not a lawful visitor. The occupier is liable for trespassers for intentional dangers such as man-traps, and for injuries caused when all that a humane person should have done for the safety of a trespasser had not been done.

British Railways Board v. *Herrington* (1972). A child trespasser was electrocuted and severely injured on the defendant's land. The fence guarding the line was broken. The House of Lords considered that there was a high degree of danger and as the defendants were aware of the possibility of such a trespass, and could easily have repaired the fence, they had not acted humanely and were liable.

The Occupiers' Liability Act 1984 is concerned with civil liability of an occupier to persons on his land who are outside the scope of the 1957 Act, namely trespassers. The aim of section 1 is to resolve points of doubt following *British Railways Board* v. *Herrington* (see above.)

An occupier has a duty to persons, other than lawful visitors, in respect of any injury suffered on his premises by reason of any danger due to the state of the premises, or to things done or omitted to be done on them.

The duty is owed by the occupier if:

(a) he is aware of the danger or has reasonable grounds to believe that it exists,

(b) he knows or has reasonable grounds to believe that there are others in the vicinity of the danger, or may come into the vicinity, and

(c) the risk is such that he may reasonably be expected to offer the other persons some protection.

The duty is to take such care as is reasonable, to see that the others do not suffer injury by reason of the danger on the premises. The duty may be discharged by giving warning of the danger or discouraging persons from taking the risk. No duty is owed by the occupier if the other persons willingly accept the risk. There is no liability in respect of loss or damage to the other person's property, only personal injury.

Section 2 of the Act deals with visitors using premises for recreational or educational purposes. Occupiers of business premises may exempt themselves from provisions of the Unfair Contract Terms Act 1977, where access is granted for purposes not connected with the business. For example, a farmer allowing a football team to play on a field normally used for pasture.

TRESPASS

Trespass is probably the oldest tort, and many other torts owe their origin to the writ of trespass, which has been described as the "mother of actions." There are three forms of trespass:

(a) trespass to the person,

(b) trespass to chattels (goods), and

(c) trespass to land.

All trespasses are actionable *per se* (by itself); that is, the plaintiff does not have to prove that the defendant caused any damage.

1. Trespass to the person
This tort consists of three separate actions:

(a) Assault
This tort is actionable when a person threatens or attempts to physically injure another, and the other person has reasonable fear that the threat will be carried out. Words are not sufficient

by themselves, they must be accompanied by actions. If a person 100 yards away shouted an abusive threat it would probably not be assault, because there would be no fear of immediate danger and no action to indicate an attack. However, if a knife or fist was raised in close proximity to a face, this would be assault as there would be good reason to be in fear of a physical attack.

It is possible for words to remove the fear of an attack. For example, if a person lifted a fist to strike another, but said "I won't hit you because it's your birthday."

(b) Battery

This occurs when an act goes beyond a threat and a person is actually touched. The attacker does not have to physically touch the other person, the injury could be caused indirectly, such as throwing a stone.

It should be noted that mere unauthorised touching is actionable, regardless of the motive. A kiss given with love and affection, is assault and battery if the receiver does not authorise the act, even if it takes place under the mistletoe at Christmas time. It is intentional bodily contact and a woman or man may claim damages if they did not voluntarily stand under the mistletoe and accept the kiss.

Assault and battery are usually joined in one action, and both are criminal offences. Conviction in a criminal court may be used as evidence when claiming a remedy in a civil action.

In *Halford* v. *Brookes* (1991), for the first time in English law a person was found liable in a civil court in respect of a murder for which he had not been prosecuted (see p. 220 for details).

(c) False imprisonment

This tort is committed when a person's liberty is totally restrained by the intentional, but unjust, act of another. The imprisonment must be for an unreasonable length of time and be total, so that if a person has reasonable means of leaving the premises it is not actionable.

In *Bird* v. *Jones* (1845) the public footpath over Hammersmith Bridge was closed. The plaintiff climbed over a fence and was stopped by the defendant from proceeding further along the footpath. The court held that it was not false imprisonment as the plaintiff could have left the bridge by the way he entered.

In *John Lewis & Co. Ltd.* v. *Tims* (1952) Mrs. Tims and her daughter were suspected of stealing and were kept in an office, against their will, until the store manager was informed. The

House of Lords held that, as the detention had not been for an unreasonable period of time, there had not been false imprisonment.

A person may have a right of action even though he did not know at the time that he had been locked in a room while he slept. *Meering* v. *Grahame-White Aviation Co.* (1919).

(d) Specific defences to trespass to the person

(i) *Parental or quasi-parental authority*. Parents or guardians may use reasonable force to chastise or imprison children. A similar authority may be given to others who take the place of parents (*quasi* means "as if"). A teacher, therefore, would not be liable for keeping pupils in school after lessons provided good reason could be shown.

(ii) *Self defence*. The force used must be reasonable, regarding the facts of the case. It may not be a good defence to shoot an attacker dead if the person was unarmed. In *Lane* v. *Holloway* (1968), the plaintiff aged 64 hit a 24-year-old man on the shoulder, and in return received a blow to the eye which necessitated 19 stitches and a month in hospital. It was held that the blow received by the older man was out of all proportion to the provocation. (The defendant had also been found guilty in the criminal courts.)

(iii) *Statutory or judicial authority*. For example, lawful arrest by a police officer.

2. Trespass to chattels (goods)

Chattels are items of tangible moveable property, such as personal possessions (pens, books, desks, cars, records, etc., and money and cheques, etc.).

This tort is committed when a person intentionally interferes with goods in the possession of another, or carries out an unjustifiable act which denies a person of the legal right to possess the goods. The merest touch of the goods without causing damage is sufficient, and it is not necessary for the defendant to dispossess the goods.

Kirk v. *Gregory* (1876). In order to place another person's jewellery in a safe place, the defendant removed the goods from one room to another. The jewellery was later stolen by an unknown party and the defendant was held liable in trespass.

The tort may also be committed without touching the goods, *e.g.* opening a farm gate and driving cows or horses out of a field.

Possession is the basis of this tort, as it is the lawful possessor of the goods, not necessarily the owner, who may bring an action. For example, a hirer of a car, not the owner, would sue for damages from the defendant who had taken possession of the car.

Most actions under this tort are brought for the intentional dispossession of the possessor's rights to the goods.

(i) Conversion arises when the defendant intentionally interferes with goods in a way that may be regarded as denying the plaintiff's rights of possession or use. If, for example, a car subject to a hire-purchase agreement is sold to a private person, the seller has given the buyer a good title (see p. 175) and denied the hire-purchase company the right of ownership of the car. The hire-purchase company could sue the seller for conversion. The usual remedies for conversion are damages and injunction.

(ii) Detinue arose when goods were wrongfully detained by another party. This tort was abolished in 1977 (see below).

(a) Torts (Interference with Goods) Act 1977

The Act abolished detinue, and section 1 defined "wrongful interference with goods" to mean:

    (a) conversion of goods,
    (b) trespass to goods,
    (c) negligence and other torts in so far as they result in damage to goods or interests in goods.

(b) Uncollected goods

If you take goods to a shop to be mended, repaired, cleaned, etc., you are the bailor and the trader is the bailee. After the goods have been mended, you have a duty to pay for, and collect your goods. The trader has a duty to return the goods. The situation often arises when you (the bailor) do not collect your goods.

This Act sets down the rights of the trader (the bailee) and the procedure to follow. In cases where the bailor has not collected the goods, the bailee has a right in certain circumstances to write to the bailor in a prescribed manner, giving notice of an intention to sell, and if the goods have not been collected within the period stated in the notice, the bailee may sell the goods (s.12).

3. Trespass to land

This tort may be defined as the intentional entering on to another person's land without lawful permission or remaining on the land after permission has been withdrawn.

The entering or interference with the land must be direct. Rubbish dumped on to another's land would be trespass, but if the rubbish was blown on to the land by gales, it would not be trespass because it was not the direct action of the defendant which caused the interference.

An invasion of air space may be a trespass of land, even though the land is not touched. The courts have held in *Kelson* v. *Imperial Tobacco Co.* (1957) that a sign erected on a building, but which protruded over another person's land was trespass, as it was in *Woolerton and Wilson* v. *Costain* (1969), where a crane swung over another person's land. In *Lord Bernstein of Leigh* v. *Skyviews and General Ltd.* (1978) it was held that an aircraft which took an aerial photograph would not be trespassing if it was at a height which did not affect the use of land.

Trespass is a civil wrong and a mere trespasser, as a general rule, is not liable for criminal prosecution, and therefore the familiar sign, "Trespassers Will Be Prosecuted," has no legal effect, except in relation to certain government undertakings where an Act of Parliament has provided a fine for trespassing.

(a) Specific defences to trespass to land

It is a defence to claim that entry on to land was justifiable. The following reasons may be used as a defence to show that entry was made:

    (a) by leave or licence granted by the occupier of the land,
    (b) by authority of law (such as a bailiff),
    (c) involuntarily (such as landing in a parachute),
    (d) where the highway was impassable, and
    (e) to retake and retain possession of one's own property.

The remedies available to the plaintiff:

    (a) Damages. If no real injury has been incurred the damages awarded may be nominal (*i.e.* 1p).
    (b) Injunction. This may be used to stop the defendant from repeating the trespass.
    (c) Forcible ejection. The occupier may only use reasonable force to move the trespasser after first requesting him to leave and giving him reasonable time to do so.

NUISANCE

There are two forms of nuisance which have quite different meanings and little in common. They are public nuisance and private nuisance.

1. Public nuisance

This wrong arises when acts or omissions have caused annoyance, inconvenience or danger to a class or part of the general public. Public nuisance includes such things as obstructing the public highway, throwing fireworks on to the road, smoke from chimneys causing damage to cars parked on the highway and quarry blasting which projects stones and dust on to the surrounding neighbourhood.

Public nuisance is a crime and the offender is prosecuted, usually by the Attorney-General. A private person who has suffered special damage of a different kind from that of the general public may sue in tort. An example would be where, in the case of blasting, an entire neighbourhood was covered in dust, but one individual was hit by falling stones.

2. Private nuisance

This tort covers the unreasonable interference with the plaintiff's enjoyment or use of his land or the disturbance of some legal interest over the land. An example of interference with the enjoyment of land would be playing music very loudly in the middle of the night so that your neighbour's sleep is disturbed. Blocking your neighbour's access from the road to his house would be to disturb his legal right of way.

3. Nuisance and trespass

Nuisance differs from trespass to land in that,

    (a)   the interference must be indirect. Therefore the smell of a garden compost heap would be a nuisance to your neighbour, the throwing of the garden rubbish on to the neighbour's garden would be trespass.

           In *Esso Petroleum* v. *Southport Corporation* (1956) a tanker ran aground and had to discharge oil at sea, which was carried by the tide and wind on to the foreshore. The Court of Appeal held the Corporation's action could not succeed in trespass as the damage was not caused by the direct act of the defendants, but by the indirect act of the wind and tide.

(b)   Nuisance is only actionable by proof of special damage.

4. Unreasonable interference
The following factors have to be considered when establishing whether or not a nuisance exists.

(a) Reasonableness
It is a good defence to claim the act was a reasonable use of one's own property. The courts take an attitude of "live and let live." What is reasonable is based on the conduct of the ordinary man.

(b) Sensitiveness
An act which would not disturb a normal person will not be a nuisance just because the plaintiff, or his property, is unduly sensitive. In *Robinson* v. *Kilvert* (1889) the plaintiff stored brown paper in the defendant's premises. The heat from the defendant's boiler damaged the paper, which was extremely sensitive to heat. The court held the defendant was not liable in nuisance.

(c) Locality
"What would be a nuisance in Belgrave Square would not necessarily be so in Bermondsey" said a judge in 1879. He was pointing out that different standards are necessary for different areas, so it is possible that noise from a club in the city centre may be reasonable, but would be unreasonable in a residential area and would be a nuisance.

(d) Continuity
The general rule is that a single event is not a nuisance and the plaintiff must show that there was some degree of repetition of the offending act. In *Stone* v. *Bolton* (1950), a ball was hit out of a cricket ground and injured a lady. It was shown that a ball had been hit out of the ground only six times in 35 years. The court held that this was not often enough to be a nuisance.

(e) Malice
The intention behind an act may be relevant in deciding whether a person's act was reasonable or not.

To shout, shriek, whistle and bang trays may be a reasonable use of your own property, but if it is done with the express purpose of spoiling your neighbour's musical evening, it may be a nuisance, because the acts would not be reasonable. (*Christie* v. *Davey* (1893).)

5. The parties to an action

The occupier of property has the right to bring an action but any other person injured on the property has no claim in nuisance. The person liable in an action for nuisance is likewise the occupier of the property from which the nuisance emanated.

In *Malone* v. *Laskey* (1907), the plaintiff, the wife of a tenant was injured when a bracket on a lavatory cistern fell on her. The defendants who leased the property owned a generator which vibrated and caused the bracket to fall. The plaintiff sued in nuisance but the court held that, as she was only the wife of the tenant and not the tenant, she had no interest in the land.

6. Remedies

The usual remedies are damages and an injunction, which are obtained from the courts. In *Kennaway* v. *Thompson* (1981), the plaintiff lived near a lake used for motor boat racing. She was awarded damages by the High Court for nuisance already suffered and damages for future nuisance. The Court of Appeal varied the award and in the place of damages for future suffering, substituted an injunction which restricted the number of races that the defendants could hold.

With regard to the remedy of injunction, it must be stressed that it is awarded at the discretion of the court.

In *Miller* v. *Jackson* (1977), the defendants, a cricket club, had played on a village ground since 1905. The plaintiffs, in 1972, moved into a house that adjoined the ground. A ball was hit into their house causing damage, and while a game was in progress there was always the danger of personal injury. The plaintiffs sought an injunction to restrain the club from playing cricket on the ground, as it interfered with their enjoyment of the land. It was held by the Court of Appeal that the interests of the public should prevail over the plaintiffs' individual suffering. The public had watched cricket for 70 years and their interest had to be guarded. The injunction was not granted.

There is an extra-judicial remedy of **abatement** which is available when the nuisance can be terminated without entering another person's land. It could be applied to over-hanging trees or roots, but it must be noted that the branches which are cut away still belong to the owner of the tree. If the nuisance cannot be abated without entering the other's land, permission must first be obtained, unless there is immediate danger to person or property.

7. Defences

(a) Statutory authority
It is a complete defence that a nuisance was expressly authorised by an Act of Parliament.

(b) Prescription
When a nuisance has been in continuous existence for not less than 20 years, the right to carry on the act may be acquired.

(c) Reasonable use of one's own property

(d) That the damage caused was minute or minimal

It should be noted that it is no defence that the plaintiff came to the nuisance. (*Sturges* v. *Bridgman* (1879).)

Liability of Parents for the Torts of Children

It is a general rule that parents are not liable for the torts of their children. A parent will be liable, however, if he is negligent in allowing his child to be in a position to commit a tort.

In *Bebee* v. *Sales* (1916), a father gave his 15-year-old son a shotgun, and the father was held to be liable when the son injured another boy.

However, the parent is not negligent if he has taken steps to lessen the risk of injury, as was the case in *Donaldson* v. *McNiven* (1952). A father showed his son how to use an air-rifle, warned him of the dangers and told him not to use it outside the house. The father was held not to be liable when his son injured another child.

Defamation

Defamation is a false, published statement, made orally, in writing or by gestures, which attacks a person's reputation. It has been defined as a statement which tends to lower a person in the estimation of right-thinking members of society generally.

Although there is the public interest of freedom of speech, the tort of defamation protects an individual's private interest in his reputation. Two points from the definition must be noted:

1. The statement must be published to a third party

It is not defamation if the statement is published only to the plaintiff. It would be defamation if a third party heard the defamatory words, even by accident. Each time a defamatory statement is repeated, it is actionable even if the maker does not know the statement is defamatory. So, if Peter made a statement to Jim about David, Jim would be liable (as would Peter) if he repeated the statement to any other person.

Post cards and telegrams are deemed to be published, even if the postal authorities have not actually read them.

2. The statement must lower the plaintiff's reputation in the minds of right-thinking members of society

A bank robber would not be liable for defamation if he informed other thieves that one of the gang had served a prison sentence for theft. This is because the gang would not disapprove, and they are not held to be right-thinking members of society.

In *Byrne* v. *Dean* (1937) a golf club had some illegal gaming machines which the police removed. A verse was placed on the notice board, which inferred that Byrne had informed the police. ("May he Byrne in hell and rue the day.") Byrne sued, but it was held that he had not been defamed, because right-thinking members of society would have approved of a person informing the police of an illegal practice.

In addition to showing that the statement was defamatory and published to a third party, a plaintiff must prove that the third party understood that the statement referred to the plaintiff. It is for the judge to decide if the statement is likely to be understood as referring to the plaintiff and for the jury (if there is one) to decide if the third party actually did so.

Not all defamatory statements are actionable. Consider the following statements and decide whether or not they are defamatory.

"All students in class 1A cheated in their examination."
(There were six students in the class.)

"Half of the Maths 'A' level class (four students) cheated in the examination."

"One or two of the law students (60 students) cheated in the examination."

The first statement would be defamatory because the class is small enough for all students to consider that they have been individually defamed.

The second statement would also be defamatory because, although it referred to only half of the class, it is small enough for any of the class to bring an action.

The last statement would not give a law student a right to sue because the class is too large for any one person to claim that it referred to him or her.

3. Innuendo

A statement may be defamatory by implication, even though the words are not defamatory in their ordinary sense, if it can be shown that another person's reputation has been affected.

In *Cassidy* v. *Daily Mirror Papers Ltd.* (1929), the newspaper published a photograph of the plaintiff's husband and another lady, and the caption announced the engagement of the couple. The plaintiff alleged that the words inferred that she had lived with the man without being married, and the court held that the picture and caption would lead a reasonable person to that conclusion.

It should be noted, however, that only a person defamed by innuendo may bring an action. If, for example, a student magazine wrongly stated a brother and sister to be illegitimate children (or words to that effect), the named persons would not be able to sue the editor, because they have not been defamed. Their parents would be able to sue, because the statement implies and infers that they are not married.

Libel and Slander

Defamation is either:

1. Libel

This is defamation in a permanent form, such as writing, or broadcasting on radio or television. It could be in a painting or cartoon, or on record, cassette or tape recorder. Libel is actionable *per se*, that is, the plaintiff does not have to show special damage. Libel may also be a crime.

2. Slander

This is defamation in a non-permanent form, such as by words and gestures. Slander is not actionable *per se*, and a plaintiff must prove special damage, except with regard to statements which:

(a) Impute that a person has committed a crime punishable by imprisonment.
(b) Impute that a person has an existing infectious disease (for example, leprosy or venereal disease).
(c) Impute unchastity of a woman.
(d) Impute against the plaintiff in respect of his office, profession, calling, trade or business.

Defences

1. Justification

It is a defence to show that the statement was completely or substantially true. Defamation must be a false statement, and a true statement which damaged a person's reputation would not be actionable.

2. Fair comment on a matter of public interest

People in public life, such as politicians, T.V. stars, footballers, etc., receive praise, and must by the same token accept criticism. Provided the comments concern their public activities, and are not made with malice or spite, they are not actionable.

3. Absolute privilege

The following carry complete protection from actions for defamation, regardless of the truth or motive behind the statement.

(a) Parliamentary proceedings

This means any statement made by a Member of Parliament in either House, and officially authorised reports on parliamentary proceedings.

(b) Judicial proceedings

This includes all statements made in court by judge, jury, counsel, witnesses, etc.

(c) Statements between solicitor or barrister and client

(d) State communications

(e) Statements between husband and wife

4. Qualified privilege

The following carry similar protection to absolute privilege, unless it can be shown that the maker of the statement acted from malice, such as an improper motive or out of spite.

(a) Reports on parliamentary and judicial proceedings

This covers newspaper and broadcasting reports and would also include reports on the proceedings of other public and international organisations (*e.g.* the United Nations).

(b) Statements made in performance of a duty

An employer has a duty to give a truthful reference concerning an employee who has applied for a position with another employer, although it should be noted that an employer is not legally bound to give a reference.

(c) Statements made to protect an interest

The interest may be to the benefit of the maker of the statement, the recipient or both, but the maker of the statement must have a duty, legal, moral or social, to protect the interest. An example would be a company director reporting to the chairman of the company about the misbehaviour of an employee.

5. Apology

A newspaper or periodical may offer this defence if it can show that the libel was published without malice or gross negligence. In addition to publishing an apology, a payment of money must be paid into court before the commencement of the case.

The Defamation Act 1952 provides that, as regards unintentional defamation, apology and amends will be a good defence.

While apology and amends is only a defence for defamatory statements in newspapers, it may serve to reduce damages if offered by a private person.

Remedies

Damages are the usual remedy in defamation cases, and are awarded by the jury. Should a jury award excessive damages they may be set aside by the Court of Appeal and the plaintiff could be involved with the expense of a retrial. In *Sutcliffe* v. *Pressdam Ltd.* (1990), a case involving the magazine "Private Eye," the Court of Appeal considered the award to the plaintiff to be excessive and ordered a retrial on the question of damages only. The Court was also of the opinion that in appropriate cases the judge should warn the jury of the consequences of an excessive award.

VICARIOUS LIABILITY

This expression is used when a person is liable for the torts of another, and mainly arises in employer/employee relationships. (It is sometimes referred to as master and servant, but it means the same relationship.)

The reasoning behind such liability is:

(a) To stop an employer hiring an employee to commit a tort.

(b) To encourage the employer to install and maintain a safe system of operation.

(c) That, as a general rule, the employer is in a better financial position to compensate the injured.

The employer is only liable for torts *committed by employees during the course of their employment.*

In *Lloyd* v. *Grace, Smith & Co.* (1912), L. asked the defendants, a firm of solicitors, for advice. All the negotiations were with a managing clerk and he persuaded L. to sign documents which conveyed property to him. The property was sold by the clerk and he kept the money. It was held that the firm was liable because the clerk was employed to give advice and convey property although in this case he did it for his own benefit.

An employer is liable if the employee commits a tort in the course of his employment, even though the latter performs his duty in a manner expressly forbidden by the employer.

In *Limpus* v. *London General Omnibus Co.* (1862) the defendants had expressly warned their drivers not to race against buses of another company. One of their drivers injured a third party while racing his bus and the court held that he was acting within the course of his employment.

An employer is not liable, however, if the employee goes on a "frolic of his own," and leaves his duties to follow a personal pursuit. For example, a driver who decides to watch a football match while on his delivery round, and damages another vehicle when parking.

If an employee performs a function for which he has no authority, the employer will not be liable. In *Beard* v. *London*

General Omnibus (1900) the conductor drove a bus and injured the plaintiff. The court held that the employer was not liable because the conductor was not acting within the scope of his employment.

An employer will be liable, however, when the employee carries out an authorised task in an incorrect way, as in *Bayley* v. *Manchester Sheffield and Lincolnshire Ry.* (1873). A porter thought a passenger was on the wrong train and pulled the person off the train, causing him injuries. The company was liable because the porter acted within the scope of his employment.

In *Harrison* v. *Michelin Tyre Co. Ltd.* (1985) S, an employee, whose duties included pushing a truck within a passage marked by chalk lines, deliberately moved the truck outside the lines as a practical joke and the plaintiff was injured. The plaintiff sued the company, arguing that S's negligence was within the course of his employment. The company contended that S was "on a frolic of his own." The court held that S's act could reasonably be regarded as incidental to the performance of his employment, regardless that the company had not authorised or condoned it. The company, therefore, was vicariously liable.

An employer is not generally liable for the torts of independent contractors, unless:

(a) They were expressly hired to commit a tort. In *Alcock* v. *Wraith* (1991) the work involved a special risk of damage to an adjoining property, and the employer was liable for damage caused by the independant contractor.

(b) The work must create a dangerous situation.

(c) The work obstructs the highway, thereby creating a public nuisance.

(d) The employer delegates a duty imposed by statute or common law.

Independent contractors are employed to do specific tasks but can choose the method of carrying out the work. An employee, on the other hand, is under the control of his employer as to what to do, and how to do it.

GENERAL DEFENCES IN TORT

There are specific defences to specific torts. Absolute privilege, for example, applies to defamation only. Often the defence may be a straight denial of the alleged facts. There are, however, the following defences which may be raised in most actions for tort.

1. Statutory authority
If a statute grants indemnity for a particular act, damages cannot be claimed unless the statute provides for compensation to be paid.

2. Consent (volenti non fit injuria)
Where there is consent, there is no injury. Consent may be given expressly or by implication. Most sporting activities involve a certain element of risk and it is common practice for organisers to make it a condition that spectators enter the grounds at their own risk. Next time you go to a football or cricket match, look for the notice as you enter the stadium.

It is usually implied that participants in sport have consented to the risk of injury. If a hockey player misses the ball and hits an opponent on the shin, no action would normally arise, because the players accept "trespasses" as part of the game. However, in *Condon* v. *Basi* (1985) the defendant was found to be negligent when he broke the plaintiff's leg in a football match, with a tackle which had been executed in a "reckless and dangerous manner," although not with malicious intent. The Court of Appeal held that all players owed a general duty of care, but what was reasonable conduct depended upon the particular circumstances of each case.

Knowledge of the existence of risk does not necessarily imply consent. If a worker knows that a crane passes dangerously overhead, he has not consented to the danger, and, if injured by a falling stone, may sue for damages. (*Smith* v. *Baker & Sons* (1891).)

In *Dann* v. *Hamilton* (1939), a young lady accepted a lift from a driver whom she knew had been drinking, and, as a result of his negligence, she was injured. The driver was not drunk when the outing began but became drunk later when it was difficult for the plaintiff to extricate herself. The court held that, although she knew of the risk, she had not consented to the driver's negligence. In *Morris* v. *Murray* (1990), Morris and Murray had been drinking together, during which time Murray had drunk the equivalent of 17 whiskies. Murray suggested that they should go for a joy-ride in his light aircraft. The plaintiff drove them to the airfield and assisted in the preparation for the take-off. Soon after take-off the plane crashed and Murray, who was the pilot, was killed. Morris was injured and sued Murray's estate. The Court of Appeal held that a passenger who agrees to travel in an aircraft when he knows the pilot is very drunk, has accepted the obvious risk of injury and has impliedly waived the right to claim damages for personal injuries caused by the pilot's negligence.

It is considered that, if a person has an alternative to riding with the drunk, the defence of *volenti* would be accepted, because the plaintiff has agreed to take the risk, rather than accept the alternative.

Rescue cases

A person who is hurt when attempting to rescue another person or to save property from damage may wish to sue the person who created the dangerous situation. The defence of consent may be invoked if there was no immediate danger to others, as the courts may consider the injured party volunteered to take the risk. In *Cutler* v. *United Dairies Ltd.* (1933), C was injured when he tried to stop a runaway horse on a quiet country road. It was held he had consented to the risk.

The plaintiff will not be a volunteer, however, if there was danger to others or if the plaintiff acted under a moral or legal duty, as in *Haynes* v. *Harwood* (1935). A police officer was injured when he tried to stop a horse that had bolted in a town and was an immediate danger to women and children. It was held that, although the plaintiff knew of the danger, he had acted under a duty and had not consented to the risk.

In *Baker* v. *T.E. Hopkins & Son Ltd.* (1959), a similar decision was made, when a doctor went down a well to help men overcome by fumes. The doctor died as a result of the fumes and the court held that the defendants who created the dangerous situation were liable.

In a more recent case, *Ogwu* v. *Taylor* (1988), the defendant negligently set fire to the roof of his house and a fireman was injured while attempting to put out a fire. The House of Lords considered that as the defendant had negligently caused the fire, it was reasonably foreseeable that a fireman would be at risk and, therefore, the defendant would be liable.

3. Inevitable accident

It is a good defence to show that the injury was caused by an accident which could not have been prevented through forethought or by taking ordinary precautions. In *Stanley* v. *Powell* (1891) the plaintiff was injured during a shooting party when a pellet glanced off a tree. It was held that the defendant was not liable as his act was neither intentional nor negligent.

4. Necessity

It may be a defence to show that the damage was caused in trying to prevent a greater evil.

In *Cope* v. *Sharpe* (1912), fire broke out on the plaintiff's land and the defendant, who was a gamekeeper, set fire to other parts of the plaintiff's land with the intention of preventing the fire from spreading to his employer's land, where there were pheasants. The fire was extinguished by other means and the plaintiff sued for damages. The court held that the defendant had carried out a reasonably necessary act and was not liable.

5. Act of God

This is an act of nature which could not have been reasonably foreseen.

In *Nichols* v. *Marsland* (1876), the defendant owned an artificial lake which overflowed as a result of a thunderstorm and caused damage to the plaintiff's land. The court held the defendant was not liable as the damage was caused by an act of God.

6. Lapse of Time

Although not technically a defence, a defendant may claim that the plaintiff's right of action is "statute barred." If after a specified period of time an action has not started the right of action is no longer enforceable. The Limitation Act 1980 provides that the right to bring an action in tort will expire after the following periods:

(a) generally, six years from the date when the cause of the claim arose;
(b) three years in cases for claims of personal injuries and in cases where both personal injuries and damage to property are claimed.

The period of time usually runs from the date when the accident, libel, assault, etc. occurs, although section 33 of the Limitation Act 1980 gives the courts power to ignore, or disapply, these periods if it appears to the court that it is equitable to do so.

In *Halford* v. *Brookes and Another* (1991) the Court of Appeal exercised this discretion. The plaintiff's daughter was murdered in 1978 and the second defendant was tried and acquitted of the murder, after accusing the first defendant of committing the crime. In 1985 the plaintiff was informed that a civil action might be brought in the tort of battery, and in 1987 a writ was issued against the defendants. The defendants alleged that the claim was statute barred as the cause of the action arose more than three years before the issue of the writ. In considering the discretion under section 33, the Court of Appeal held that the plaintiff did not know her legal rights until 1985 and had acted promptly from then on, and any prejudice to the plaintiff in preventing an action far outweighed any prejudice to the defendants in disapplying the limitation period. This was the first case in English legal history of a civil court upholding a claim against an alleged murderer who had not been convicted of the crime.

REVISION TEST

1. What three things must a plaintiff prove to succeed in the tort of negligence?

2. What is the Latin phrase to show that the defendant must prove he was not negligent?

3. Name the three forms of trespass.

4. Who may sue in the tort of nuisance?

5. Name three remedies for nuisance.

6. What is the name given to a permanent form of defamation?

7. Name the five categories of defences for defamation.

8. Name the general defences in tort.

9. What does "actionable *per se*" mean?

SPECIMEN EXAMINATION QUESTIONS

1. Explain the general defences available in tort.

2. Explain the nature of the defence of "*volenti non fit injuria.*"

3. Distinguish the torts of nuisance and trespass to land.

4. (a) What factors must a plaintiff prove in order to succeed in the tort of negligence?
   (b) Steve, by negligent driving, injured Paul and his son Mark, aged five. Paul's wife was immediately informed of her family's accident and suffered shock and a consequent nervous breakdown. What are Steve's legal liabilities to the wife?

5. Elizabeth invited Richard to her house for tea. Richard hurt his knee as he tripped on a loose carpet. Robert entered her garden to take a short cut to the shops and fell into a ditch. Explain to Elizabeth whether she will be liable to pay damages to Richard and Robert.

6. (a) Explain the effect of *res ipsa loquitur* in the law of tort.

(b) Terry slipped on fruit juice which had spilled on to the floor of Debbie's shop by Gareth, a customer. Will Terry be able to sue Debbie for his injuries?

7. In a negligence action, the plaintiff must prove that he was owed a duty of care. In *Donoghue* v. *Stevenson*, Lord Atkin said that we owe a duty of care to our neighbours, *i.e.* persons (who we could reasonably foresee would be) affected by our actions.

   In each of the following situations, explain whether or not a duty of care would be owed, giving reasons for your answer.

   (a) Harriet is a barrister defending Ron on a charge of manslaughter. Ron is convicted. However, he is convinced that Harriet presented his case badly in court. He would like to sue her for negligence.

   (b) James is at work when a police officer calls to tell him that his wife and children have been involved in a bad car accident caused by another driver. James suffers nervous shock when he later visits his family in hospital. He wishes to sue the other driver for negligence.

S.E.G. 1991

8. Explain the principles of contributory negligence and vicarious liability. In the following situations explain how the principles work:

   (a) Elizabeth is employed as driver. While delivering goods for her employer she runs down and injuries Richard.

   (b) Ashley is driving his own car when he negligently injures David, who crossed the road without looking.

9. Smith was driving his employer's van to deliver goods to a customer when he negligently crashed into Jones' car. Inform Jones as to whom he may sue. Would the information be different if Smith was using the van to attend a football match?

10. Explain the differences between libel and slander in the tort of defamation.

11. The Daily Echo correctly reported that "Jack Jones of Richmond was yesterday convicted of theft and fined £50." Another Jack Jones also lived in Richmond and he

wished to sue the newspaper. Discuss Jack's chances of obtaining an award of damages for defamation.

SUGGESTED COURSEWORK TITLES

Distinguish between criminal and tortious liability. As some torts are also criminal offences, is there justification for considering them separately?

Explain the law of libel. Famous people are now receiving larger sums of damages for defamation of character, than received by some members of the public, seriously injured by the negligence of large organisations. Discuss the different attitudes of the law in this respect.

Chapter 10

Criminal Law

DEFINITION

There are as many definitions of a crime as there are textbooks on criminal law. This is because it is difficult to attach an exact definition to something which has many aspects; from motoring offences to murder; from theft to treason; from bigamy to blackmail and so on. From these examples it is possible to see the great variety and difference in gravity of the offences, although they are all crimes.

Earlier in the book, criminal law was classified as public law, because it is an offence against the State and is punished by the State. It would appear, therefore, first that a definition of a crime must show that an offence is against the public, although it might affect only one person, and, secondly, that the person who committed an offence either by a positive act or by omitting to do something which was a legal duty will be punished in some manner prescribed by the State. A definition which contains these points arose in the House of Lords when Lord Tucker, in *Board of Trade* v. *Owen* (1957) considered that the correct definition of a crime in the criminal law was the following passage from Halsbury's Laws of England. "A crime is an unlawful act or default which is an offence against the public and renders the person guilty of the act or default liable to legal punishment."

Classification of Offences

Crimes may be classified in several ways as follows:

1. Method of trial

In order to establish the method of trial, offences are classed as:

(a) Indictable offences

These are serious offences, triable by judge and jury, for which a Bill of Indictment sets out the charges alleged to have been committed by the person(s) sent to the Crown Court for the trial.

(b) Summary offences
These are offences which are subject to trial by magistrates' courts. The cases are decided in these courts.

(c) "Hybrid" offences
These are offences created by statute and may be tried either summarily or on indictment.

2. Power to arrest
A new classification of offences was introduced by the Criminal Law Act 1967, which is important with respect to the power to arrest without a warrant (see p. 241).

(a) Arrestable offences
These are offences established by The Criminal Law Act 1967, "...for which the sentence is fixed by law or for which a person (not previously convicted) may...be sentenced to imprisonment for a term of five years." The Police and Criminal Evidence Act 1984 extended the list by including certain offences under Customs and Excise law, Official Secrets Act, Sexual Offences Act, Theft Acts and offences of corruption in office. For a more detailed summary see p. 242. This classification is important in that arrestable offences are subject to the power to arrest without a warrant.

(b) Non-arrestable offences
Although this class is not defined by the Act, it relates to all other offences which are not arrestable offences.

ELEMENTS OF A CRIME

A person is generally guilty of a crime (but not always) if two elements are present. First, there must be a wrongful act which would be a crime and, secondly, there must be the intention to do the wrongful act, knowing it to be a crime.

Therefore, in most crimes there must be the physical element; a wrong act (the *actus reus*) and the mental element; a guilty mind (*mens rea*), and if both elements are not present there is no crime. It should be noted that there are some crimes for which both elements are not necessary. These crimes are committed by the act, and the intention is not necessary (see strict liability below).

1. Mens Rea

Mens Rea means the guilty mind or wrongful intention and, obviously it differs from crime to crime. The wrongful intention of a person committing a theft is completely different from that of a person committing treason. To be criminally liable, a person must have intended to do wrong or have acted in such a reckless and negligent manner that a reasonable person must have realised that a crime would be committed. If a terrorist leaves a bomb in a train and kills a passenger, it would not be a defence to claim that there was no intention to kill anyone. Such an act is so reckless, and the likelihood of death so foreseeable, that the wrong or criminal intention is present.

The House of Lords have ruled that intent to kill or inflict serious bodily harm is necessary to establish malice aforethought and even the foresight of the probable consequences of an act does not automatically mean the consequences were intended.

In R. v. *Moloney* (1985) the accused received a friendly challenge by his step-father to see who was "quicker on the draw" with shotguns. Both men were drunk, but good friends. Moloney shot and killed his step-father, although he claimed he had no intention to do so and did not appreciate that the gun was aimed at the victim. The House of Lords held that Moloney was not guilty of murder as a person only intends the result of an act if his purpose is to bring about that result. As Moloney did not intend to kill his step-father he was not guilty of murder. He was, however, guilty of manslaughter.

In R. v. *Hancock and Shankland* (1985) the defendants were striking miners. They pushed blocks of concrete from a bridge above a road, which landed on a windscreen of a taxi carrying a miner to work. The driver of the taxi was killed and the defendants were charged with murder. They claimed that they had not intended to kill or injure anyone, but merely to block the road. The House of Lords ruled that in such cases the probability of death or injury arising from the act done is important, because "if the likelihood that death or serious injury will result is high, the probability of that result may be seen as overwhelming evidence of the existence of the intent to kill or injure." The men were found not guilty of murder but guilty of manslaughter.

This decision was followed by the Court of Appeal in *R.* v. *Nedrick* (1986), where the court considered that in such cases a person would only be guilty if his actions will inevitably result in death or serious harm, regardless of intent.

Certain offences have **strict or absolute liability**, and *mens rea* is not essential. For example, the Health and Safety at Work, etc., Act provides that certain machines must have safety covers, and if these covers are not fixed, the employers are strictly liable. In one case, the employers asked an outside contractor to supervise the safety regulations but the employers were still liable when the contractors did not comply with the statutory requirements. Strict liability arises when the crime consists of performing a forbidden act or not performing a statutory duty (the *actus reus*); the wrongful intention (the *mens rea*) is irrelevant here.

In *Meah* v. *Roberts* (1977) two children were served with glasses of caustic soda instead of lemonade. Meah was found guilty of selling food unfit for human consumption, contrary to the Food and Drug Act 1955, even though another person was responsible for the cleaning fluid being in the lemonade bottle.

When interpreting statutes, there is a general presumption that *mens rea* is necessary in all crimes. This rule can only be replaced if an Act of Parliament expressly or impliedly excludes the necessity of *mens rea* (*Sweet* v. *Parsley* (1970)).

2. Actus Reus

This element includes all circumstances relating to a crime other than the *mens rea*. It is the wrongful act or omission which leads to a crime. For example, burglary is committed when a person enters a building as a trespasser with intent to steal, or to inflict grievous bodily harm on any person, or to rape a woman, or to do unlawful damage to the building.

The *actus reus* of burglary is the entering into a building without the right to do so. The *mens rea* is the intention of committing certain crimes when in the building. It is not burglary to enter a building without this intention, but merely the tort of trespass. The crime is committed when both elements are present. The *actus reus* of entering the building and the *mens rea* of intending to commit the other crimes, even though the other crimes were not actually committed. The above is only a part of the definition of burglary, see p. 235 for the complete definition.

SPECIFIC CRIMES

Offences Against the Person

1. Unlawful homicide

Homicide is the killing of a human being by another human being and it is not necessarily a crime. To kill as a means of lawful self-defence is not unlawful homicide and is not a crime. The following are examples of unlawful homicide, and are crimes.

(a) Murder

Murder is unlawful homicide, and it is defined as unlawful killing with malice aforethought, with the death taking place within a year and a day of the attack or event that caused the death.

Malice aforethought may be defined as the intention to kill or cause grievous bodily harm to the other person. It could be murder if the killer intended to murder one person, but killed another instead.

When a person kills whilst committing a crime or avoiding arrest, it would not be murder unless there was an intention to kill or inflict serious bodily harm (R. v. *Hancock and Shankland* (1985), see p. 227).

The punishment for murder is imprisonment for life, and, when sentencing, the judge may recommend a minimum term to be served.

The specific defences to a murder charge are:

(i) **Diminished responsibility.** The defence is that the killer was suffering from an abnormality of the mind at the time of the crime, that impaired the mental responsibility for committing the act or omission. If this defence is accepted the charge would be manslaughter. In the "Yorkshire Ripper" case the jury did not accept this defence, and found Peter Sutcliffe guilty of murder.

(ii) **Provocation.** To plead this defence a defendant must show that the actions and behaviour of the dead person was such that any reasonable person would lose control of the mind, and that the loss of self control was sudden and temporary. If accepted the charge is changed from murder to one of manslaughter. The defence is not available to a defendant who, after the provocative acts or assault, has time to think and reflect before committing the murder.

In *R.* v. *Thornton* (1992), the defendant had received a series of serious domestic violence and abuse from her husband. After one such incident she went to the kitchen to calm down, looked for a weapon and took a carving knife, sharpened it and returned to the living room where she stabbed her husband to death. The Court of Appeal confirmed her conviction of murder, holding that there had not been a sudden loss of control. This case has raised the question whether this defence makes allowances for such victims of domestic violence, and for the different temperaments and characteristics of men and women.

It should be noted that the House of Lords in *R.* v. *Howe, etc.* (1987), declared that duress (where a person is forced by another person to commit the crime) is no defence to murder (see p. 247).

(b) Manslaughter

Manslaughter is unlawful homicide without malice afore-thought. Manslaughter occurs when:

    (a)   A person acts with gross negligence and kills another person.

    (b)   A person kills another person whilst carrying out an unlawful act which would not normally kill or seriously hurt that other person.

    (c)   A person is directly the cause of another's death, although the actual killing was the act of a third party. For example, where a person involved in a shooting incident with police uses the victim as a shield as protection against the police bullets.

    (d)   The defences of provocation, suicide pact or diminished responsibility are pleaded successfully.

Examples (a), (b) and (c) above are classed as involuntary manslaughter because of the absence of malice aforethought. The last example is classed as voluntary manslaughter because the crime would have been murder but for the specific defences. The maximum punishment for manslaughter is imprisonment for life.

(c) Suicide

Suicide and attempted suicide are not crimes, but it is a criminal offence to aid, abet, counsel or procure the suicide of another. (Suicide Act 1961, s.2.) A suicide pact occurs when two or more persons agree that they shall be killed by some means. Survivors of such a pact are charged with manslaughter, whether they killed another or whether the dead person killed himself.

It should be noted that, as with murder, death by suicide must take place "within a year and a day" of the injury (*R.* v. *Inner West London Coroner* (1988)).

(d) Infanticide
Infanticide is committed when a child under the age of 12 months is killed:

(a) by its mother, and
(b) at the time of the killing, the mother was mentally disturbed as a result of not fully recovering from the effects of the child's birth.

The maximum punishment is the same as for manslaughter.

(e) Causing death by reckless driving
This offence is committed when a motorist does not drive with due care and attention and causes the death of another. It is punishable by imprisonment of up to five years and/or a fine.

2. Assault and battery
It is common to hear these two charges joined as one. They are, however, separate offences.

(a) Assault
This is an act which causes another person to be in immediate fear of an unlawful physical attack. It is generally considered that mere words are not sufficient but that they must be accompanied by some positive action. An action which arouses fear, although there was no intention to harm, would still be an assault.

(b) Battery
This is the actual unlawful force on another person, without lawful reason or just cause. The force may be the merest touch which caused no physical harm or injury.

It is usual for both offences to occur at the same time, but assault is not committed if the person is unaware that the battery is to take place. For example, if an attack takes place behind a person's back.

Defences include lawful consent, parental or quasi-parental authority and reasonable self-defence.

Offences Against the Person Act 1861, s.47, provides the offence of assault causing *actual* bodily harm, which would be less serious than grievous bodily harm (see below).

3. Wounding with intent

This offence is committed when a person, *with intent*, unlawfully and maliciously wounds or causes grievous bodily harm to another person. (Offences Against the Person Act 1861, s.18.) Section 20 of the Act has similar wording to section 18, but does not require *intent*. It is only possible to make this charge if there has been serious bodily harm or wounding by a breaking of the skin.

A bruise, burn or scratching of the skin is not wounding in this sense, nor would the breaking of a bone be so if the skin was not broken. It would appear, therefore, that bleeding from the wound is necessary for this offence. In *C*. v. *Eisenhower* (1983) a pellet from an airgun did not break the skin, but caused internal bleeding. The court held the defendant to be not guilty of unlawful wounding as there had not been a breaking of the skin.

4. Rape

This offence occurs when a man has unlawful sexual intercourse with a woman without her free consent. It would still be rape if consent was given by a trick, such as a man pretending to be the woman's husband (see p. 246).

The House of Lords, in *R*. v. *R*. (1991) held that a husband who rapes his wife can be prosecuted, as all rapes (even in marriage) are unlawful.

Boys under 14 may not be charged with rape but they could be liable in a civil case involving affiliation proceeding, where a boy is the father of a child (*L*. v. *K*. (1985)). A woman who forces a male to have unlawful sexual intercourse would be liable to the charge of indecent assault.

Offences Against Property

The Theft Acts 1968 and 1978 provide many offences against property. The main crimes are as follows:

1. Theft

"A person is guilty of theft if he dishonestly appropriates property belonging to another with the intention of permanently depriving the other of it."

The punishment for theft is a maximum of 10 years' imprisonment. The definition of theft, set out above, which is found in section 1(1) of the 1968 Act contains certain words or phrases which need to be explained.

(a) Dishonestly appropriates

This could be considered the "*mens rea*" of stealing, so that if a person did not intend to be dishonest, there would be no theft. For example, if I took another person's coat from a rack, thinking it was my own, there would be no theft, but if I took it knowing it was not my coat, it would be dishonest. If I took the coat thinking it was mine, but later discovered it belonged to another person, it would be theft if I decided to keep it.

The Act does not define "dishonestly" but gives examples of when the appropriation of another's property would not be dishonest.

(a) If a person believes in law that he has the right to deprive the other person of the property.

(b) If a person believes he would have the owner's consent. For example, borrowing £5 from a friend's locker.

(c) If a person (other than a trustee) believes that, after taking reasonable steps, the owner of the property which he holds cannot be found. This example would apply to the finding of lost property.

Appropriation takes place when a person assumes or takes over the rights of an owner. In *R. v. Morris* (1983) the defendant took articles from shelves in a supermarket and substituted the price labels with labels from lower priced goods. The House of Lords held that there had been a dishonest appropriation.

(b) Property

The term includes all things which can be owned, money, goods, rights of action and, in certain circumstances, land. As a general rule, it is not theft to pick mushrooms, flowers, fruit or foliage from a plant or trees growing wild, provided that the picking is not done for sale or other commercial purposes. It would not be stealing to pick flowers growing wild and give them to a friend (it would be the tort of trespass), but it would be stealing to sell them for gain.

(c) The intention of permanently depriving

This phrase is essential to the definition of theft. If I take a book intending to return it to the owner, I have not committed theft. In *R. v. Lloyd* (1985) a cinema projectionist took films from his employer's cinema and made "pirate" video copies for sale. The films were returned to the cinema within an hour or two. The Court of Appeal held that there was no intention permanently to deprive the owner of the property.

It is, however, possible to "steal" the book while it is still in my possession if, after borrowing it, I later decide to keep it. Theft takes place at the time I decide to keep the book permanently. Section 6(1) provides that in certain cases, although there was no intention to permanently deprive the owner of the property, borrowing goods would be theft. It would be theft in the following cases:

(a)   to take a train ticket from British Rail with the intention of returning it to them when arriving at the station of destination;

(b)   to take a football club season ticket and return it to the owner at the end of the football season;

(c)   to take a sack of potatoes from a farmer and sell it back to him by pretending to be the owner of the potatoes.

In these cases the true owners were not permanently deprived, but they were cases of theft, because there was an intention by the borrowers to treat the property as their own, and to deprive the owners of their rights to the property. It is the period of time that is important in (a) and (b) above, because it amounts to an outright taking of the goods.

2. Robbery

Section 8(1) provides that: "A person is guilty of robbery if he steals and immediately before or at the time of doing so, and in order to do so, he uses force on any person or puts or seeks to put any person in fear of being then and there subjected to force." The maximum punishment is imprisonment for life.

The principal elements of this offence are:

(a)   Stealing;

(b)   Using force; or

(c)   Fear, on the victim's part, of force being used.

A person does not commit robbery if there is no theft. The force used must be more than a gentle push, or more than is needed to take the property from a passive victim. It has been considered that merely snatching a handbag from a woman who did not resist would not be using force as required by the Act.

3. Burglary

Section 9 of the Theft Act 1968 provides that this offence occurs when a person:

- (a) enters any building or part of a building as a trespasser and with intent to commit an offence of theft, inflicting grievous bodily harm, rape or unlawful damage, or
- (b) having entered a building as a trespasser, steals or attempts to steal anything in the building or inflicts or attempts to inflict grievous bodily harm upon any person therein.

The maximum punishment is 14 years' imprisonment.

The main elements of this offence are: (i) entering as a trespasser; (ii) the intention of entering the building to commit one of the offences mentioned in (a) above; or (iii) having entered without intention to commit any offence, the commission or attempted commission of one of the offences mentioned in (b) above.

Section 10 provides that a person is guilty of an aggravated burglary if he commits burglary while he has a firearm or imitation firearm, any offensive weapon or explosive. The maximum penalty for aggravated burglary is imprisonment for life.

The Theft Act 1968 sets out many more offences against property, of which the following will be of interest:

(a) Section 12

This makes it an offence to *take a conveyance*, other than a pedal cycle, without the consent of the owner, or to drive or travel in the conveyance knowing it has been taken without the owner's consent. When the conveyance is a pedal cycle, it is far less serious, but still an offence. It is not an offence if the person believed he had the owner's consent, or would have had it if the owner had known he was taking the conveyance. It is not an offence if permission to use the conveyance is obtained by fraud. In *Whittaker* v. *Campbell* (1983), W., who did not have a driving licence, hired a van by showing a licence belonging to another person. The court held he was not guilty of this offence because he took the van with the owner's consent, although he obtained this consent by fraud. The "conveyance" includes anything constituted to carry persons on land, sea or air.

The offences carry a maximum punishment of three years' imprisonment. The penalty for the offence when the conveyance is a pedal cycle is a maximum fine of £50.

(b) Section 13

This provides for the *dishonest use of electricity*. It is theft to dishonestly use, divert or waste electricity.

(c) Section 15

This provides that it is an offence to dishonestly obtain *property* belonging to another by deception. It carries a maximum of 10 years' imprisonment. For example, it would be an offence to obtain a T.V. set on rental by showing the owner a means of identity which belonged to another person.

(d) Section 16

This provides that it is an offence for a person to dishonestly obtain a pecuniary *financial advantage* by deception. The maximum penalty is five years' imprisonment. Examples of pecuniary advantages would be obtaining an overdraft, or insurance policy, or obtaining employment or advancement at work, or winning money by betting. The deception may be by words or conduct. This offence would be committed, for example, if a person applying for a job falsely claimed to have a certain qualification (say two "A" levels) and was employed as a result of the deception.

In *R. v. Callender* (1992), the Court of Appeal held that the defendant, who obtained employment and earned remuneration by the deception that on his curriculum vitae he falsely claimed to have professional qualifications, had dishonestly obtained a pecuniary advantage by deception, contrary to section 16.

(e) Section 21

This provides that it is the offence of *blackmail* when a person with a view to profit, makes an unwarranted demand with menaces. Menaces may be expressed threats of violence, or threats of action that would be detrimental or unpleasant to the person addressed, or the conduct of the accused may justify the opinion that a demand with menaces has been made. The maximum punishment for blackmail is imprisonment for 14 years.

(f) Section 22

This makes it an offence to *handle stolen* goods, if a person knows or believes them to be stolen and dishonestly receives the goods, or helps or arranges for the goods to be removed or sold. This offence has a maximum sentence of 14 years' imprisonment.

(g) Section 25

This provides that it is an offence for a person, when not at his place of abode, to have any article for use in the course of, or in connection with, any burglary, theft or threat. Any person may arrest without warrant a person whom he reasonably suspects to be committing this offence. It is sometimes referred to as "going equipped for stealing." The maximum penalty is three years' imprisonment.

In the following case, the court had to decide if the car of the accused was a "place of abode."

In *R. v. Bundy* (1977) the police stopped the appellant's car and found articles for use in the course of theft. Bundy claimed that his car was his place of abode and therefore he had not committed a crime under section 25 of the Theft Act 1968. The Court of Appeal held that "a place of abode" meant a place in which the occupier intended to stay, and as a car was a means of transport, it was not a place of abode within the meaning of the Act.

4. The Theft Act 1978

The Theft Act 1978 introduced three offences.

Section 1 makes it an offence to dishonestly *obtain services* by *deception*, and it applies when services are obtained where the other person is induced to confer a benefit on the understanding that the benefit has been or will be paid for.

This section would apply when a person paid for a service by cheque knowing that the cheque was worthless.

Section 2 provides for the offences of *evasion of liability* by deception. It applies where a person by any deception:

(a) dishonestly secures the remission of the whole or part of any existing liability to make a payment, whether his own liability or another's; or

(b) with intent to make permanent default in whole or in part on any existing liability to make a payment, or with intent to let another do so, dishonestly induces the creditor or any person claiming payment on behalf of the creditor to wait for payment (whether or not the due date for payment is deferred) or to forgo payment; or

(c) dishonestly obtains any exemption from or abatement or liability to make a payment.

Examples of the above offences are:

(a) Jones owed the butcher £100 and falsely informed him that he was out of work and, as a result, the butcher reduced the debt.

(b) Smith had a car on hire and owed the rental for one month. Robinson, the owner of the car, demanded payment of the arrears or the immediate return of the car. If Smith needed the car for another day and gave Robinson a cheque for the overdue rental, knowing that she was leaving the country in two days and had closed her bank account, it would be an offence under this section because she had intended to permanently default the payment of an existing liability by deceiving Robinson into thinking the cheque was good.

(c) Barclay had a period contract on the railways and his friend Lloyd borrowed the contract and used it to obtain a free journey, although the contract was not transferable.

Section 3 creates an offence of *making off without payment*. It applies where a person knows that payment on the spot is required for any goods supplied or services done, and dishonestly makes off without paying with the intent to avoid payment.

This offence would apply in cases such as leaving a café, or a petrol station or bus or train without paying. In *R. v. Allen* (1985) the defendant left a hotel without paying the bill. He claimed that he genuinely intended to pay at a later date. The House of Lords considered that to be liable under this heading a person must act dishonestly and intend to evade payment altogether. Therefore, the defendant was not guilty.

The section does not apply when the payment cannot be legally enforced.

Criminal Damage

(1) The Criminal Damage Act 1971, s.1 provides that it shall be an offence to unlawfully destroy or damage any property belonging to another, either intentionally or recklessly.

Section 1(2) provides that it is an aggravated offence to unlawfully destroy or damage property with the intention of endangering the life of another, whether the property belongs to the offender, or to another. Section 1(3) provides that if the damage or destruction to property in the above offences is by fire, the charge shall be arson.

The maximum penalty for offences under sections 1(2) and (3) is life imprisonment.

"Property," for the purposes of this Act, means real and personal tangible objects, including money and wild animals.

Misleading Trade Descriptions

The Trade Descriptions Act of 1968 and 1972 provide that it shall be an offence carrying criminal sanctions for a person to make a false or misleading trade description. Under the 1968 Act the offence is committed when, in the course of business, a person makes a false description of goods with regard to such matters as price, size or quantity and method or place of manufacture.

In *Wings Ltd.* v. *Ellis* (1984), a holiday brochure was published with false information. The brochure was later amended but a customer booked a holiday relying on the original brochure. The House of Lords held that it is no defence that the defendant did not know at the time of publication that the statement was false. In *R.* v. *Nash* (1991), the Court of Appeal upheld a sentence of imprisonment on the defendant who, when selling a car, described it as being in excellent condition when it was in fact a potential death trap.

Section 24 provides that it would be a defence to show that:

(a) The misleading description was caused by information supplied by a third party, or through some fault of a third party, over which the defendant had no control.

(b) The defendant did not and could not know, after reasonable inquiry, that the goods did not correspond with the description, or that the goods had been so described, and

(c) The defendant took all reasonable precautions to ensure that the offence was not committed by himself or by persons under his control.

The 1972 Act makes it an offence not to indicate the origin of goods which bear certain United Kingdom names and trade marks and have been produced or manufactured outside the United Kingdom.

There have been many prosecutions under the 1968 Act. A typical example would be selling a motor car with the mileage meter showing a mileage far less than the car has actually travelled. It should be noted, however, that, as a result of this Act many garages now sell cars expressly stating that they do not guarantee the mileage shown to be correct.

It should be noted that the provisions of the Acts do not give buyers a right to enforce a contract as, unfortunately, the Acts only carry criminal sanctions.

THE POWERS OF ARREST

In an earlier chapter, the functions of the criminal courts were discussed and in this chapter some specific crimes have also been covered. It is now necessary to see how persons accused of a criminal offence are called or brought before a particular criminal court. There are three ways by which a person suspected or accused of committing a crime may be brought to court.

    (a) By summons,
    (b) By warrant for arrest,
    (c) By arrest without a warrant.

The first two methods are known as "process."

1. Summons

A summons is a document which orders the accused to attend court. It is issued and signed by a magistrate and states the nature of the offence and the time and place at which the accused should attend court. The summons is served or sent to the accused, who remains at liberty until the court hearing. A summons must be issued unless the offence is indictable or subject to punishment by imprisonment.

2. Warrant

This document is an order for the arrest of a particular person and is addressed to police officers in the area concerned. The accused person must be named or described in sufficient detail to be recognised as that person. It is unlawful to issue warrants that do not state the name or description of a person.

A warrant has a statement of the offence and is signed by a magistrate and it empowers the police to arrest the accused in order to bring him before the court. It is not necessary for a police officer to possess the warrant at the time of arrest but, if the accused demands, it must be shown as soon as is practicable.

A person arrested by warrant is not automatically at liberty until the time of trial, as he would be under a summons.

However, the magistrate may endorse the warrant at the time of issue so that the person named may be released on bail on an undertaking that he will appear in court at the specified time and place. This is referred to as "backed for bail," and the accused is released as soon as he has complied with the conditions of the undertaking.

Basically, a warrant may only be issued for offences which are indictable or punishable by imprisonment. In addition, however, warrants may be issued if a person does not appear in court to answer a summons, or if the address of the accused is not sufficiently established or known to enable a summons to be served.

3. Arrest without a warrant

The Police and Criminal Evidence Act 1984 provides powers of arrest by the police and lessens the powers of arrest by a private citizen as follows:

(a) Police officers

Police officers may arrest without a warrant, when they have reasonable grounds for suspicion, any person who:

(a) (i)   has committed an arrestable offence,
    (ii) is committing an arrestable offence, or
    (iii) is about to commit an arrestable offence

If there are no reasonable grounds for the above suspicion, the arrest is unlawful. The arrest would also be unlawful unless the person arrested is informed of the reason for the arrest at the time of the arrest, or as soon as is practical afterwards.

(b) has committed or is committing any offence which is not an arrestable offence and the police officer has reasonable grounds for suspecting that (i) the service of a summons is impracticable or (ii) inappropriate because:
    (i)   the person arrested is unknown to the police or
    (ii) is likely to cause injury or damage to other persons or property, or
    (iii) a child or other vulnerable person needs protection from the person arrested.

(b) Private citizens

Private citizens may arrest a person when an arrestable offence is being committed or has been committed and the private citizen suspects that other person of committing the offence.

An arrestable offence is:

(a) an offence which carries a penalty fixed by law, (an example would be murder for which the penalty has to be a sentence of life imprisonment.),

(b) an offence for which a person aged 21 or more, not previously convicted, may be sentenced to imprisonment for five years or more,

(c) an offence under certain Customs and Excise legislation, Official Secrets Act, Sexual Offences Act, Theft Acts and corruption in office and,

(d) to attempt, or to conspire, incite or procure the commission of, the offences listed in (c) above.

A new classification was introduced, of "serious arrestable offence" which gives the police extended powers of investigation, with regard to offences such as murder, rape, causing an explosion and other arrestable offences which might become "serious" depending on the circumstances.

4. Stop and search

Section 1 of the 1984 Act provides that the police may search anything which is in or on a vehicle, for stolen or prohibited articles (burglary tools, offensive weapons and the like), and detain a person or vehicle to carry out the search, if there are reasonable grounds for suspecting that such articles will be found. The search must take place in a public place. A person may also be searched, although the police may only request the removal of a coat or jacket. Before making a search the police officers must identify themselves or, if in plain clothes, show a warrant card. As soon as practical after the search, the police officer must make a written report of the time, date, place of the search and any information regarding articles found, injuries to persons or damage to property as a result of the search.

5. Entry and search

Police officers may enter private premises to search for evidence and seize items connected with an arrestable offence. The Code of Practice provides that the search should be at a reasonable hour and with due consideration for property and the occupants' privacy. A police officer may enter and search, with the occupiers' written permission, to:

(a) execute a warrant,

(b) arrest for an arrestable offence (without a warrant),

    (c)   arrest a person unlawfully at large.

In addition, when a person has been arrested for an arrestable offence, a police officer may search that person's premises provided the officer has reasonable grounds for suspecting that evidence of that, or some other, offence will be discovered.

6. Seizure

In addition to all the powers mentioned above, a police officer, lawfully on premises, may seize any article or items which is reasonably believed to be evidence of an offence and, if not seized, would be lost, destroyed, concealed or damaged.

Complaints Against the Police

The Act set up the Police Complaints Authority which has the power to investigate complaints against the police. Complaints may be made by anyone in writing or in person.

BAIL

In the previous section, it was shown that a magistrate may endorse a warrant that the accused may be released on bail, which means that he is at liberty and not in custody. On other occasions the decision to grant bail is made in court or by the police. Bail is a security given by other persons that the accused will attend court on the appointed day and time. If bail is granted, the accused may carry out the normal functions of a free person and will not be in custody for the period between the arrest and the magistrates' hearing, and between trial in the magistrates' court and the Crown Court.

The sureties (the persons who give the security) usually promise to pay a sum of money into court if the accused does not attend the hearing. In addition, the court may require the accused to surrender his passport. If the court or police are satisfied that the sureties are able to meet their promised commitment, the accused is handed into their custody. The Bail Act 1976 abolished the accused's own recognisance but introduced a new offence of absconding whilst on bail. The sureties have the right of arrest if they consider that the accused will not attend court on the appointed day and the police also have power to arrest the accused if he is not following the conditions of his release on bail.

When an accused has been committed by the magistrates for trial to the Crown Court, he may apply for bail for a period up to the trial. The Bail Act 1976 provided that there is a presumption that bail will be granted and, therefore, the accused is entitled to bail unless a good reason can be shown why it should not be granted.

The magistrates will ask the police if they oppose the application, and if there is no objection, they will grant bail. The value of the security will depend on the seriousness of the offence but if the terms of bail are unreasonable, the accused may appeal to a High Court judge. Bail is very rarely granted for murder and may not be granted for other offences if the accused:

(a) cannot obtain the necessary sureties;
(b) has previously been granted bail and did not attend court as ordered;
(c) is likely to commit other offences;
(d) does not have an established address;
(e) is suspected of committing a violent offence or was in possession of firearms or other offensive weapons;
(f) is likely to leave the country and avoid the trial.

GENERAL DEFENCES

There will be specific defences to all crimes, even if it is simply "I didn't do it," or "I was in another place at the time of the offence." Sometimes a specific defence may be more technical, and with a charge of theft, the defence may be that there was no intention to permanently deprive the owner but merely to borrow for a short period of time.

There are certain defences, applying generally to criminal charges, under which the accused will not deny performing the offence but will claim one of the following as a reason why he or she is not guilty:

1. Insanity
The defence of insanity in criminal cases is based on the M'Naghten Rules. In 1843, Daniel M'Naghten, motivated by an insane delusion of persecution by Sir Robert Peel, killed Edward Drummond who was Peel's secretary. M'Naghten was acquitted on the grounds of insanity, and the House of Lords, in its

Parliamentary role, produced the following rules which still apply today.

(a) Every person is presumed sane until the contrary is proved.

(b) The defence must show that the accused was labouring under a defect of reason caused by a disease of the mind, and that he did not know the nature and quality of his act, or, if he did know it, he did not know that he was doing wrong.

(c) Where a person commits a crime under an insane delusion, he is considered to have the responsibility that he would have had if the facts as he imagined were real.

If a man had insane delusions that another man was about to kill him, and in self-defence he killed the other man, there would be no criminal liability. If, however, his delusions were that the man was making friendly advances to his girl friend, and he killed him, he would be liable for punishment, because his delusion did not warrant the action he took.

It should be noted, (i) that the defence has to prove insanity, (ii) the verdict is "not guilty by reason of insanity."

Diminished responsibility is not a general defence, as it specifically applies to charges of murder.

2. Automatism

This is an act done by the muscles of the body without any control of the mind. It could be a reflex action, a blackout, an act done when sleepwalking, or any other involuntary movement, provided the person's physical and mental state was not caused by his own negligence.

The defence is based on a general rule that an offence is not punishable if the action of the defendant was involuntary.

3. Mistake

A mistake of law is no defence, but a person may claim that, had he known the true facts, the crime would not have been committed. In *R. v. Tolson* (1889) a woman remarried during the lifetime of her husband. It was shown that she honestly believed her husband to be dead, and the court upheld her defence to the charge of bigamy.

Mistake when pleaded must be reasonable. In *Tolson*'s Case, the plea was accepted because the husband had been reported drowned at sea and had been missing for five years.

4. Intoxication (by drugs or alcohol)

Although it is not a defence in itself, and in some cases it is an offence, the plea may be used to show that the *mens rea* required for the offence was not present.

In *R. v. Hardie* (1985) the defendant was under the influence of valium, which had not been prescribed for him, and he set fire to a friend's flat, endangering lives. The Court of Appeal held that he did not have the *mens rea*, and considered that while intoxication cannot usually be pleaded as a defence to offences of recklessness, the rule will not generally apply to drugs which are merely sedative. Obviously, this defence could not be used in cases such as reckless driving.

It may also be a defence to show that intoxication produced insanity and that the M'Naghten Rules are relevant.

A person who forms the intention of committing a crime whilst sober and becomes drunk to acquire "Dutch courage" will not be able to use this defence. In *Att. Gen. for Northern Ireland v. Gallagher* (1963) a man planned to kill his wife and drank a bottle of whisky before committing the crime. His defence of drunkenness was refused by the House of Lords. In *R. v. Fotheringham* (1989), a husband and wife expected to be returning late and informed the baby-sitter to sleep in their bed. When the couple returned home the husband, who was drunk, got into the bed and raped the baby-sitter. His defence was that he was drunk and thought he was in bed with his wife. The Court of Appeal held that intoxication which is self induced is no defence to rape.

5. Necessity

There is no general defence of necessity, except in cases of self-defence or prevention of violent crimes. It would appear that the defence cannot be used for the murder of an innocent person. In *R. v. Dudley & Stephens* (1884) two seamen who had been shipwrecked for nearly three weeks killed and ate the cabin boy, who was the only other survivor. The defence of necessity was rejected and they were found guilty of murder, even though the jury considered that they would have died from starvation had they not killed the boy.

6. Duress

Duress may be raised as a defence when a person is threatened that, unless he commits a certain crime, he or another person may be killed or suffer serious personal injury. Threats may also arise from circumstances, such as, for example being chased by a rioting mob and driving the wrong way down a one way street. In *R. v. Conway* (1988), the Court of Appeal recognised the defence of "duress of circumstances." In *R. v. Martin* (1989) the Court of Appeal again recognised this defence when the defendant, while disqualified from driving, drove his stepson to work. He claimed that his wife, who had suicidal tendencies, threatened to kill herself if he refused to do so. This type of situation has also been considered as a defence of necessity (see above).

The House of Lords in *R. v. Howe* (1987) ruled that duress is not a defence in murder. In *R. v. Gotts* (1992), a 17-year-old man caused serious injuries when he stabbed his mother with intent to kill her. He was charged with attempted murder but alleged that his father told him to do so and threatened to kill him if he did not carry out his wishes. The House of Lords, following the decision in *R. v. Howe*, held that as duress is no defence to murder, it would be illogical to apply this defence to attempted murder.

A wife may plead the defence of coercion if she commits a crime, other than murder or treason, under the coercion of and (most important) in the presence of her husband. Marital coercion may cover threats of physical injury and mental pain, such as the threat to leave the family.

REVISION TEST

1. Name the class of offence which is decided in the magistrates' court.

2. Name four crimes of unlawful homicide.

3. Name the two elements usually required for a person to be guilty of crime.

4. What is the name given to offences which only require one of these elements to be present?

5. Name five general defences to criminal charges.

6. What are the three ways by which a person suspected or accused of committing a crime may be brought to court?

SPECIMEN EXAMINATION QUESTIONS

1. Explain the terms *actus reus* and *mens rea*.

2. Murder is defined as the unlawful killing of a reasonable creature in being, under the Queen's Peace, with malice aforethought expressed or implied, the death occurring within a year and a day.

    In each of the following examples, explain whether or not the named person would be convicted of murder, and give reasons for your answer.

    (a) Fiona is driving her car at 60 m.p.h. in a 30 m.p.h. zone and runs over and kills Brian.
    (b) David is walking home late one night and is attacked by a man with a knife. During the struggle which follows, David grabs the knife, stabs his attacker and kills him.
    (c) John breaks into Paul's flat at night and shoots Paul while he is lying in bed. Paul had died 30 minutes earlier of a heart attack.

    S.E.G. 1990

3. Murder is described as "an arrestable offence." Explain what is meant by the phrase "an arrestable offence."

4. When does a policeman without a warrant have the power to arrest a person? Do other persons have the power to arrest?

5. Under the Theft Act 1968, theft is defined as the dishonest appropriation of property belonging to another with the intention of permanently depriving the other of it.

   In each of the following situations, explain whether or not theft has occurred, and give reasons for your answer.

   (a) Sarah and Alice are flatmates. Sarah borrows Alice's scarf, thinking Alice will not mind because she has lent it to Sarah before. Later, Sarah realises that Alice thinks she has lost her scarf. Sarah then decides to keep it.

   (b) Bill has a season ticket for his local football club. Barnard, without permission, takes his ticket near the start of the season and then returns it a week before the end of the season.

   (c) Mary finds a wallet in the street with the initials J.W. on the outside and £50 inside. She decides to keep the wallet and money as she does not think she can discover the owner.

   S.E.G. 1991

6. (a) Explain the defences to a charge of murder of
      (i) diminished responsibility, and
      (ii) provocation.

   (b) What is the effect on the charge of murder if either defence is successful?

7. Anne has been charged by the police with taking a car without the owner's consent.

   (a) What crime has Anne committed?
   (b) What specific defences could she plead?
   (c) Would it be the same offence if she had taken a pedal cycle instead of a car?

8. Explain the general defences to a criminal charge.

9. There is a range of non-fatal criminal offences against the person. These include assault (an attempt or threat which produces fear of an unlawful physical attack), battery (the application of unlawful force), wounding (which involves the breaking of the skin), and grievous bodily harm (defined as serious bodily harm).

   In each of the following situations identify what criminal offence(s) may have been committed, giving reasons for your answer.

    (a)   Michael and Alan are having an argument. Michael aims a punch at Alan. Alan ducks and Michael hits Bernard in the face, breaking his nose.

    (b)   Kylie and Jason are at a Christmas party. Jason sneaks up behind Kylie with a piece of mistletoe and gives her a kiss. Kylie is annoyed because she does not like Jason, a fact of which Jason is well aware. Kylie slaps Jason across the face, cutting his face with her ring.

S.E.G. 1992

SUGGESTED COURSEWORK TITLES

Explain the present system of sentences for criminal offences and discuss the purposes for them. Suggest other ways of punishment which you think would be more appropriate for today's society.

Explain the concepts of "mens rea" and "actus reus," and strict liability. Do you think that there should be strict liability for a crime where there was no prior intention to commit the offence?

Chapter 11
Family Law

MARRIAGE

The standard definition of marriage is "The voluntary union for life of one man and one woman to the exclusion of all others." (*Hyde* v. *Hyde* (1866).)

In this country marriage is monogamous, which means, as the definition above indicates, one man and one woman. When a party is allowed to have more than one spouse at the same time, it is polygamy. In certain countries polygamy is allowed.

Before looking further into the definition, with all the obligations and legal duties which marriage brings upon the parties, it is helpful to consider the legal consequences of the preliminaries that may lead to marriage, such as engagement and co-habitation.

1. Engagement
There is now no action for "breach of promise." Until the Law Reform (Miscellaneous Provisions) Act 1970 abolished this right of action, a party (usually the woman) could sue for damages for breach of contract if the other party refused to marry.

Engagements are usually formalised by the man giving the woman an "engagement" ring. The ring remains the property of the woman should the engagement be broken, unless at the time it was given the man made it clear that in the event of the marriage not taking place the ring was to be returned. In *Mossop* v. *Mossop* (1988), where an engaged couple cohabited for five years but never married, it was held that engaged couples do not have the same rights as married couples to claim under legislation specifically provided for married couples.

2. Cohabitation
The legal status of an unmarried couple living together as man and wife is very complex, as the law does not recognise such a "marriage." Parliament has recognised, however, that in certain

251

matters these partners have similar duties and problems as legally married partners and has provided appropriate legislation.

For example a woman may claim against the estate of her deceased partner as a dependant, and the Supplementary Benefits Act 1976 treats the partners as though they were married.

The Requirements of a Valid Marriage

1. Both parties must be 16 years of age or over

If either is under 18, consent must be given by both parents, if alive. If the parents refuse to give permission, the minor may apply to the magistrates' court where the magistrates will make a decision based on what they consider to be in the best interests of the minor. A marriage which is formally solemnised without this permission will be valid. A marriage where one of the parties is under 16 years is void.

2. The prohibited degrees

The parties must not be closely related, as marriage is not allowed between parties within the prohibited degrees. This means that certain persons who are closely related, either by blood or marriage, may not marry each other. The obvious relations that are not allowed to marry are parents to their children (*e.g.* father and daughter, mother and son) and brothers and sisters. The Marriage Act 1949 as amended by the Marriage (Enabling) Act 1960, provides two complete lists of the prohibited degrees; a list showing the relations a woman may not marry, and a list of relations a man may not marry. Generally, uncles may not marry nieces, nor aunts their nephews, but first cousins may wed, and a woman may marry her husband's brother, uncle or nephew if her marriage has ended by death or divorce. A man has a similar right to marry his former wife's sister, niece or aunt. The Marriage (Prohibited Degrees of Relationship) Act 1986, makes further provision for the marriage of persons related by infinity (or marriage). For example, a man could now marry a woman who is the daughter of a former spouse of his (and who is obviously not his daughter), provided that they are both 21 or over and the younger party had not been a child of his family at any time before attaining the age of 18.

The reason for these prohibitions is, first, public policy, and, secondly, the genetic risk which might produce un-desirable side-effects or characteristics in a child born of a marriage between blood relatives.

3. Neither party must be in an existing marriage

A person who marries for a second time whilst the first marriage is in existence may commit the crime of bigamy, although the following defences may be pleaded:

(a) that in good faith and on reasonable grounds, it was believed the spouse was dead.

(b) That in good faith and on reasonable grounds, it was believed that the first marriage was annulled or dissolved.

(c) That the first spouse had been missing continuously for seven years, and there was no reason for supposing that partner to be alive.

4. The formalities required by statute

A marriage ceremony must be performed and solemnised as provided by the Marriage Acts 1949 and 1983.

Void and Voidable Marriages

A void marriage means that, as far as the law is concerned, no marriage has existed and the parties are in a single state. On the other hand, a voidable marriage is regarded as legally valid until a court of competent jurisdiction pronounces it a nullity. Marriages are void because of some defect which is so fundamental that it is considered the marriage never existed.

Voidable marriages are valid, but, because of certain circumstances after, or at the time of the wedding, they may be annulled by the courts:

1. Void marriages

The Nullity of Marriage Act 1971, as now consolidated in the Matrimonial Causes Act 1973, provides that marriages shall be void for the reason that a valid marriage had not taken place because:

(a) one or both of the parties—
  (i) were under 16 years old (see p. 252)
  (ii) were within the prohibited degrees (see p. 252)
  (iii) were already married (see p. 253)
  (iv) had entered a polygamous marriage whilst being domiciled in England or Wales (see p. 251)

(b) there was a basic defect in the marriage ceremony (see p. 255).

(c)   the parties were not respectively male or female (see p. 251).

2. Voidable marriages

Section 2 of the Nullity of Marriage Act 1971, as consolidated in the Matrimonial Causes Act 1973, provides that marriages are voidable for the following reasons:

(a)   the marriage had not been consummated, owing to incapacity or the wilful refusal to consummate, by either party. This means that one party was incapable of having sexual intercourse or refused to do so.

(b)   either party did not validly consent to the marriage because of duress, mistake, unsoundness of mind or otherwise. Parties to marriage must give their consent freely. Similarly, an insane person cannot give a valid consent because he does not know the consequences of what he is saying. This situation may also exist if one of the parties is drunk or under the influence of drugs.

(c)   either party was, at the time of the marriage, suffering from a mental disorder within the Mental Health Act 1983, which makes them unfitted for marriage.

(d)   one party was suffering from venereal disease in a communicable form and the other party did not know.

(e)   at the time of the marriage, the man did not know that the bride was pregnant by some person other than him.

A petition for nullity of a marriage may be made to the court immediately. There is no need, as with divorce, to wait for a period of time. Petitions for reasons (c), (d) and (e) above, must be made within three years but this period may be extended if the petitioner has been suffering from a mental disorder. The court has the discretion to refuse to grant a decree if it considers it would be unjust to do so.

It must be noted that children born of a voidable marriage are legitimate, even if the marriage is later declared void by the court, and children born of a void marriage are legitimate, if, at the time of conception (or the marriage, if later), the parties reasonably believed the marriage to be valid.

The Formalities of a Marriage

A marriage may be solemnised by a Church of England ceremony, by ceremonies of another religion or in a Registrar's Office. The formalities of each ceremony are different.

1. Church of England

(a) Banns have to be published. Banns are a public announcement that the marriage is to take place and they must be published on three Sundays in the churches of either or both of the parties.

(b) A common licence has to be issued by a Bishop for the marriage to take place within the parish of one of the parties, or the Archbishop of Canterbury has to issue a special licence which permits the parties to marry anywhere.

(c) A superintendent registrar's certificate has to be issued, which authorises the church to solemnise the marriage.

(d) The wedding must take place between the hours of 8 a.m. and 6 p.m. within three months of the banns being published, and there must be two or more witnesses.

2. Marriages solemnised by a superintendent registrar's certificate
The certificate authorises a marriage to take place:

(a) in the superintendent registrar's office, or

(b) in a registered building (usually a church of a non-Anglican religion) except in marriages between two professing Jews or between members of the Society of Friends (Quakers),

(c) between the hours of 8 a.m. and 6 p.m. before open doors and witnessed by at least two persons (except Jewish or Quaker marriages).

(d) within three months of the issue of the certificate.

(e) The Marriage Act 1983 enables marriages of housebound and detained persons to be solemnised at the place where they reside.

The Duties of Husband and Wife

The legal consequence of marriage is that certain duties fall upon the parties. Some of the duties are laid down by statute, while others are provided by the common law.

The principal duties are as follows:

(a) A spouse has a duty to maintain his or her partner, but this right is lost if a partner commits adultery or desertion. A husband has a common law duty to maintain his wife, but a wife will have to maintain a husband who is ill and incapable of earning an income. Although the old rule by which a deserted wife had authority to obtain credit against her husband's account, as an "agent of necessity," was abolished in 1970, a wife who lives with her husband has the implied authority to pledge the husband's credit (buying goods on credit on his account) for necessary household goods. This authority is based on the presumed, implied consent of the husband that she is his agent. This presumption may be rebutted by the husband informing the trader not to give credit to his wife, or by showing the court that the wife had a sufficient supply of the goods in question, or that she had a sufficient allowance to pay for them herself.

(b) Both parents normally have custody of their children until they are 18, although it can be lost earlier if the children marry or leave home. Parents may lose the right of custody should the marriage end in divorce, or if the children are taken into care because they are considered to be in danger.

(c) Both parents have a duty, depending on the age of the children, to;
  (i) financially support and maintain their children;
  (ii) educate their children, and this usually means sending them to school;
  (iii) protect them from dangers in the home (*e.g.* unguarded fires);
  (iv) protect them from many other dangers likely to harm their health and moral welfare (*e.g.* introduction of alcohol or prostitution).

THE CHILDREN ACT 1989

This Act tries to bring together all public and private law relating to children into one Act of Parliament. It is very wide ranging and detailed, and brings about radical changes and improvements in the law relating to the care, upbringing and protection of children, and provides a single and consistent statement of the law.

The following notes are an indication of the principles of the Act and the new orders available to the courts.

The Act considers that children are generally better looked after within the family, with both parents taking a full part without resorting to legal proceedings.

Section 1 of the Act provides three main principles to guide a court when making decisions under the Act, which are of general application.

1. The Welfare Principle

When a court decides any question with respect to the upbringing of the child or the administration of a child's property, or the application of any income arising from it, the child's welfare shall be the court's paramount consideration.

2. A Presumption of No Order

Where the court is considering whether or not to make one or more orders under the Act, with respect to a child, it shall not make the order or any other orders unless it considers that doing so would be better for the child than making no order at all.

3. Delay

A court shall have regard to the general principle that any delay in determining the question of the upbringing of the child, is likely to prejudice the welfare of the child. The Court is required to draw up a schedule or timetable for deciding such matters without delay. Any delay that takes place will have to be justified on the basis that it safeguards or advances the welfare of the child concerned.

New Orders Available to the Courts

Section 8 provides the following orders (referred to as section 8 Orders) which are available in all proceedings relating to children. The courts, however, must consider the above principles when making an order.

(a) A Contract Order

This order requires the person with whom a child lives, or is to live, to allow the child to visit or stay with the person named in the Order, or for that person and the child otherwise to have contact with each other.

(b) A Prohibition Order

This Order provides that no step which could be taken by a parent in meeting his parental responsibility for a child, and which is of a kind specified in the Order, shall be taken by any person without the consent of the court.

(c) A Residence Order

This important Order settles the arrangements to be made as to the person with whom a child is to live. It is aimed to replace orders for custody, care and control.

(d) A Specific Issue Order

This Order gives directions for the purpose of deciding a specific question which has arisen, or which may arise, in connection with any aspect of parental responsibility for a child.

DIVORCE

The Matrimonial and Family Proceedings Act 1984 provides that either spouse may petition for divorce after one year of marriage. The courts have no discretion to shorten this period.

The only reason for petitioning for divorce is that "the marriage has broken down irretrievably." The basis of the law on divorce is the Divorce Reform Act 1969, now consolidated into the Matrimonial Causes Act 1973. A petitioner for divorce must prove to the court any one of five "facts" which can establish that the marriage has irretrievably broken down. Even if one or more of these facts are established, however, the court will not grant a divorce if it remains unconvinced about the breakdown of the marriage. The five facts which can establish the breakdown of the marriage are:

1. Adultery

Adultery is voluntary sexual intercourse between two persons, one or both of whom are married, but not to each other. The petitioner must prove that the other spouse committed adultery and that this act makes it *intolerable* to continue living with the respondent.

2. Behaviour

The petitioner must show that the respondent's behaviour was such that the petitioner could not reasonably be expected to live with the respondent.

It is a question of fact in each case, but the court would obviously expect to see evidence of very unreasonable behaviour, such as violence, extreme bad temper, drunkenness, obsessive jealousy and so on.

3. Desertion

It must be shown that the respondent deserted the petitioner for a period of two years or more. Generally desertion means living apart, but if the parties live in the same house, not as man and wife but following completely separate lives, this might be considered sufficient to prove desertion. It would be desertion if the respondent acted in such a way that the petitioner had to leave the family home.

4. Living apart for two years

The petitioner must show that the parties have lived apart continuously for more than two years immediately before presentation of the petition and that the respondent consents to the decree being granted.

5. Living apart for five years

It is sufficient under this heading to show that the marriage has broken down and the consent or otherwise of the other party is irrelevant to a spouse's right to petition.

Divorce Decrees

When a petition is successful the court grants a "decree nisi." The effect of this decree is not to dissolve the marriage immediately but it will be dissolved unless good cause be shown to the court, within six weeks, why the decree should not be made absolute.

After six weeks have elapsed, the party who was granted the decree may apply to the court for a "decree absolute." Until this decree has been granted the parties are not divorced and may not remarry. It would be committing bigamy if they did so.

Undefended Divorces

Well over 90 per cent. of petitions are undefended and procedure for such cases has been simplified and made slightly impersonal because neither party nor their lawyers need attend the hearing. It is commonly known as the "postal divorce."

JUDICIAL SEPARATION

There are occasions when the parties to a marriage do not wish to live together as man and wife, but do not want to obtain a divorce. The reasons for petitioning for a judicial separation and not for divorce are usually religious or because children are involved. There are less than 1,000 petitions each year for judicial separation.

The petition may be made at any time, based on one of the five grounds for divorce outlined above. Its main effect is to release the parties from their obligation to cohabit.

MAINTENANCE

A wife whose husband neglects to maintain her or the children of the marriage, may apply to the courts for a matrimonial order for maintenance. Maintenance is a financial payment or settlement from a husband to maintain a wife and family. An order for maintenance may be obtained from the magistrates' court, county court or High Court. It is possible for a man to apply for maintenance from his wife, but, because it is more common, the text that follows refers to wives claiming from husbands, although it would apply to the reverse situation.

Maintenance is usually claimed when the married parties do not live together, because of a breakdown in the marriage. A party may claim as a result of a judicial separation or divorce or when the parties are separated but no legal action has been taken.

1. Maintenance claims made before or after divorce or legal separation

(a) *Before the divorce or legal separation*, the courts may award periodical cash payments to be paid by the spouse. The amount payable is what the court considers reasonable in the circumstances; and it is provided to enable the claimant to maintain herself until the court action. Maintenance for children may also be claimed at this time.

(b) *After legal proceedings*, the courts may award in addition to a periodical cash payment:
　(i)　a lump sum for the wife and children, or
　(ii)　a part of the husband's capital (usually no more than one-third) to be secured for the benefit of the wife and children, or
　(iii)　a transfer of property belonging to the husband or which was owned jointly.

The court has discretion as to the size and nature of an award, but where the court makes an award of a periodical payment order, the Matrimonial and Family Proceedings Act 1984, provides power to the courts to implement "the clean break principle." The court should consider whether it would be appropriate to either award a lump sum payment or to limit the duration of the periodic payments for a time considered sufficient to enable the recipient to adjust to the termination of financial dependance from the other party.

The court should consider:

(a) the income, earning capacity and financial resources of both parties,
(b) the financial needs and obligations the parties have or are likely to have,
(c) the standard of living enjoyed by the family before the breakdown of the marriage,
(d) the age of the parties, and the length of the marriage,
(e) any disability of either of the parties, physical or mental,
(f) the contribution each party made to the welfare of the family. (In *Gojkovic* v. *Gojkovic* (1990), the Court of Appeal considered that the wife's share should not only be calculated on the wife's reasonable needs, but her contribution to the family should also be taken into consideration.)
(g) after a divorce or nullity, the value of the loss of some benefit (such as a pension) which cannot be acquired because of the termination of the marriage.

In addition, the Matrimonial and Family Proceedings Act 1984, requires:

(a) that first consideration should be given to any child of the family under the age of 18, and
(b) the court should consider whether it may exercise its power so that the financial obligations of each party to each other might be terminated as soon as is just and reasonable after the decree of divorce.

The courts have power to vary the awards on the application of either party. The amounts may be increased or reduced or the method of payment varied or the payment stopped. For example, in *Cann* v. *Cann* (1977) a wife obtained a matrimonial order from the magistrates' court and a year later, in 1961, the couple were divorced. In 1974, the wife successfully applied for a variation and the order was increased to £7 per week. Two years later the husband retired and applied for a reduction. His weekly income was £23 and the wife's income was £13. The court reduced the order to £5 per week, and considered that the one-third rule was inappropriate in this case. The result of the variation was that both the husband and wife had weekly incomes of £18.

In *Clutton* v. *Clutton* (1991), the parties' sole capital asset after divorce was the family home, in which the wife and their daughter lived and which was in the husband's name. When considering an order to transfer the house to the wife as a "clean break," the Court of Appeal held that the transfer of the house would be unfair to the husband and ordered that the sale of the house be postponed until the wife remarried or cohabited with another man, when the proceeds of the sale should be divided on the basis of two-thirds to the wife and one-third to the husband.

2. Maintenance claims when there are no judicial proceedings for divorce or separation

A wife may apply to the courts (magistrates or superior courts) for maintenance on the grounds that her husband has neglected to provide maintenance for her and her children (if any). The claim may also be made on the grounds that, because of the husband's desertion or behaviour, the wife could not reasonably be expected to live with him. This behaviour could include such acts as adultery, cruelty, violence, drunkenness, and the like.

Maintenance paid to claimants is a weekly sum and is loosely based on one third of the gross total income of the parties. For example, if a husband earned £120 and the wife had no income, the wife would receive £40 a week. However, if the husband earned £60 and the wife earned £60 per week, the wife would receive nothing because she earned more than one-third of the total income. A county court or High Court may award a lump sum.

An important factor when assessing maintenance is the payment of income support. Anyone receiving income support will have the payments reduced by the amount of maintenance received.

REVISION TEST

1. What is the minimum age for marriage?

2. If a minor marries over this age but under 18, is the marriage valid?

3. Name the only reason for petitioning for a divorce.

4. What are the five facts which establish the reason for divorce?

5. What are the decrees granted by the court to a successful petitioner for a divorce?

SPECIMEN EXAMINATION QUESTIONS

1. In each of the following situations explain what the legal consequences would be if the marriage were to take place.

   (a) Mary obtains a decree nisi of divorce from Malcolm. She intends marrying her cousin George four weeks after the decree nisi.

   (b) David, aged 16, has been going out with Louise, aged 18, for about a year. Louise has just discovered that she is pregnant and Louise's father has threatened David with physical violence if he does not marry his daughter.

   S.E.G. 1992

2. A court will not grant a divorce unless it is satisfied that the petitioner has proved, by one of five "facts", that the marriage has irretrievably broken down. Explain the facts which have to be proved.

3. What is the legal position of minors if they wish to marry?

4. Distinguish between void and voidable marriages.

5. What is judicial separation and how does it differ from divorce?

6. Explain what maintenance is and how it may be claimed.

7. Describe the duties and responsibilities of a man and wife when they marry.

SUGGESTED COURSEWORK TITLES

Explain the present situation in English law with regard to marriage for people under the age of 18 years. Argue for and/or against the position that minors below this age should be able to marry without consent of adults.

Describe the position of maintenance for a divorced spouse. Discuss the suggestion that the aim of maintenance should be that both parties should eventually be able to maintain themselves.

Chapter 12

Law of Succession and Property

Death comes to all and the law of succession deals with the ways by which property of a dead person is transferred to the new owners. The duty of transferring the property falls to personal representatives, called executors and administrators depending on whether or not the dead person left a will. The law allows (with some exceptions as shown later) for a person to decide the destination of his property after death by leaving a will. If, however, a will is not made a dead person's possessions are distributed according to rules laid down by statute.

Ownership

Property is anything that can be owned, and is either real property (freehold land) or personal property (all moveable things, such as clothes, furniture, personal belongings, etc.; leasehold property, as well as legal rights over things such as copyrights). These things may be bought and sold and may be left in a person's will.

As a house or flat is usually the most valuable part of a dead person's estate, students should be aware of the different forms of home ownership and the different methods of buying a house or flat.

House ownership falls under two headings; either freehold or leasehold.

1. Freehold land

This form of ownership has the technical name of "fee simple absolute in possession" and it gives the owner the right to reside in the property or to receive or collect rents from other persons who may reside in the property. "Fee simple," means that the property is an estate of inheritance and may be left in a will to whoever the owner wishes, without any restriction; "absolute" means that it is not subject to any condition of length or period of time; and "in possession," means that the owner has the right of possession, or to receive rents, immediately.

2. Leasehold land

It is not complete ownership of the land, but gives the holder the right to enjoy the "ownership" of the land for the period of the lease. Its technical name is "term of years absolute," and the term can be for a very small period of time, say one week or one month to say 999 years. Leasehold land may be sold or inherited during the term of years as may freehold, but at the end of the term of the lease, the land reverts back to the freeholder, together with any house or other buildings that have been erected on the land. There is statutory provision for leaseholders to purchase the freehold under certain conditions and within the period of the leasehold.

Means of Purchasing Houses

Mortgage

The vast majority of house buyers do not have the money to buy a house or flat, and they borrow the money from institutions. A loan is made on the security of the house, and a mortgage is created. A mortgage is a conveyance of real property (freehold) or personal property (leasehold) as security for the repayment of the money borrowed. If the owner does not or will not repay the loan, the mortgagee (the lender) may take possession of the property. Building Societies are the most common lenders of money for house purchases. The borrower usually but not always has to provide a proportion of the cost of the house and the balance is repaid, plus interest, over a given period of time, usually between 20–30 years.

Insurance companies, local councils and banks will also make loans to assist home buyers. An insurance company may make the loan on the security of a life assurance policy. This method means the borrower has to repay the interest, plus the premiums of the life assurance policy, and in some cases, the loan.

It should be noted that home ownership does not give unrestricted rights over the property, as it will be subject to many restrictions contained in covenants, local by-laws and government statutes.

WILLS

A will is a declaration by a person about the distribution after death of his property, both real and personal. It must be noted that a will has no legal effect, and does not come into operation, until the death of the testator. A person named in the will, therefore, has no claim or right to any property until the testator's death, and until that occurs, the testator may do what he likes with the property. It could be sold, destroyed or given away to someone not named in the will. It is desirable for a person with a large estate to make a will, although for those who have little property the need is not so great. A will is necessary, however, when it is the intention to leave property to persons who are not members of the testator's immediate family, or on the negative side to ensure that a specific near relative does not inherit anything. For example, a wife may not wish a husband who deserted her to inherit her property, so she may make a will leaving the property to someone else.

Anyone aged 18 or over and of sound mind may make a will, provided it complies with the requirements of the Wills Act 1837 and the Administration of Justice Act 1982. There is no need to have it drawn up by a solicitor, although it is not usually expensive if professional services are required. Wills in blank form may be bought from most stationers, and, provided the testator's intentions are straightforward, there should be no difficulty. It is impossible to know how many adults make wills, but it is estimated that it is less than 25 per cent. of those entitled to do so.

Requirement of a Valid Will

A man making a will is called a testator and a woman is called a testatrix.

A will must be in writing, and must be signed by the testator. The writing can be on any type of paper or parchment (a will has been accepted which was written on an egg shell), and the will may refer to several other documents, provided that they are capable of being identified and were in existence at the time of making the will. The testator's signature should normally be at the end of the writing but if it is, say, at the top of a will, it would be effective if it appears that the testator intended his signature to make the will valid. The intention could be shown by evidence, such as independant witnesses.

In *Wood* v. *Smith* (1992), a testator made a handwritten will which was headed, "My Will by Percy Winterbone." The witnesses were informed by the testator that he had not signed at the end of the will because his signature was at the top of the page. It was contended that while a signature need not be at the foot of the will, there needs to be a will in existence when the signature is made. The Court of Appeal held that the signature could precede the contents of the will provided the signature and the preparation of the will were all part of one operation.

If the testator cannot write, a "mark" (usually a cross) or an ink thumb-print will be sufficient provided the "mark" can be identified as the testator's. Another person may sign if the testator cannot, say for reasons of infirmity, sign himself. The will must be signed by the other person in the presence of the testator, who must acknowledge to the witnesses that the other person signs on his behalf.

The testator's signature must be witnessed by a least two witnesses who are present at the same time. Witnesses do not have to be present when the signature is made, provided the testator acknowledges the signature as his. The witnesses must sign the will, testifying that the signature of the testator was made or acknowledged in their presence. If the witnesses are not present together at the time of the signature or acknowledgement the will is generally void. The Administration of Justice Act 1982, provides that if only one witness is present when the testator signs a will, both the testator and witness may acknowledge their signatures at a later date, when a second witness is present and adds the second signature. This provision would not apply when an attestation clause is used (see p. 277).

Witnesses must reasonably understand that they are witnessing a signature, but it is not necessary to know the nature or contents of the document. A competent witness could be a person under 18 or over 80, or an illiterate, provided that he or she had sufficient understanding. A blind person would not be a competent witness because he would not be able to observe the signature or acknowledgement.

It is not necessary for the will to have an attestation clause, but it is usual (see p. 277). The witnesses may sign or make their marks immediately below the testator's signature.

Witnesses, or their spouses, generally cannot benefit from a will, but *it must be stressed* that provided there are other beneficiaries named, the will would not be invalid, but only the gift to the particular witness or spouse would be void. The Wills Act 1968 provides that, if there are two or more disinterested witnesses, gifts to additional interested witnesses will be valid. See *Re Bravda* (p. 3).

It is usual to date a will although it is not essential to the validity of the will. A dated will would be evidence when deciding which of two wills is the later one and therefore the valid last will.

Soldiers' Wills

It has been recognised that in times of emergencies or war, there may not be the opportunity to comply with the requirements needed to make a valid will. A sailor, for example, could not be expected to have his signature attested while his ship was sinking into the sea. Witnesses may be difficult to find in such circumstances.

The strict rules for making a will as stated above are relaxed for soldiers, sailors and airmen on actual military service, or for any seaman at sea.

An informal or nuncupative will may be made by the above if they are aged 14 or over. If a will is in writing witnesses are not needed, although if made orally there obviously must be witnesses.

In *Rapley* v. *Rapley* (1983) a 15-year-old sailor wrote an unwitnessed will while on shore leave. When he died more than 40 years later the court held that as he was not at sea when the will was made, it had no effect and he died intestate (see p. 274).

Whether or not the forces are on actual military service depends on the nature and activities of the force to which they are attached. In *Re Jones* (1981), Jones was a soldier stationed in Northern Ireland. In 1978 he was shot and on the way to the hospital and before two officers said "If I do not make it, make sure Anne gets all my stuff." (Anne was his fiancee.) Jones died on the following day. It was held by the court that this statement be accepted as his last will even though he had previously made a formal will in favour of his mother. The court considered that he was on actual military service at the time of making the statement although there was no state of war and the forces to which he belonged were not engaged against a regular or uniformed enemy (see p. 21.)

An informal will remains valid even after the hostilities or emergencies have ended.

Revocation

The absence of the necessary formalities makes a will invalid and this usually means that the intentions of the testator are ignored by law and the property distributed as an intestacy. A testator may change, vary or completely revoke a will. A will may be revoked expressly, or impliedly from the conduct of the testator.

1. By expressly revoking the will

An express revocation has to be made in exactly the same way as making a will, *i.e.* in writing, signed and witnessed.

2. By making a new will or codicil

A new or subsequent will revokes all previous wills which are not inconsistent or different. It is usual to start a new will with a statement revoking all previous wills, thereby making an express revocation. If this statement is not made, any gifts in a previous will would still be effective if not accounted for in the subsequent will. For example, if a will provided, "my money in the bank to Peter, my car to Michael, my dog to Linda," and a subsequent will provided, "my money to David, my car to Nicholas and my boat to James," and there was no clause revoking previous wills, Linda would be entitled to the dog, because the second will made no provision for this property. Without the express exclusion clause it would be necessary to study all previous wills to find the testator's intentions.

Sometimes a will is amended or varied by a codicil, which is inserted in or attached to the will. It is necessary to have a codicil signed and witnessed.

In *Re White (Deceased)* (1990), the testator dictated amendments to his original will, which were handwritten on to the original will. At the foot of the last page of the will the testator wrote, "Alterations to will dated 14.12.84. Witnessed," and two witnesses duly signed below, although neither the testator nor the witnesses signed or initialled the alterations. It was held that the original will, without the amendments, was the valid will, because neither the testator nor the witnesses of the alterations had signed in the prescribed manner.

3. By destroying a will

A will is only revoked if it is intentionally destroyed by the testator or by someone else in the testator's presence and as instructed by the testator. It may be destroyed by burning, tearing or any other means, but it must be done with the intention of destroying the will. A will destroyed accidentally would still be valid. In such a case, the personal representative would refer to other material, such as a copy of the will or oral evidence, to find the testator's intentions.

In *Re Adams (Deceased)* (1990), the testatrix informed her solicitors to destroy her will. The will was returned to her with the advice to destroy it herself. After her death the will was found and it had been heavily scribbled on with a ballpoint pen. It was impossible to read the signatures on the will but other parts of the will could be read. It was held that as the signatures were destroyed with the testator's clear intention to revoke, meant the will as a whole had been revoked.

4. By subsequent divorce

A divorce or nullity of a marriage revokes any gift to the former spouse, and revokes the appointment of the spouse as executor or executrix. If another person or persons are also named as beneficiaries in the will, it would remain valid and only the gift to the former spouse would be invalid. If the spouse was the only beneficiary the dead person's estate would be distributed under the rules of intestacy (see p. 274).

5. By subsequent marriage

A will of a man or woman is revoked by a subsequent marriage, but a will will not be revoked if it is made in contemplation of marriage. It is not sufficient to state in the will that the testator intends to marry, the will would still be revoked by a subsequent marriage unless the name of the intended spouse was also stated and the testator intended that the will would not be revoked by the marriage.

FAMILY PROVISION

Before 1938 a man could leave his property to whomsoever he wished, and there was no requirement to provide for his family. A man could give his entire estates to charity and leave his wife penniless. The Inheritance (Family Provision) Act 1938 gave the court power to make a financial provision out of the husband's estate to a wife and certain other dependants if they had not been provided for in the will. Further and more extensive powers were given to the courts by the Inheritance (Provision for Family and Dependants) Act 1975. This Act provides that the court has a discretion to make an award out of the dead person's estate to dependants who have not received "reasonable financial provision," from a will or intestacy, or from both. The following persons may apply to the court for family provision:

1. The husband or wife of the dead person and former spouses who have not remarried.

2. Children of the deceased, whether they be illegitimate, adopted, or treated as a child of the family. There is no restriction as to age, incapacity, sex or whether married or not.

In *Re Callaghan (Deceased)* (1984), a married man, over 40, made a successful claim to be treated as a child of the family and was awarded a lump sum because the deceased, who died intestate, had treated him as a son from the age of 12.

3. Any other persons who immediately before the death of the deceased were being maintained, either wholly or partly, by the deceased. This heading would cover other relatives such as sisters, brothers, mothers and fathers, friends, common law wives and mistresses who were receiving substantial financial support before the deceased's death.

"Reasonable financial provision" means:

(a) In the case of a spouse, financial provision as would be reasonable in all the circumstances, whether or not that provision is needed for maintenance,

(b) In the case of other persons, such financial provision, as would be reasonable in all the circumstances, needed for their maintenance.

The applications must be made within six months of grant of probate or letters of administration being taken out. The court would consider the value of the estate and the provision already made to the applicant. In the case of a spouse, consideration would be given to age, duration of marriage and the contribution made by the applicant to the family and its welfare.

With regard to young children, educational needs would be considered and with older children, the ability to reasonably maintain themselves. The court would also take into consideration statements made by the deceased as to the reasons why certain provisions were made or were not made.

The court may award lump sums or periodical payments, transfer certain property, such as the family house, and make settlements of other property.

LEGACIES

The legal terms for the gifts named in a will differ according to the property. A transfer of real property (freehold land) is called a devise, and the transfer of personal property (chattels) are called legacies or bequests.

Types of Legacies

1. General legacy
This is a gift where no specific thing is named, "I leave a car to..." or "I give a boat to..."

2. Specific legacy
As the name suggests, a specific thing is given. "I leave my Rover car..." or "I leave my boat the 'Skylark' to..."

3. Residuary legacy
After all the debts have been paid and the general and specific devises and legacies distributed, the residue is what is left.

It should be noted that if a general or specific gift is not in the testator's ownership at the time of death, the gift "is adeemed" and there is no inheritance. Should a person named in a will die before the testator, the gift lapses and goes into the residue, unless the person is the child of the testator and he dies leaving an issue (see below), or the will provides for another to receive it. For example, it is quite common to leave property to X, if X dies before the testator, it is left to Y.

4. Children of testator
When a testator leaves property to sons or daughters, the gifts shall not lapse if they die before the testator, provided they die leaving an issue (children). The property passes *per stirpes*, to the issue living at the time of the testator's death. If, for example, a gift was to a son or daughter who died childless before the testator died, the gift would lapse and pass to the residuary estate, but if the son or daughter had one or more children alive

at the time of the testator's death, the issue would take, in equal shares, the gift intended for their father or mother.

PERSONAL REPRESENTATIVES

Property of a deceased person vests in personal representatives who have a duty to collect all money and property due to the deceased, pay all debts owed by the deceased, including funeral expenses, and sell or convert property as is necessary.

An executor is usually named in the will and has the above duties to perform immediately upon the death of the testator. Before an executor may deal with the estate, it is necessary to apply to the court for a grant of probate. It is normally a formal exercise in presenting the will and giving details of the property and value of the deceased's estate. Provided that there are no complications, probate should be granted in a comparatively short period of time. A beneficiary may be appointed executor, and frequently more than one executor is named in the will. Solicitors and banks often act as executors.

As soon as probate has been granted, an executor may collect and pay off debts, and then distribute the estate according to the terms of the will.

An administrator is appointed if an executor is unwilling or unable to act, or not named in the will, or if there is no will and the deceased died "intestate."

Administrators are appointed by the court (usually the spouse or children of the deceased) and they apply for Letters of Administration in a similar way as an executor applies for probate. They distribute the estate according to the will or if there is no will, according to the rule of intestacy (see below).

INTESTACY

When a person dies without making a valid will, he or she is said to die intestate, and the property is distributed according to the rules laid down by the Administration of Estates Act 1925, as amended by other Acts. These rules also apply to a partial intestacy which occurs when all the testator's property has not been disposed of by a will.

For convenience, the following rules assume that it is a man that has died, but the rules are similarly applied when a woman is deceased.

1. A surviving wife only

If there are no children to the marriage and the deceased has no living parents, brothers or sisters, or their issue—the wife receives the whole estate.

2. A surviving wife and children

The wife receives the personal chattels (furniture, etc.) and the first £75,000 of the estate, plus interest at seven per cent., from the date of death to the time of payment. The balance of the estate is then halved. The wife receives interest on one half for life; the children share the other half immediately, and the mother's half on her death.

The share for children under 18 is kept in trust until they reach that age. A grandchild of the deceased would receive the share of its parent who had predeceased the intestator (*e.g.* a grandchild would inherit if its parent had died before the grandparent).

An illegitimate child has full rights of inheritance and may claim against the estates of both his or her parents on the same basis as legitimate children.

3. A surviving wife with no children, but a surviving parent, brother or sister, or their issue

The wife would receive the chattels, the first £125,000 with interest at seven per cent. as above, and the absolute ownership of half of the remaining balance. Surviving parents would equally share the other half, but if there were no surviving parents, the deceased's brothers or sisters (or their issue if they predeceased the intestator) would share this half of the residue.

4. Surviving children but no wife

The children take absolutely all the estate, but if under 18 the property would be held on trust. They take the estate regardless of all other relatives.

5. Surviving parents, but no wife or children

The parents share absolutely the whole estate.

6. No surviving wife, children or parents

The following relations will be entitled to the estate in the following order:

    (a)   brothers and sisters of the whole blood,
    (b)   brothers and sisters of the half blood,

    (c)   grandparents,
    (d)   uncles and aunts of the whole blood,
    (e)   uncles and aunts of the half blood.

If none of these relations survive the intestate, the estate passes to the Crown as Bona Vacantia. The property which comes the way of Bona Vacantia is disposed of and the proceeds paid into the Exchequer. It is possible to recover the proceeds at a later date if an unknown relative makes a belated claim.

Forfeiture Rule

It is a general rule of law that a person who unlawfully kills another is stopped from benefitting as a consequence of the killing. The "forfeiture rule" arises from public policy. Obviously, a person named in a will cannot benefit from the will if he murders the testator.

The Forfeiture Act 1982 was created to enable certain persons found guilty of unlawful killing (other than murder),

    (a)   to obtain relief from forfeiture of inheritance,
    (b)   to enable such persons to claim for financial provision out of the deceased person's estate, and
    (c)   to receive certain pensions and social security benefits.

The Act allows persons convicted of unlawful killing (manslaughter, death caused by reckless driving, suicide pacts, infanticide, etc.) to make a claim, within three months of conviction, to the court to modify the "forfeiture rule." The court will only do so if the justice of the case requires it to do so. It must be stressed that convicted murderers do not come within this Act.

In *Re K. (Deceased)* (1985) (the first case under this Act) a wife, during a quarrel, killed her husband with a shotgun. She pleaded guilty to manslaughter, and as she had been subject to unprovoked violent attacks by the husband, she received a two year probation order. The court held that although the "forfeiture rule" applied on the facts of the case it would be unjust if she was stopped from receiving benefit under the will, and ordered that the effect of the "rule" should be modified accordingly.

SPECIMEN FORM OF A DRAFT WILL

This is the Last Will and Testament of James Doe, 4 Somerset Street, Manchester.

1. I HEREBY REVOKE all former wills made by me and declare this to be my last will.

2. I APPOINT MY SON JOHN DOE as the executor of my will.

3. I BEQUEATH to my son John Doe my car and £5,000.

4. I DEVISE AND BEQUEATH all the residue of my estate both real and personal whatsoever and wheresoever to my wife Jane Doe.

IN WITNESS WHEREOF I have hereunto set my hand this thirty-first day of July One Thousand Nine Hundred and Ninety Four.

SIGNED by the above named James Doe as
and for his Last Will and Testament in
the presence of us both present
at the same time who at his   James Doe
request in his presence and in   (signature).
the presence of each other have hereunto
subscribed our names as witnesses.

Uriah Heap—(signature)
Solicitor,
Manchester.

Ebenezer Scrooge—(signature)
7 South Street,
Manchester,
Secretary.

NOTE. The writing opposite the signature of James Doe is the attestation clause. You will note that the witnesses sign as being "both present at the same time". (See p. 268.)

REVISION TEST

1. What is the minimum age that a person may make a formal will?

2. What is the name of a person who makes a valid will?

3. May a person claim a legacy before the person making the will dies?

4. May a blind person be a witness to a will?

5. Name the five ways by which a will may be revoked.

6. What is the name given to a personal representative

    (a) named in a will,
    (b) where there is no will?

SPECIMEN EXAMINATION QUESTIONS

1. What are the requirements of a valid will? When are these formalities not required?

2. A will is a declaration by a person about the distribution of property after death. In order to be valid, the will must be in writing, signed by the testator and witnessed.

    In each of the following situations, explain whether or not the wills are valid, and give reasons for your answer.

    (a) Mary types her will on the back of an old shopping list. She signs it at the bottom. The will is then correctly witnessed by two people.
    (b) Tom, who cannot read or write, asks a friend, Bill, to write out his will for him. Tom then makes his mark with a cross in the margin because there is not enough room at the bottom of the will. The will is then correctly witnessed by two people.
    (c) Jane writes out her will and then signs it at the bottom. Her witnesses are James, aged 16, and Steve, who is blind.

    S.E.G. 1990

3. Discuss the validity of the following wills:

    (a) Joyce signed her will in the presence of Tim (who is blind) and David (aged 17), both of whom signed as witnesses. At a later date Nick also signed the will as a witness.

(b)   By his will Henry left his estate to Fred and Perry. Henry's signature was witnessed by Fred, Perry and their two secretaries.

4.   What are the legal titles and duties of personal representatives of a deceased person?

5.   Explain how the estate of a dead person is distributed when he dies without leaving a will.

6.   Explain the present position of the law with regard to family provision.

7.   Ivy Smith, aged 40, wrote and signed a will in which she left £5,000 to her daughter-in-law, Gail; £2,000 to her friend, Vera. The remainder of her estate was divided between her two grandchildren, Nicholas aged 18 and Sarah-Louise aged 15. Ivy also has a sister, Mabel aged 75, who lives in a nursing home. Ivy has for many years contributed towards the costs of Mabel's care in the nursing home.

   Ivy's will was witnessed by:
(1) Ivy's next door neighbour, Jack, who is Vera's husband;
(2) Martin, Gail's new boyfriend;
(3) Kevin and Sally, a handicapped young married couple who live in Ivy's street. Kevin aged 18 is blind; Sally, aged 17, is deaf.

(a)   Explain whether or not each of the above persons is competent to witness the will.

(b)   Explain whether or not a valid will exists after all four witnesses have signed the will. In your answer, explain whether or not all Ivy's bequests will be received by her beneficiaries.

(c)   Why do you think the law is so reluctant to allow a witness also to be a beneficiary?

(d)   If Ivy had died without making a will, the intestacy rules would have applied to her estate. How would the estate be distributed in this case?

(e)   Ivy left nothing to her sister in her will even though Mabel was dependent on her. On the facts, it looks very likely that Mabel may be able to claim against Ivy's estate. Do you think it is right that the testator's wishes are ignored in this way? Give reasons for your answer.

S.E.G. 1992

SUGGESTED COURSEWORK TITLES

Explain the requirements to make a valid will and consider whether or not the present position of witnesses is suitable for today's methods of recording data.

Describe the method of distribution of a person's estate under the rules of intestacy. Could you suggest a fairer method of distribution?

Chapter 13

Welfare Law

SOCIAL SECURITY

Social security is a system of State financial assistance to persons aged 16 and over. The aim of social security is to ensure that persons who do not have sufficient income to maintain themselves or their dependants will receive a minimum income.

1. National insurance

Most employed and self-employed persons pay a national insurance contribution, and employers also pay a contribution for every employee. The scheme is administered by the Department of Social Security (D.S.S.). The scheme aims to reduce the risk of workers suffering financial loss through occurrences such as:

(a) sickness,
(b) unemployment,
(c) maternity.

Most national insurance benefits are subject to contributions being kept up-to-date. A break in payment of contribution could mean a reduction of benefit.

2. Income support

Income support is a social security benefit to help people who do not have enough money to live on, and it is intended to meet regular weekly needs.

People who do not have sufficient money to live on may claim income support if they are:

(a) unemployed or aged 60 or over, or
(b) bringing up children on their own, or
(c) too sick or disabled to work, or only able to work part-time, or

(d) staying home to look after a disabled relative.

Anyone who works for more than 24 hours a week cannot normally claim, unless they work at home as a childminder or are so disabled that they cannot earn a living wage.

The amount of income support which persons may receive depends mainly on how much the government considers they need to live on, taking into account how much money they already receive from other social security benefits and part-time work, and their savings.

People who receive income support do not have to pay for NHS prescriptions or dental treatment, and will receive help towards the cost of glasses.

3. Family credit

This is a benefit for working people who work for 24 hours or more each week and who support at least one child, living with them. A single person or married couples may not claim this benefit if they have a combined savings of over a prescribed amount.

The amount paid depends on the number of children in the family; the amount of money coming into the home from wages and other social benefits and total savings.

People receiving Family Credit are also entitled to free NHS prescriptions, dental treatment and help with the cost of glasses.

REVISION TEST

1. Who may be able to receive Income Support?

2. What is the largest amount of savings a person may have to qualify for Income Support?

3. What is the maximum number of hours a person may work each week and still qualify for Income Support?

4. Is Family Credit available to unemployed people?

5. What is the maximum amount of savings a person is allowed to have to qualify for Family Support?

SPECIMEN EXAMINATION QUESTIONS

1. Discuss the various social security benefits that are available.

2. What is:

   (a) income support,
   (b) family credit.

   Explain which persons are entitled to claim for these benefits.

SUGGESTED COURSEWORK TITLE

Explain the social security benefits available to the general public. Discuss the need for them and give your comments on their suitability. Would you suggest the need for other benefits?

Chapter 14

Examination Technique

Many candidates do not make the most of their knowledge when answering examination questions. In law examinations, questions which describe hypothetical situations cause the greatest concern.

An examiner may set a question which asks the candidate to write on a given topic, or the question may be set in the form of a problem. In either case the examiner wishes to know if the candidate understands a particular aspect of law. The question could be: (i) "Distinguish an offer from an invitation to treat," or it could be (ii) "Jane saw a coat in a shop window marked £5. She offered to buy the coat at this price, but was told it should have been £25, but the 2 in the sign had fallen. Can Jane enforce the contract?"

The first answer would contain the definition of an offer and invitation to treat. Reference would be made to leading cases—*Boots Cash Chemists*, the "flick knife" in *Fisher* v. *Bell*, *Harvey* v. *Facey's Bumper Hall Pen*, etc. Most well prepared candidates would experience little difficulty.

What should the answer to the second question contain? The examiner is again requiring an explanation of the difference between an offer and an invitation to treat. This time, however, the candidate must reveal knowledge by advising Jane.

As a guide to answering problems or situation questions, follow these rules:

1. Discuss the law to which the situation relates, but forget about the problem at this stage, and write an account or discussion of the law.

2. Support your discussion with the authority of the law, bringing in statutes and cases which are the source of this particular aspect of law. There is generally no need to give details of cases. The names will usually be sufficient, but if you feel the need to explain the case, confine your answer to the principle involved (the *ratio decidendi*).

3. From what has been written under the other two rules, argue the problem, if possible come to a decision and support your decision with the authorities already stated. If you have stated the law correctly, and argued and discussed the problem fully, it will not matter if you come to the wrong decision. In many examinations for legal qualifications, the problems set have no correct answer because they have not come before the courts in the particular form posited.

GENERAL COMMENTS

Always read the paper carefully before attempting any questions and jot down facts or cases which immediately come to mind. When you have decided to answer a question, write down on rough paper all your thoughts in note form and then arrange them into a plan for your answer. By following such a course of action, you should ensure that your answer is complete and you have not forgotten to include any relevant information.

Do not write for too long on any one question as it restricts the time available for the last questions. Remember, it is always considered easier to obtain the first five marks for an answer than it is to earn the last five. Always answer the required number of questions and try to write neatly and legibly. An examiner cannot give marks if there is nothing to mark or if the writing cannot be read.

Never leave the examination room before the end of the examination unless you are completely satisfied that you have answered every question to the best of your ability. Have you noticed the sheepish look on the first candidate to leave the room and how happy he or she is when another candidate also leaves early? If the examination appears hard, stay in the room and give your brain a chance to show its powers of recall. Once a candidate has left the examination, there is no second chance to go back and write down any thoughts that have just come to mind. You have paid your money, so stay and fight for your marks. Good luck.

Appendix

LIST OF ADDRESSES WHERE INFORMATION MAY BE OBTAINED

Consumer matters
National Associations of Citizens Advice Bureaux,
    115 Pentonville Road, London N1 9LZ
        (for your local branch—see local telephone directory)
The Office of Fair Trading,
    Field House, Breams Buildings, London EC4A 1PR
National Consumer Council,
    20 Grosvenor Gardens, London SW1W 0BD
Consumers' Association,
    2 Marylebone Road, London NW1 4DF
National Federation of Consumer Groups,
    12 Mosley Street, Newcastle upon Tyne NE1 1DE
British Standards Institution,
    2 Park Street, London W1
British Tourist Authority,
    Blacks Road, London W6 9EL
Design Council,
    28 Haymarket, London SW1Y 4SU

Professional associations
The British Insurance Brokers' Association,
    Biba House, 14 Bevis Marks, London EC3A 7NT
Solicitors Complaints Bureau,
    Portland House, Stag Place, London SW1E 5BL

General business
The Stock Exchange,
    London EC2
There are also Stock Exchange Offices in Belfast, Birmingham, Bristol,
    Liverpool and Manchester
Banking Information Service,
    10 Lombard Street, London EC3V 9AT
Banking Ombudsman,
    5 Fetter Lane, London EC4

Building Societies Association,
  3 Savile Row, London W1X 1AF
Building Society Ombudsman,
  35 Grosvenor Gardens, London SW1X 7AE
The Insurance Ombudsman,
  135 Park Street, London SE1 9EA
Confederation of British Industries,
  103 New Oxford Street, London WC1
Chambers of Commerce, Industry and Trade
  see local directories
Companies Registration Office,
  Maindy, Cardiff SF4 3UZ

Legal Aid
See local directories.

County court office
Check local telephone directory for address

Other useful addresses
Parliamentary Ombudsman,
  Office of the Parliamentary Commissioner for Administration,
  Church House, Great Smith Street, London SW1P 3BW
Commissioner for Local Administration in England,
  21 Queen Anne's Gate, London SW1H 9BU
Commissioner for Local Administration in Wales,
  Court Road, Bridgend, Mid Glamorgan CF31 1BN
Office of the Health Service Commissioner for England,
  Great Smith Street, London SW1P 3BW
Office of the Health Service Commissioner for Wales,
  Greyfriars Road, Cardiff CF1 3AG
Police Complaints Authority,
  10 Great George Street, London SW1 3AE
Age Concern
Oxfam
Samaritans
Gingerbread Groups
  see local telephone directories and yellow pages
Health Education Authority,
  Hamilton House, Mabledon Place, London WC1H 9TX
Commission for Racial Equality,
  10 Allington Street, London SW1E 5EH
National Council for Civil Liberties,
  21 Tabard Street, London SE1 4LA
Rights of Women,
  52 Featherstone Street, London EC1Y 8RT

Equal Opportunities Commission,
  Quay Street, Manchester M3 3HN
Advisory, Conciliation and Arbitration Service (ACAS),
  83 Euston Road, London NW1
Industrial Tribunals (Central Office),
  93 Ebury Street, London SW1W 8RE

SUGGESTED BOOKLIST

The following list consists of books that may help students who require additional reading for a piece of coursework on a particular topic, and sources, where other material may be found, which will update students with recent changes in the law and current legal issues.

Most of this material should be obtainable from the public libraries, if it is not available in school or college. It must be stressed that students should obtain the latest edition available.

BOOK	AUTHOR	PUBLISHER
Davies on Contract	Upex	Sweet & Maxwell
Consumers, Society and the Law	Borrie and Diamond	Penguin
Sale of Goods and Consumer Credit	Dobson	Sweet & Maxwell
Consumers and the Law	Cranston	Weidenfeld & Nicolson
Business Law	Shears	Hulton Press
Tort	Baker	Sweet & Maxwell
The Law of Torts	Street	Butterworths
Elements of Family Law	Cretney	Sweet & Maxwell
Freedom, the Individual and the Law	Street	Penguin
Parents and Children	Hoggett	Sweet & Maxwell
Social Workers, their Clients and the Law	Zander	Sweet & Maxwell
The English Legal System	Walker and Walker	Butterworths
Eddey on The English Legal System	Darbyshire	Sweet & Maxwell
A First Book of English Law	Phillips and Hudson	Sweet & Maxwell
Smith and Bailey on The Modern English Legal System	Bailey and Gunn	Sweet & Maxwell
The Motorist and the Law	Wickerson	Oyez
The Penguin Guide to the Law	Pritchard	Penguin
Labour Law	Davies and Freedland	Weidenfeld & Nicolson
Criminal Law	Seago	Sweet & Maxwell

BOOK	AUTHOR	PUBLISHER
Updating Material		
Law Notes	Monthly	The College of Law
Modern Law Journal		Stevens
Law reports and columns in newspapers		(*The Guardian*; *The Times*; "*The Daily Telegraph*"; "*The Independent*," etc.)

Index